# AFRICA AND THE INTERNATIONAL POLITICAL SYSTEM

Edited by
## Timothy M. Shaw
## 'Sola Ojo

UNIVERSITY
PRESS OF
AMERICA

LANHAM • NEW YORK • LONDON

Copyright © 1982 by

**University Press of America,™ Inc.**

4720 Boston Way
Lanham, MD 20706

3 Henrietta Street
London WC2E 8LU England

Printed in the United States of America

**Library of Congress Cataloging in Publication Data**
Main entry under title:

Africa and the international political system.

    1. Africa–Politics and government–1960– –
Addresses, essays, lectures. 2. Africa–Foreign relations –
1960– –Addresses, essays, lectures. 3. Africa –
Economic conditions–1960– –Addresses, essays,
lectures. I. Shaw, Timothy M. II. Ojo, Sola. III.
University of Ife. Dept. of International Relations.
DT30.5.A35         320.96        80–6242
ISBN 0–8191–2233–5         AACR2
ISBN 0–8191–2234–3 (pbk.)

84-9947

Published by University Press of America for the Department
of International Relations, University of Ife, Ile-Ife, Nigeria

The Editors wish to acknowledge the generous assistance of the
Ford Foundation in the development and preparation of this book.

# TABLE OF CONTENTS

iii

iv

# PREFACE

The dawning of the decade of the eighties constitutes a turning-point for African international affairs for reasons of both actuality and analysis. First, in terms of actuality, the new decade represents the half-way mark between the optimistic independence mood of the early 1960s and the pessimistic scenario forecast for the end of the century. As we suggest in the introduction, the very gloom of present predictions may lead, hopefully, to their avoidance.

And second, in terms of analysis, the new decade coincides with a milestone in the development of indigenous scholarship on African foreign relations and international politics. For in 1981 the Department of International Relations at the University of Ife became fully Africanized and its first Professor -- holding the only Chair of its kind in Black Africa -- delivered his augural lecture. Happily, Professor Aluko's work, along with that of four of his colleagues at Ife, is included in this collection.

This book is being published for the Department of International Relations at Ife: a symbol of its intellectual and institutional development. One indication of its influence on the study of international affairs in Africa is the fact that all of the individual contributors, whether presently resident at Ife or not, are associated with the Department, either through the Nigerian Institute for International Affairs and the Nigerian Society for International Affairs or through the connection between Ife in Nigeria and Dalhousie University in Canada. One important event in the latter linkage was the series of joint workshops on the future of Africa held from May to November this year. This present collection represents, then, a major milestone -- but by

no means the end of the road -- in the development
of international relations in both practice and
analysis in Africa, centered appropriately on a
unique department with the same name.


Timothy M. Shaw and 'Sola Ojo
Halifax and Ife, October 1981

Chapter One

Introduction: Africa and the international
political system

Timothy M. Shaw and 'Sola Ojo

Although studies of African international
politics have increased in scope and sophistication in recent years, according to one leading
student of the area there are still many "weaknesses and lacunae in the scholarly production on
African international relations." Mark W.
DeLancey concludes his contemporary overview of the
state of the field by arguing that "there remains
much research, debate and writing to be done."[1]
This collection represents one attempt to respond
positively to DeLancey's lament. It is also
intended as a corrective to the complaint of Chris
Allen that "most international relations work on
Africa can be safely neglected."[2]

The present collection was stimulated not
only by apparent deficiencies in the literature to
date. It was also prepared to mark the first
twenty years of Africa's renewed participation in
the international system. For whilst decolonization is a limited process (see Chapter Three) -
one which by itself does not ensure Africa's development or independence - nevertheless, it did
restore Africa's international presence and personality. And although individual African states may
be quite powerless in the global milieu, the
collectivity of 50 members of the Organisation of
African Unity (OAU) has considerably more status
and influence. By the end of the century, this
number of participating countries is likely to
grow with the independence of Namibia and South
Africa and so the role and impact of Africa in
international affairs may be further enhanced.

Therefore, this volume has two purposes;
one is heuristic, the other historic.  First, it
seeks to review and advance the state of the field
of African international studies.  And second, it
seeks to mark Africa's first 20 years in the
international system and anticipate its next 20
years, that is, until the end of the current
century.  In other words, the collection is concerned both with analysis and with practice, with
explanation as well as with prescription and
prediction.

The dominant theme of these nine chapters
is change:  change in both existential and intellectual worlds.  Together they review and preview
i) existential change - within African states,
within the African continent, and within the world
system - and ii) intellectual change - from more
traditional and borrowed modes of analysis to more
contemporary and indigenous forms.  In turn, these
have generated change in prescription as well as
explanation, so producing a new generation of
activists as well as analysts who are distinguished
by a concern for fundamental rather than superficial issues.

i)   Africa in the international system: factor
     and/or actor

Africa has always been a _factor_ in international relations: a place for "discovery," a
source of slaves, a market for exports, a store of
raw materials, and territory over which to fight.
Before informal and formal colonialism it was also
an _actor_, albeit a weak and marginal one.  "Independence" has restored this lost status and per-
mitted it to begin to play a more effective and
extensive international role than ever before.  As
we have noted elsewhere, "Africa has a much longer
and more distinguished history of involvement in
international politics than is indicated by the
recent celebration of the first decade of the
OAU."[3]

As indicated in most of the chapters in

this volume, Africa's present position and problems are, in part, an inheritance of its place as
a factor in the world system over the last few
centuries. But although this inheritance is
largely unhelpful, Africa's independence may enable the continent to overcome some of it through
the adoption of more appropriate and autonomous
development policies. As an actor, Africa is
attempting to reassert its own interests through
national and collective foreign policies. As
Olajide Aluko and Amadu Sesay indicate in Chapters Two and Seven, Africa has used the United
Nations (UN) system, for instance, both before and
after independence to advance political and economic decolonization throughout the continent.

Many of the chapters in this collection
treat Africa now as an effective actor rather than
as a passive actor. They are concerned with the
ways in which individual states and the continent
as a whole relate to extra-African states, institutions, and issues. Ironically, because of the
relentless participation of African leaders and
groups in the international system, Africa has
become not only a major actor but also a more
salient factor than ever in global affairs. Given
the diversity and complexity of these interactions
it is important to distinguish amongst different
levels and actor types as they relate to Africa's
participation in world politics.[4]

ii) Levels of interaction: national, regional
    and global

Africa as a collective actor can clearly
only play a role in extra-continental affairs. At
the global level, both African states and African
continental institutions constitute actors in their
own right, whereas at other, more exclusive, levels
of interaction only states or regional organizations are active. Most states on the continent
are most involved at the regional rather than
other levels - one indicator of relative weakness
and dependence - although all have links with
major industrial and strategic powers and are

members of major political and economic institutions.

As indicated by the four chapters in Part One of this volume, Africa as a collectivity is most concerned with development and with participation. Having been both underdeveloped and excluded during the colonial period, it is anxious to enhance its developmental prospects and its political influence. It has attempted to do so particularly through the UN system, via the non-alignment movement, and within the debate about a New International Economic Order. Whilst individual states and leaders have advanced Africa's visibility in these fora, it is at this global level that the continent qua continent has been most active.

At the regional level, as indicated in Part Two of this collection, particular countries and coalitions have been most influential. Individual states like Nigeria in the OAU, or groups of countries like the Front Line States (FLS) in Southern Africa have advanced continental order and liberation, respectively. Moreover, at the inter-regional level, as in the Middle East, OAU members have become part of an Afro-Arab alliance opposed to Israeli expansionism (see Chapter Six).

At these regional, inter-regional and continental levels, non-state actors affect inter-state relations. For instance, Chapters Four, Five and Nine all refer to the ubiquitous activities of multinational corporations in retarding African development and integration. And Chapters Six, Seven and Eight refer to the central role of liberation movements in advancing change in the Middle East and Southern Africa. At no level of interaction involving Africa is the role of the state an exclusive one; non-state interests and actors intrude at each of them. The intra-national aspects of such actors' activities draw attention to the national level of interaction. For the making of foreign policy in Africa is no longer the exclusive preserve of presidents or ministers.

Rather, a variety of sub-national and international interests and institutions affect the
making of both national and continental policies.

The African international system is increasingly complex, not only because of the emergence of its component countries as actors as well
as factors but also because of the involvement of
sub-national, trans-national and inter-national
forces. And the pattern of relationships amongst
this set of interests and institutions will have a
marked impact on the developmental and diplomatic
effectiveness of the continent in the remaining
two decades of the twentieth century. Concern
with this pattern is reflective of a shift from
more superficial to more fundamental issues, to
which we return in the final section of this
introduction: the existential and the intellectual
are always intertwined.

iii) Africa's future in the international system:
     incorporation or self-reliance?

As several of the contributions to this
collection suggest, Africa's past incorporation
into a world system over which it had minimal
control is a major factor in its present problems
and predicaments. Indeed, movements throughout
the continent for political and economic nationalism were direct responses to its historical inheritance of colonialism and underdevelopment.
Moreover, the continuing oppression of the blacks
in Southern Africa and the Arabs in Israel is a
legacy of a world order in which African interests
were hardly a factor let alone an actor. Over its
first 20 years of recaptured independence, Africa
has begun to deal with some, mainly the political
and superstructural, aspects of its dependence and
underdevelopment. In the next 20 years up to the
year 2000, Africa may be expected to deal with
other, mainly the economic and sub-structural,
features of its inheritance (as indicated in the
final sections of Chapters Five and Seven).

Most authors of the following chapters

indicate ways in which the international system
has changed over the past two decades: towards,
for instance, multipolarity, regional conflict and
co-operation, multinational corporate penetration,
and increased interstate inequalities. During the
remainder of this century, such global features
are likely to erode the stability of Africa's
political economies. Indeed the tendency towards
"cold-war"-type strategic tensions and towards
"mercantilist"-type economic policies poses a
profound challenge to decision-makers on the continent as indicated in Chapters Eight and Five
respectively.

Even before the particular problems of the
1980s were apparent it was clear that Africa's
mid-term future would probably be a troubled one.
For given its unpromising inheritance at independence its first 20 years have been characterized by
considerable disappointment. As the Executive
Secretary of the Economic Commission for Africa
(ECA), Dr. Adebayo Adedeji, has warned:

> There is no gainsaying the fact that
> Africa cannot afford to continue to
> perform in the field of development
> during the next decade or two at the
> same rate as in the last 15 years or
> so. If it does, the Africa region
> will be a much poorer relation of the
> rest of the world than it is now; the
> gap between it and the rest of the
> world will be wider, and its economic
> and technological backwardness will
> be much more pronounced. I shudder
> to think of the implications of this
> for social and political stability in
> the region.[5]

ECA data point to two salient features of
Africa's past and projected performance. First,
its overall rate of growth has been disappointing
and inadequate - less than 5% per annum and
falling. And second, even this growth has been
unevenly distributed: "In only nine African

countries have the growth rates achieved during
the past 15 years been such as to bring about a
relatively substantial increase in real <u>per capita</u>
income."[6]  For the mid-term future, whilst no
dramatic improvement in continental growth is
envisaged, ECA "estimates reveal prospects of even
greater disparities in incomes and levels of development among the countries."[7]  Only the minority
of middling rich (mainly OPEC members and NICs)[8]
will get richer; the majority of very poor will
get even poorer.  Such inequalities will have a
marked impact on patterns of regional interaction
as noted in Part Two of this book.

This unpromising picture is clouded further by the prospects of increasing conflict both
within and between states (see Chapter Seven) as
well as by the potential for extra-continental
involvement in such conflict (see Chapter Two).[9]
Many non-African countries and corporations
already identified can be expected to play an
increasing role in African affairs unless the
continent can turn adversity to advantage (see
Chapter Four).  For the very tenuousness of most
African political economies may yet lead to their
transformation; not through external intervention,
but rather through disengagement from the international system.

For if Africa's inheritance of dependence
is the major factor in its lacklustre performance
and its considerable vulnerability then in the
transcendence of incorporation may lie its salvation.  As Adedeji has proposed on behalf of the
ECA:

> . . . if we are to reverse the past
> and present trends of low development
> and accelerate the rates of socio-economic
> advancement, we will need to install,
> first, at the national level, a new
> economic order based on the principles
> of self-reliance and self-sustainment
> . . . (and, second) regionally, there
> is an urgent need for concentrating on

achieving an increasing measure of
collective self-reliance among
African states.[10]

But given the history of extroverted
economies and uneven growth rates, some African
leaders are more likely to opt for national and
collective self-reliance than others. The richer
and more powerful states may be able to maintain
a relatively profitable relationship with metropolitan interests, while the poorer and weaker
countries may move towards more socialism and
self-reliance. Such a divergence would serve to
exacerbate inequalities and tensions between
"semi-periphery" and "periphery" and expose the
continent to further foreign intervention and
manipulation.

The prospects of such centrifugal trends
developing in Africa are enhanced by i) the
established and dominant interests of "bourgeois"
forces inside many of Africa's political economies
and ii) the appearance of more radical regimes as
successive Southern African territories are liber-
ated.[11] And, in turn, these internal and regional
possibilities are affected by the emergence of
multipolarity and neomercantilism amongst the
more advanced industrialized states.[12] Therefore
we come full circle and have to recognize the
continuing interrelationship between center and
periphery (as well between center and semi-
periphery): until Africa achieves a greater
degree of self-reliance, factors such as international polarity and protectionism will continue
to influence its rate of development and its role
as an actor.

Hence the two parts to this volume: the
first on the extra-continental setting and the
second on the continental situation. Because of
Africa's past inheritance and present position
both global and regional levels of interaction
and analysis are likely to continue to be integral
to any description or explanation of African international relations for the rest of this century

at least.

Hence also the intellectual trends displayed by most of these contributions. Old political and policy assumptions are being discarded as the myths of decolonization are being eroded (see especially Gilbert Sekgoma's investigation of American interests in independence and "free trade" in Chapter Three). The limits of formal decolonization along with the threats of unpromising projections have combined to produce a new emphasis on both political economy and futures studies among both analysts and activists.[13] Scholars as well as statesmen are now searching for underlying trends through which to explain change: change within African states, within the African continent and within the world system.

The new concern with economic as well as with political liberation, reflected by political and intellectual leaders alike, is reflective of an attempt to evaluate change to date and to control change in the mid-term future. More "radical" analysis and advocacy have been entertained as a way of responding to previous deficiencies and emerging dilemmas. The study of international relations in Africa is beginning to reflect this new spirit - the assertion of autonomy in both intellectual and political realms. The present set of essays is intended to reinforce this trend in both explanation and prescription.

## Notes

1. Mark W. DeLancey "The study of African inter-
   national relations" in his collection on
   Aspects of International Relations in Africa
   (Bloomington: Indiana University African
   Studies Program, 1979) 22.

2. Chris Allen "A bibliographical guide to the
   study of the political economy of Africa" in
   Peter C. W. Gutkind and Immanuel Wallerstein
   (eds) The Political Economy of Contemporary
   Africa (Beverly Hills: Sage, 1976) 298.

3. Timothy M. Shaw and Kenneth A. Heard "Africa
   and international politics" in their collection on The Politics of Africa: dependence and
   development (London: Longman and New York:
   Africana, 1979) 265.

4. For an attempt to do this see Timothy M. Shaw
   "The actors in African international politics"
   in ibid. 357-396.

5. Adebayo Adedeji "Africa: the crisis of development and the challenge of a new economic
   order. Address to the Fourth Meeting of the
   Conference of Ministers and Thirteenth Session
   of the ECA, Kinshasa, February-March 1977"
   (Addis Ababa: ECA, 1977) 3-4.

6. Ibid. 9.

7. Ibid. 12. See also Timothy M. Shaw (ed)
   Alternative Futures for Africa (Boulder:
   Westview, 1981) and "On projections, prescrip-
   tions and plans: towards an African future"
   Quarterly Journal of Administration 14(2),
   July 1980.

8. That is, Organisation of Petroleum Exporting
   Countries (OPEC) and Newly Industrializing
   Countries or Newly Influential Countries (NICs).

11

9.  On this see Anirudha Gupta "Africa in the
    1980s" India Quarterly 35(3), July-September
    1979, 326.

10. Adedeji "Africa" 16.

11. On these contrary tendencies see Timothy M.
    Shaw "From dependence to self-reliance:
    Africa's prospects for the next twenty years"
    International Journal 35(4), Autumn 1980,
    821-844.

12. See Timothy M. Shaw "Towards an International
    Political Economy for the 1980s: from depend-
    ence to (inter)dependence" (Halifax: Centre
    for Foreign Policy Studies, 1980).

13. See Timothy M. Shaw "Foreign policy, polit-
    ical economy and the future: reflections on
    Africa in the world system" African Affairs
    79(315), April 1980, 260-268 and "Class,
    country and corporation: Africa in the
    capitalist world system" in Donald I. Ray
    et al. (eds) Into the 80s: proceedings of
    the 11th annual conference of the Canadian
    Association of African Studies, Volume 2
    (Vancouver: Tantalus, 1981) 19-37.

PART ONE


Global Level of Interaction

Chapter Two

Africa and the Great Powers

Olajide Aluko


It is easy for cynics to say that there
is very little or nothing that can be said about
Africa and the great powers· Peregrine Worsthorne
has recently stated  i) that without Western aid
and technology most African states would collapse
within weeks and  ii) that Africa is only useful
as a source of raw materials.[1]  A decade earlier,
Nigel Lawson had asserted that in times of international crises the roles of Africa (and other
minor powers) are "at best a nuisance, and at
worst a positive menace to world peace."[2]  And in
the mid-seventies Professor F.S. Northedge said
that the intrusion of African (and Asian) states
has injected "noise" into the international system
thereby creating friction among the great powers.[3]

But even if Africa has not "significantly
affected" the "political balance in the world" to
the extent Arnold Rivkin once envisaged,[4] the role
of the continent has been far from passive and
negative.  While Africa does receive aid from the
great powers, the value of aid for the whole of
the continent over the past two decades has been
less than that received by Israel and South Korea
from the Western powers alone.  Yet Africa provides markets not only for raw materials but also
for the capital and consumer goods and services
produced by the industrial countries.  Indeed in
many respects, the relationships among Africa and
the great powers are those of interdependence in
an increasingly shrinking world.

This is not to say that there are no difficulties in writing about this subject. The
first is the sheer number of states in Africa: 50
of them at the time of writing. These countries
display differences in socio-economic arrangement
and ideological orientation as well as differences
in colonial history and legacy. Africa can be conveniently divided into three language groups, viz:
Anglophone, Francophone, and Arab-speaking
Africans. Further divisions are possible. On the
one hand, for instance, Arab-speaking North Africa
is split by some industrial powers such as the US,
the UK and even the USSR into the Maghreb states
of Morocco, Algeria, and Tunisia, while Libya and
Egypt are grouped with the Middle Eastern countries
of Jordan, Syria, Israel and Lebanon. On the
other hand, Dennis Austin grouped the whole of
tropical Africa outside the areas under white
supremacist regimes into more or less one category.[5]

However, despite all these differences,
the continent has some common features which will
be dealt with below in some detail. Another
obvious difficulty which needs to be pointed out
is the fact that the great powers themselves are
not a monolithic entity. While they are all industrial states with a high level of technological
development they are broadly split into two blocs
in terms of socio-economic systems, with the Sino-
Soviet rift leading to a further division.

The aim of this chapter is three-fold.
First, it attempts to examine the nature of Africa's
relationships with the great powers. Second, it
assesses the extent to which these relationships
have changed since independence, especially since
the year 1960 when 17 states became independent
during what the UN General Assembly depicted as
"Africa's Year." Third, it examines how these
relationships may change in the rest of this decade.
However, before doing this I will identify basic

facts about the African states as well as the
international system in which they found themselves on independence.  For both of these factors
have gone a considerable way to shape relationships with the great powers.  Indeed, in some
real sense, Africa's relationships with the powers
have flown from two main sets of variables -
internal and external.

i)   Basic facts about Africa

        Among the most notable of the basic facts
common to most African states are the following:
i)   their newness to the international system;
ii)  their geographical distance from the great
powers;  iii) their poverty and underdevelopment
which make them militarily  and economically weak;
iv) the fragility of most of their regimes as
well as consequent endemic political instability;
and v) their location in Africa, the only continent with pockets of white supremacist regimes.
All the African states outside South Africa and
Namibia are members of the OAU.  Indeed, as far
back as 1958 the African Group in the UN had been
set up to coordinate common African positions on
major international issues.  All of them except
Ethiopia and Liberia were former colonies of
seven West European powers, viz: UK, France,
Belgium, Italy, Germany, Spain and Portugal.
I will say something briefly about each of these
facts or characteristics below.

        First, the newness of Africa to the inter-
national system is too obvious to require any
detailed discussion.  Tracing the emergence of the
modern state system, F. S. Northedge has put the
arrival of African (and some Asian) states as the
seventh and last stage in the evolution of the
modern international system.[6]  Largely because of
their newness on the international scene most of
the African states have lacked established tra-

ditional external interests. It is mainly because
of this that it has been easier for some of them
to swing from one end of the cold war spectrum to
the other; for example in close relations with
the Western powers to the Eastern powers as in the
case of Ethiopia, Ghana and Libya, or vice versa
in the case of Egypt and Somalia.

Second, another important factor that has
continued to shape the external relations of the
African states is the fact that, with the exceptions of i) Liberia, which was more or less an
appendage of the U.S. from 1847 until recently,
and ii) Ethiopia, which came under Italy from
1935 to 1941, all of them were former colonies of
West European powers. While colonial legacies
left them with heavy ties to the former rulers,
the demonstration of independence has been found
in their conscious attempts to diversify their
external ties from the West to Soviet bloc
countries and to China. Admittedly only a few
African states have in reality succeeded in doing
this, for a number of obvious socio-economic and
political reasons. Yet there is no doubt that
most of them are genuinely committed to reducing
their dependence on their former colonial masters.
While a few francophone states have continued to
rely on French military assistance for their own
security and survival, most of the countries of
Africa would be happier without such dependence.[7]

Third, paradoxically, although Africa is
well-endowed by nature, having plenty of agricultural and mineral resources, the continent is
economically poor. With a population of about
4 billion in 1975, or 10 per cent of the world's
population, and covering an area of about
26,123,000 sq. km, or about 20 per cent of the
world's land, Africa's GNP in 1973 of $95,971
million was less than 2 per cent of the global
total for that year.[8] Indeed by 1976 the African

share of the world's GNP had declined to about 1.2
per cent.[9] Over the past decade the economic performance of Africa has moved from bad to worse
with public debt quadrupling, rising from $7
billion in 1965 to $28 billion in 1975. Agricul-
tural output has declined sharply, while inflation
and widespread unemployment have been wreaking
havoc on the continent. The situation was so
serious that Executive-Secretary of the Economic
Commission for Africa (ECA) had to state in 1977
that "Africa more than any other region in the
Third World is faced with a development crisis of
great portent."[10] Of the 25 least-developed
countries in the world identified by the UN
Economic and Social Council (ECOSOC) in the
early seventies, 16 were in Africa. The level
of industrialization in Africa is also very low.
The continent's economy has remained a colonial
one based largely on the export of primary products and the import of finished goods and
services.

In terms of military capability Africa
is very weak. The size of the armed forces in
African countries between 1966 and 1970 did not
show any appreciable increase except in a few
cases such as in Egypt, Ethiopia, Nigeria, and
Somalia which in any case were in response to
local conflicts. Very few arms are produced in
Africa. All the African states are heavily dependent on the great powers for the importation
of military hardware and equipment for their
national armies. A few African countries such
as Central African Republic, Gabon, Ivory Coast
and Senegal have their security underwritten by
formal military arrangements with France. Local
conflicts in Southern Africa and in the Horn of
Africa have brought army personnel from some of
the industrial powers into such areas of the
continent.

A few African countries such as Botswana,
Lesotho, Swaziland, and Gambia have no national
armies at all. Even some that do, such as Zaire,
have armies that are so hopelessly demoralized
and undisciplined that they could not really defend their countries against internal subversion
and external aggression without help from some of
the great powers; this was the case during the
Shaba "invasions" I and II in 1977 and 1978
respectively.

The implications of this economic and
military impotence for Africa's relationship
with the great powers are serious. These are
two-fold: first, unequal relationships; and
second, paradoxically, greater dependence on the
great powers after independence than before.


## ii) Implications of economic and military weakness

As indicated above, since the African
states are under-developed economically and rely
almost exclusively on the same great powers for
the satisfaction of their needs for military equipment and even training, the relationship is
asymmetrical and unequal. So the continent has,
as a whole, little or no bargaining power with
the powers on these two vital areas: economic
and strategic. So in most cases, the states of
Africa are bound to take more or less the diktats
from the industrial powers on these issues.

Another aspect is that since the African
states need economic and military aid and cooperation from the great powers, the end-result
has been a deepening of their dependence on these
industrial powers. Almost all African regimes
have been committed to meeting the rising ex-
pectations of their peoples through the provision
of food, shelter and clothing, and through massive
investment in the agricultural and industrial

sectors. Since they have been unable to provide all these on their own, the only viable alternative has been to turn to the industrial powers; very few of the other Third World states could meet such demands in view of the fact that most African states are "in a hurry to catch up" with the industrial powers. This has led to the request for economic aid from and to unequitable trade ties with the great powers.

Although some of the African states have sought aid and trade opportunities from both East and West, "nonalignment" has not reduced their dependence. Rather than lessening their dependence on these industrial powers, paradoxically it has increased Africa's reliance on them now more than ever before. For example, African indebtedness to the industralized world has risen from about $7 billion in 1965 to over $43 billion in 1981.[11] Apart from this, although the precise figure is difficult to come by, there are more expatriate experts working in the continent today than at the point of independence in 1960.

Likewise, the military weakness of Africa has made the continent more dependent on the great powers than was the case in the early sixties. Then most African states were committed to excluding the troops of the powers from the continent as evidenced by the Congo (now Zaire) operation, 1960-64; at worst individual governments sought troops from other African states, such as those from Nigeria during the army mutinies in East Africa in 1964. However, since the seventies some, if not many, African states have openly welcomed the introduction of troops from the great powers into some parts of Africa such as Angola, Ethiopia, Morocco, and Zaire. Moreover, Africa is mainly dependent on the powers for the importation of arms and ammunition, and even for the training of officers and men.

The upshot of this dependence is that no
African state can seriously engage in any pro-
longed, active military campaign if the great
powers are not prepared to provide them with the
military equipment and hardware necessary for
such an operation. For instance, if France and
the US were to stop their arms supply to Morocco,
King Hassan would be forced to withdraw from the
Western Sahara. Similarly, without Soviet military equipment, Angolan troops with the support
of Cuban forces could not for long resist the
South African military thrust into that territory.
This is also true for some other countries such
as Central African Republic, Ivory Coast, and
Zaire that are heavily dependent on the military
support of one or other of the Western powers.
All in all, then, the consequence of the economic
and military weakness of the continent has been
greater dependence on the great powers than ever
before.

Fourth, another important factor influencing the relationship of Africa to the great
powers has been the basic question of the fragility
of African regimes. Political instability is
endemic in Africa. There is a lot of uncertainty
because of what Michael Leifer has called the
"inheritance elites"[12] giving way to ruling
military juntas and in some cases vice versa.
This sudden replacement of regimes coupled with
the "newness" of most of the states, as noted
earlier, have accounted largely for vicissitudes
in relations with the powers.

iii)  Vicissitudes of policies towards the great
      powers

Largely as a result of the frequent and
sudden change of governments in Africa, especially

by the military, and given the lack of established
traditional interests by most of them, it has
been usual to find coups d'etat in Africa being
accompanied by some changes in external ties with
the great powers. Another factor that has contributed to this instability in foreign affairs
has been the predominantly personalized nature of
the foreign policies of most African states.
Whether sensible or not there has been a general
tendency among new regimes in Africa to change
the external orientation of their predecessors.
This has resulted in the vicissitudes of policies
towards the great powers.

To cite some random examples of such
changes, the replacement of the Nkrumah government
by that of General J. Ankrah in 1966 led to a
shift in Ghana's policies from rather close ties
with the Soviet bloc countries to a pro-Western
stance. Likewise, the Amin coup in 1971 immediately shifted Uganda's relations away from close
ties with the Communist countries and towards
something of an entente with the West, especially
with Israel and the UK until the enforced ex-
pulsions of the Asians with British passports
from Uganda in 1972. Soon after this the Amin
government turned against the Western powers
while relying on the Soviet bloc for military
and political support. Similarly, Ethiopia
moved from being a near-satellite of the US
early in the seventies to being a bastion of
anti-Americanism during the second half of
seventies. On the other hand, Somalia moved from
being more or less a client state of the Soviet
Union in 1977 to a pro-Western position soon
after. Likewise, Egypt shifted from being almost
a protege of the USSR in 1973-4 to being almost
a US ally in the Middle East. Such examples can
be multiplied. What is important is to state
that such vicissitudes in policies have brought
little credit to the African states among the
great powers whether East or West. For a policy

to be respected, it has to be consistent, coherent and effective rather than changing according to the whims and caprices of incumbent leaders, especially when there are doubts about the survival of some of the new regimes.

Still another factor that has shaped relationships between African states and the great powers has been the sheer size in their number: 50 of them, or about one-third of the total membership of the UN. Although as shown above Africa is economically and militarilly weak, it has numbers on its side. Largely because of this neither the Western group of powers nor the Eastern group of states has indulged in taking on all of the states of Africa against themselves. The possible exception has been the presidency of Nixon (1969 to 1974) and now that of Reagan (since January 1981). Even then during these periods, the US did try to stave off conflict between herself and Africa. Apart from this, the African countries have on some occasions used their collective votes through the African Group at the UN to make the General Assembly take decisive actions.

Examples of this are abundant. It was the African states that played a major role in preventing some countries from recognizing the Rhodesian rebel regimes of Ian Smith from 1965 until 1978 and of Bishop Muzorewa from 1978 to April 1980. African pressures on the great powers have led to the expulsion of South Africa from most of the UN agencies and to the application of some limited sanctions on the apartheid republic. They have also prevented some countries of the world from dealing directly with the puppet government of the Turnhalle alliance in Namibia.

Even outside Africa, it was the over-

whelming support of the African states at the UN
that led to recognition of the Palestinian Liberation Organization (PLO) by the General Assembly
in the early seventies.[13]  Another question to
which the African states have contributed immensely
has been the efforts of the Third World to sell
the proposals for a New International Economic
Order to the majority in the UN.

And finally, fifth, still another factor
that has sorely affected Africa's policies and
attitudes to the great powers has been the continuing existance of apartheid in South Africa
and the illegal occupation of Namibia by
Pretoria.  While the continuing existence of the
white supremacist regimes has provided the most
potent single rallying point for the African
states, their policies and attitudes to the great
powers are within limits determined by the policies
of these industrial powers towards South Africa
and Namibia.  Thus some African states such as
Angola, Mozambique, and Tanzania regard the Soviet
bloc countries as their natural allies in the
struggle against apartheid and the enslavement
of black people in Southern Africa.  On the other
hand the relationships of such African states with
the Western powers have been cool if not intensely
hostile because of what they consider to be
Western collusion and support for the apartheid
regime and its continuing defiance of the UN over
Namibia.

iv)    International setting

Much of the behavior of the African states
has been influenced by the international environment in which they found themselves on independence.
In 1960 when most African states became independent
the cold war was at its iciest.  The international
system was cleft into two,dominated by two powerful and antagonistic blocs that had competing

socio-economic systems buttressed by military
pacts:  NATO, and the Warsaw Treaty Organisation.

Although Africa is geographically remote
from either of the super powers the cold war has
had reverbeations throughout the world.  Indeed,
from 1960 until 1964 the Congo (now Zaire) was
a major cold war theater.  Since the seventies
the cold war has moved from Europe to the Southern
hemisphere, especially from the Red Sea through
the Gulf to the Indian Ocean.  The heavy American
naval and military buildup in Diego Garcia in the
Indian Ocean has resulted from and reinforced
this development.  As a counter-measure the
Soviet Union has acquired some naval facilities
along the coast of Ethiopia and in Aden.  And
in turn this has been followed by the American
acquisition of naval bases in Kenya and Somalia.

In these circumstances, most African
countries have little choice other than to be
uncommitted to either of the cold war blocs.
It has to be remembered that the principle of
non-alignment is one of the principles enshrined in the Charter of the OAU.  It is true
that this principle for most of the 97 members
of the nonaligned movement means hardly more
than nonparticipation in either of the super-
power-led multilateral military alliances.
Most African states like their counterparts in
Asia and Latin America have tended in practice
to follow any brand of nonalignment which their
local circumstances permitted.  Thus, while
Kenya and Somalia with American bases claim to
be nonaligned, so does Ethiopia with a Soviet
base,  and so do Ghana and Nigeria without any
foreign military base.  Despite all this, however, it is assuredly the case that most African
states wish to remain independent of the super-
powers rather than being their satellites .  It
is this goal that has accounted for the efforts

of most African states to maintain cultural,
economic, military, political and technical ties
with both the East and the West. While because
of historical links and structural deficiencies
the bulk of their ties have remained with the
Western powers, it is also true that most of
them have since independence made conscious
efforts to establish some links with the Soviet
bloc countries and China.

From the above it is clear that Africa
is to a large extent dependent on the great
powers especially those in the West for economic,
financial and military assistance. However, in
some respects the African states have used their
numerical strength to put pressures on the powers
on issues that have been of primary concern to
them in particular and to the rest of the Third
World as a whole.

v)  Change in nature of relations since independence

In some areas Africa is more heavily dependent on the great powers today than at independence. This is true in the area of indebtedness as well as in the field of military assistance and technological transfer. Edem Kodjo,
the OAU Secretary-General, said in August 1981
that the external debt of Africa was over $43
billion which was over six times that of 1973.[14]
And, as pointed out earlier, there are more
expatriate experts working in Africa now than was
the case on independence. This can partly be
explained by the fact that many African states
want to speed up the rate of their socio-economic
development in a situation where there is a
dearth of local experts. Although more schools
and health facilities have been established,they
have been inadequate to support the rate of
development envisaged in different national development plans.

One of the tragic ironies of independence is that most African states have become more dependent on the great powers for the import of food than during the immediate years after independence.[15] Countries such as Cameroon, Kenya, Liberia, Nigeria, and Uganda that were self-sufficientin food on independence - and some were even exporting foodstuffs to other countries at the time-have since the early seventies become net importers of food. This is partly due to misrule, mismanagement, inefficiency and corruption, and partly due to natural disasters such as drought and famine.

In terms of commercial ties with the great powers there has been a slight change in the sense that most African states have been trying to diversify their trade and commercial ties as can be seen in Table One. Yet the bulk of Africa's trade has continued to be with the West. This is partly because of the nature of the African economy and partly because of the Lome Convention that has tied Africa to the EEC.[16]

In terms of military links Africa is perhaps more dependent on the great industrial powers today than on independence. This is partly because very few arms are produced in the continent and partly because of the pressing security requirements of some African countries such as Angola, Egypt, Ethiopia, Libya, Morocco, Mozambique, and Somalia. Even in this issue area, the Western powers have remained the largest suppliers of arms to Africa.

However, in the diplomatic sphere many African states have diversified their ties. But more connections still remain with the Western powers. For instance, there are more African diplomatic missions in the West than in the East and China.

Table 1  Africa's Trade with the Great Powers
(in million US dollars)

| TRADE WITH | ALGERIA | | | | LIBYA | | | |
|---|---|---|---|---|---|---|---|---|
| | 1961 | | 1975 | | 1961 | | 1975 | |
| | Imports | Exports | Imports | Exports | Imports | Exports | Imports | Exports |
| United Kingdom | 6.8 | 16.1 | 205.7 | 166.3 | 29.0 | 7.8 | 194.8 | 272.7 |
| % of world trade | 0.7 | 4.4 | 3.4 | 3.9 | 19.5 | 36.4 | 5.5 | 4.0 |
| France | 832.9 | 299.4 | 2,004.2 | 632.9 | 5.5 | .6 | 313.1 | 252.6 |
| % of world trade | 82.4 | 82.0 | 33.5 | 14.7 | 4.3 | 0.3 | 8.8 | 3.7 |
| West Germany | 10.7 | 10.6 | 695.8 | 816.8 | 19.5 | 1.0 | 429.9 | 1,331.1 |
| % of world trade | 1.08 | 3.0 | 11.6 | 19.0 | 13.5 | 4.5 | 12.1 | 19.5 |
| Japan | 2.0 | 1.4 | 220.2 | 38.9 | 2.9 | N.A. | 293.3 | 232.1 |
| % of world trade | 0.2 | 0.3 | 3.7 | 0.8 | 2.0 | N.A. | 8.3 | 3.4 |
| USSR | 7.3 | 1.3 | 73.8 | 96.6 | 1.5 | 0.6 | 22.3 | N.A. |
| % of world trade | 0.7 | 0.3 | 1.5 | 2.2 | 1.4 | 0.27 | 0.7 | N.A. |
| China | N.A. | N.A. | 26.2 | 33.9 | N.A. | N.A. | 71.5 | N.A. |
| % of world trade | N.A. | N.A. | 0.5 | 0.8 | N.A. | N.A. | 2.0 | N.A. |

(cont'd)

| TRADE WITH | IVORY COAST 1961 Imports | Exports | IVORY COAST 1975 Imports | Exports | SENEGAL 1961 Imports | Exports | SENEGAL 1975 Imports | Exports |
|---|---|---|---|---|---|---|---|---|
| United Kingdom | 3.7 | 3.6 | 38.0 | 29.2 | 2.8 | 3.3 | 22.6 | 22.9 |
| % of world trade | 2.6 | 2.3 | 3.4 | 2.5 | 1.9 | 2.4 | 2.3 | 4.5 |
| France | 108.0 | 91.3 | 440.5 | 320.0 | 103.1 | 94.4 | 290.2 | 207.2 |
| % of world trade | 70.1 | 51.4 | 39.1 | 27.1 | 66.4 | 75.7 | 30.5 | 31.5 |
| West Germany | 7.1 | 8.0 | 59.2 | 104.5 | 5.7 | 2.0 | 40.4 | 6.8 |
| % of world trade | 4.5 | 4.5 | 5.3 | 8.8 | 3.9 | 1.6 | 4.3 | 1.0 |
| Japan | 0.1 | 0.7 | 44.6 | 18.8 | N.A. | 1.2 | 5.8 | 7.3 |
| % of world trade | 0.07 | 0.4 | 4.0 | 1.6 | N.A. | 0.8 | 0.7 | 1.1 |
| USSR | N.A. | N.A. | 22.3 | 16.7 | N.A. | N.A. | 17.3 | N.A. |
| % of world trade | N.A. | N.A. | 1.10 | 1.4 | N.A. | N.A. | 2.0 | N.A. |
| China | N.A. | N.A. | 5.4 | N.A. | 3.3 | N.A. | 1.8 | 2.8 |
| % of world trade | N.A. | N.A. | 0.5 | N.A. | 1.9 | N.A. | 1.9 | 0.4 |

(cont'd)

| TRADE WITH | GHANA 1961 Imports | Exports | GHANA 1975 Imports | Exports | NIGERIA 1961 Imports | Exports | NIGERIA 1975 Imports | Exports |
|---|---|---|---|---|---|---|---|---|
| United Kingdom | 145.1 | 92.6 | 116.1 | 112.6 | 238.5 | 214.4 | 1,387.9 | 1,126.7 |
| % of world trade | 36.4 | 28.7 | 14.7 | 15.3 | 38.4 | 44.0 | 23.0 | 14.1 |
| France | 7.9 | 1.7 | 30.3 | 4.9 | 16.4 | 27.2 | 501.0 | 871.8 |
| % of world trade | 2.0 | 0.6 | 3.8 | 0.7 | 2.6 | 5.6 | 8.3 | 10.9 |
| West Germany | 30.2 | 39.8 | 90.0 | 66.6 | 46.2 | 37.1 | 882.2 | 542.8 |
| % of world trade | 7.5 | 12.4 | 11.4 | 9.0 | 7.4 | 7.6 | 14.6 | 6.8 |
| Japan | 30.9 | 4.6 | 5.13 | 57.8 | 85.0 | 9.4 | 595.1 | 279.6 |
| % of world trade | 7.8 | 1.6 | 6.5 | 7.8 | 13.7 | 1.9 | 9.9 | 3.5 |
| USSR | 6.2 | 8.6 | 8.2 | 55.1 | N.A. | N.A. | 24.4 | 121.4 |
| % of world trade | 1.5 | 2.8 | 1.0 | 7.5 | N.A. | N.A. | 0.4 | 1.5 |
| China | 2.4 | .2 | 15.5 | 12.5 | N.A. | N.A. | 69.9 | 7.9 |
| % of world trade | 0.5 | 0.6 | 2.0 | 1.7 | N.A. | N.A. | 1.2 | 0.10 |

(cont'd)

| TRADE WITH | KENYA 1961 Imports | KENYA 1961 Exports | KENYA 1975 Imports | KENYA 1975 Exports | TANZANIA 1961 Imports | TANZANIA 1961 Exports | TANZANIA 1975 Imports | TANZANIA 1975 Exports |
|---|---|---|---|---|---|---|---|---|
| United Kingdom | 85.4 | 26.1 | 187.1 | 60.4 | 33.3 | 49.2 | 107.1 | 47.2 |
| % of world trade | 34.3 | 22.2 | 20.5 | 13.2 | 36.5 | 34.8 | 14.9 | 13.7 |
| France | 6.8 | 1.2 | 25.9 | 3.9 | 1.9 | 2.4 | 11.4 | 2.5 |
| % of world trade | 2.8 | 0.9 | 2.9 | 0.8 | 2.3 | 1.4 | 1.6 | 0.7 |
| West Germany | 12.0 | 16.5 | 72.9 | 51.7 | 4.2 | 11.0 | 59.3 | 32.3 |
| % of world trade | 6.5 | 14.5 | 8.0 | 11.3 | 4.5 | 7.8 | 8.3 | 9.4 |
| Japan | 23.7 | 5.5 | 81.1 | 12.3 | 8.8 | 6.7 | 48.1 | 6.0 |
| % of world trade | 9.6 | 5.1 | 8.9 | 2.7 | 10.0 | 4.9 | 6.7 | 1.7 |
| USSR | N.A. | N.A. | N.A. | N.A. | N.A. | N.A. | 4.0 | 3.6 |
| % of world trade | N.A. | N.A. | N.A. | N.A. | N.A. | N.A. | 0.6 | 1.0 |
| China | N.A. | 0.1 | 3.8 | 3.8 | N.A. | N.A. | 79.0 | 15.1 |
| % of world trade | N.A. | 0.09 | 0.4 | 0.8 | N.A. | N.A. | 11.0 | 4.4 |

(cont'd)

| TRADE WITH | MOROCCO 1961 Imports | Exports | MOROCCO 1975 Imports | Exports | ZAMBIA 1961 Imports | Exports | ZAMBIA 1975 Imports | Exports |
|---|---|---|---|---|---|---|---|---|
| United Kingdom | 13.4 | 24.2 | 83.2 | 103.3 | N.A. | N.A. | 183.9 | 181.1 |
| % of trade with | 2.9 | 7.0 | 3.3 | 6.7 | N.A. | N.A. | 19.8 | 22.5 |
| France | 220.4 | 125.7 | 774.4 | 335.6 | N.A. | N.A. | 15.9 | 67.8 |
| % of trade with | 48.9 | 36.8 | 30.4 | 21.7 | N.A. | N.A. | 1.7 | 8.4 |
| West Germany | 23.8 | 39.8 | 203.7 | 100.7 | N.A. | N.A. | 68.2 | 14.4 |
| % of trade with | 5.3 | 11.7 | 8.0 | 6.5 | N.A. | N.A. | 7.3 | 14.2 |
| Japan | 2.0 | 2.4 | 30.1 | 35.4 | N.A. | N.A. | 83.3 | 141.3 |
| % of trade with | 0.4 | 0.6 | 1.3 | 1.6 | N.A. | N.A. | 9.0 | 17.6 |
| USSR | 4.1 | 4.6 | 73.6 | 46.0 | N.A. | N.A. | 0.1 | N.A. |
| % of trade with | 0.9 | 1.5 | 2.9 | 3.0 | N.A. | N.A. | 0.01 | N.A. |
| China | 8.7 | 3.8 | 27.8 | 6.4 | N.A. | N.A. | 26.5 | 20.1 |
| % of trade with | 2.0 | 1.2 | 1.0 | 0.4 | N.A. | N.A. | 2.9 | 2.5 |

Sources: UN Yearbook of International Trade Statistics, 1977, Volume 1 (New York, 1978. ST/ESA/STAT/SER.G/20).

IMF Direction of Trade, Volume 3, 1961-65 (Washington, 1965).

Yet in terms of political understanding and sympathy, most African states have tended to be closer to Soviet bloc countries and to China than to the Western powers. This is mainly because on issues that are of direct concern to Africa such as the questions of decolonization and the elimination of racism and apartheid from Southern Africa - all of which are essential features of African nationalism - the African states have continued to receive diplomatic, material, military, moral and political support from the Soviet Union, other East European countries and China. On the other hand, the Western powers have at best shown sympathy and verbal support, and at worst indifference and even outright support for the white supremacist regimes in South Africa and Namibia. The efforts of the Reagan administration to seek closer ties with South Africa and to abort UN Security Council Resolution 435 on Namibia have further worsened the relationship between most African states and the Western powers in general, and the US in particular.

Likewise, the intransigent attitudes and policies of the US towards the Palestinian Liberation Organization (PLO), and the right to a separate Palestinian homeland, as well as rather unlimited American support for Israel, have since 1973 gone a long way to poison America's relationship with most OAU member states. Conversely, the consistent support for, and the continuing encouragement of, the cause of the Arabs in the Middle East and North Africa have enhanced the prestige and the standing of the Soviet Union in many African capitals. Similarly, the uncompromising attitude of the US to demands from the Third World in the North-South dialogue since the early seventies has done much damage to the position of the US not only in Africa but also in most of the Third World countries.[17]

Strategically, until very recently, Africa was quite marginal to the great powers. However, with the theater of the cold war moving from Europe to the area stretching from the Red Sea through the Gulf to the Indian Ocean, Africa has become of considerable strategic importance. Apart from great power rivalry in the Horn of Africa and in the Indian Ocean, the fact that over 60 per cent of the West's oil supply from the Middle East has to pass around the Cape has given added strategic importance to the continent. Similarly, the fact that some scarce strategic goods of great importance to the Western powers such as antimony, chromium, platinum, uranium, vanadium and industrial diamonds are found in some African countries such as Namibia, South Africa, Zaire and Zimbabwe has served to underline the strategic importance of Africa to the powers.

Yet despite this strategic importance of Africa, most African states have chosen to remain nonaligned. Although questions may be raised about the nonalignment of those that have granted military bases to any of the great powers, the fact is that only a very few of them have allowed foreign military installations on their territories. Indeed, considerations of both domestic and external politics make the commitment to nonalignment more meaningful and sensible to African states than ever before.

From the above I can say that few changes have occured in the areas of commercial, cultural, economic, and technical ties of Africa with the great powers. However, in political-security matters some considerable changes have occurred. Unlike the immediate years after independence, the attitudes and policies of most African states to the powers have since the seventies been determined largely by the attitudes and policies of the great powers to issues that are of direct concern of Africa. The granting of facilities by some African states to some of the powers for the establishment of military installations dates back only to the seventies. This is also true of the introduction of extra-African troops and other military personnel into Africa.

vi) Future trends

It is not easy to speculate about the future of Africa's relation with the great powers. However, since the future is a function of the past and present in terms of social science analysis, I can say something about the likely future trends in the relationship.

Unless there is a major structural change in the socio-economic order of the African states, which seems unlikely in the foreseeable future, and unless the various regional and sub-regional economic groupings in Africa really become viable, the bulk of their cultural, economic, financial and technical ties will continue to be with the great powers especially with the Western powers. Indeed, for the foreseeable future, Africa may be more rather than less dependent on the great powers for capital and consumer goods and services to develop. Likewise, unless greater emphasis is given to agriculture in all its ramifications, the dependence of Africa on food imports from the powers will be greater in the foreseeable future than was the case before. As indicated earlier, the great powers too, are to some extent dependent on the African market for raw materials, including mineral and strategic goods, but also for their finished goods and services. This trend is likely to continue.

Unless there is a technological break-through on the continent, especially in military technology, Africa's dependence on the powers for the importation of military hardware will be greater in the immediate future. Indeed, given the explosive, and dangerous situation in Southern Africa and the frequent border conflicts in the rest of the continent - compounded at times by traditional hatreds and hostilities - and given the helplessness of the OAU to effect peaceful solutions to inter- and intra-African conflicts, the chances are great that more arms and ammunition will be imported from the powers by Africa than ever before.

Unless the strategic value and importance of Africa were to alter in a major way - which is unlikely in the foreseeable future - the great powers will continue to show a keen interest in Africa, especially in Central Africa, Southern Africa and the Eastern coast of Africa up to the Red Sea. In actual fact, given present trends, the US and the USSR are likely to increase their military presence in these areas, especially in the Indian Ocean. In such circumstances, there is very little the African states can do. They are too weak to halt or to restrict the military expansion of the super-powers into these areas. However, if revolutionary Marxist governments were to come to power in Kenya and Somalia, such regimes might switch from a pro-Western military posture to a pro-Soviet military stance. While this development might mean some change in the contest between the super-powers, it would make little difference to Africa. For if such regimes were to offer the USSR military bases it would only serve to maintain or even increase Africa's dependence on the great powers for their military requirements.

Largely as a result of colonial history, with its web of tangible and intangible ties with the West, the number of African diplomatic missions in the West will continue to be higher than that in the Soviet bloc countries and China.

However, there may be some change in
political relations in the future. For instance,
if the Western powers led by the US were to show
greater understanding of African problems such
as those of racism, _apartheid_, the Palestinian
question, poverty and disease, Africa's political
relations with the West might improve appreciably.
But on the contrary, if the Western powers were
to continue to show little or no regard for
African opinion, and were to see African issues
in the context of an East-West contest as
Ronald Reagan and Mrs. Thatcher have tended to do,
then Africa's political relationships with them
will sour further. Political relations with the
USSR and with other East European countries and
China would then be likely to grow stronger. For
the Communist countries have consistently
supported the African position on almost all the
issues that have been of direct relevance to
Africa. There is nothing to indicate that these
Communist countries will relent in their support
for African nationalism. Indeed, there is every
likelihood that they may increase their support
for African causes in the years ahead. If this
were to happen then the USSR and her allies and
China would enhance their prestige and position
in Africa further.

Though the foregoing analysis I have tried
to examine the nature of Africa's relationship
with the great powers, the extent to which this
has changed since 1960, and the likely trend in
the foreseeable future. What is clear is that
while in some issue areas Africa has been
heavily dependent on the great powers, it is also
true that the major industrial powers are dependent on the continent in some respects. I
speculate that in the foreseeable future some of
these relationships may change. But whatever
happens elsewhere it is clear that Africa and the
great powers will continue in the future to depend on each other in a world that is increasingly
becoming small and interdependent.

Notes

1. Sunday Telegraph (London), 14 December 1980.

2. Sunday Times (London), 20 June 1971.

3. F. S. Northedge The International Political System (London: Faber, 1976) 66.

4. Arnold Rivkin The African Presence in World Affairs (New York: Free Press, 1963) 244.

5. See Dennis Austin "Ex Africa Semper Eadem?" in Roger Morgan (ed) The Study of International Affairs (London: OUP, 1972) 156-174.

6. Northedge The International Political System 76.

7. It should be noted that the number of francophone states having military pacts with France has dropped sharply since 1960.

8. For details see Colin Legum (ed) Africa Contemporary Record: annual survey and documents, Volume 9, 1976-1977 (London: Rex Collings, 1977) C170 and C210.

9. See Martin M. McLaughlin et al. The US and World Development: agenda 1979 (New York: Praeger, 1979) 174.

10. "Africa: the crisis of development and the challenge of a new economic order. Address to the Fourth Meeting of the Conference of Ministers and Thirteenth Session of the ECA, Kinshasa, February-March 1977" (Addis Ababa: ECA, July 1977) 8.

11. The Punch (Lagos) 21 August 1981.

12. See Michael Leifer "South-East Asia" in

Christopher Clapham (ed) Foreign Policy-
Making in Developing States (Farnborough:
Saxon House, 1977) 25.

13. See Tom J. Farer "The US and the Third World:
a basis for accommodation" Foreign Affairs
54(1), October 1975, 79-97.

14. The Punch 21 August 1981.

15. For details see Hugh M. Arnold "Africa and
the New International Economic Order" Third
World Quarterly 2(2), April 1980, 295-304.

16. See Robert L. Rothstein The Weak in the
World of the Strong (New York: Columbia
University Press, 1977) 152.

17. The extent to which the intransigence of the
US under Nixon to issues that are dear to
the hearts of the Third World undermined
America's position was well dealt with by
Farer in his "The US and the Third World."
Unless the Reagan administration changes
its current policies and attitudes it will
succeed in doing greater damage to America's
standing in Africa and the rest of the Third
World.

Chapter Three

Decolonization:   towards a global perspective,
1940-1978

Gilbert A. Sekgoma


The debate over decolonization remains current in international relations, and may continue
to be lively for some time to come, because it lies
at the core of the relations between the industrialized and the developing countries.  Indeed, it
can be argued that the present center-periphery
dichotomy is but a major feature of the process of
decolonization that took place in the last three
decades (1940-1970) following a century or more of
integration into the world capitalist system.  The
global economic negotiations that have taken place
under different titles, and are still continuing,
are but moderate attempts to remedy international
inequalities (which intensified after political decolonization) and thus bring about international
economic interdependence (i.e. economic decolonization).  Whether these ideals will eventually be
realized remains an open question in international
relations.

As used in this chapter, "decolonization"
designates the transfer of political power to the
local bourgeoisie of the various colonies who could
be trusted to preserve and/or extend some of the
colonial relationships, either with the former
colonial powers in particular or with international
capital in general.  In a word, the concept "decolonization" as conceived by the colonial powers was
limited to self-government.  Therefore, it may be
appropriate to contend that decolonization actually
means the creation of neo-colonial relationships
with former colonies.  It means, more or less, a
return to pre-colonial style informal control relationships, since the colonial powers in many ways
continue to influence and dominate the politico-

economic policies of their former colonies, albeit
to different degrees.

However, subsequent developments in the former colonies have affected the broadening of the
definition of the concept of decolonization to
embrace the economic aspect of independence. Thus,
at the international level, the concept of decolonization implies the transfer of both political
and economic independence through negotiations in
global forums such as the United Nations (UN),
United Nations Conference on Trade and Development
(UNCTAD), the New International Economic Order
(NIEO) and the North-South Dialogue. In other
words, in theory, decolonization envisages equality
and international interdependence as the ultimate
goal. Technically, however, the real or effective
political and economic independence of the former
colonies or the so-called Third World or underdeveloped countries appears to be inconceivable
given their present dependence on and integration
into the global capitalist economy. The present
peripheral status of the Third World stems from
the kind of political decolonization which took
place after the end of the war, in which Third
World economies were left conditioned by developments in the metropolis and/or the international
economic system.[1]

This chapter is designed to provide a purview of the processes of decolonization from the
1940s-1970s from an international perspective. An
attempt will be made to situate the origins of progressive colonial policies within the broader context of changes in superpower configurations in
the global economy. Emphasis will be laid on the
United States' pressure on Britain to relinquish
the empire; on the impact of the Second World War;
on the Anglo-French economies; and on the emergence
of Pax Americana, through the establishment of the
Bretton Woods system after the war and into the
1970s. Last, though by no means least, the impact
and results of the mainstream of nationalist forces

in the Third World will be considered.

The chapter concludes with an examination of
the results of decolonization in the Third World.
The major argument in the conclusion is that, given
the character and nature of the global capitalist
economy, economic decolonization through the
various international economic forums aimed at
equitable participation (production and distribution) in the international economy is doomed to
failure.  Any substantial successes in such negotiations would, in my view, be tantamount to the
destruction of the capitalist economic system;
this will not be tolerated by the central capitalist countries and corporations.  To date, history
has shown the futility of such global negotiations,
though some people - especially national elements
within the transnational bougeoisie - still have
faith in them.  The best that can be achieved in
these international forums will be marginal com-
promises between the Third World states and the
industralized countries, and the current tempo of
negotiations will continue for some time to come
if the Third World continues to seek changes within the system through the decolonization approach.

It would appear that the only option open to
the Third World states, if they want to develop
meaningfully,is disengagement from the
capitalist economy.  To be effective, this disengagement has to be accompanied by a qualitative
ideological reorientation and a clear definition
of new strategies for restructuring the economy.
To this extent the new system will have as its
objective the introduction of self-reliant economies geared towards the needs of the people.  However, since some of the countries may be less endowed with economic resources, it will be essential
to form regional groupings and functional structures to facilitate commodity exchanges at parity.

a) American and metropolitan perspectives on decolonization

        The historiography of colonial politics in-
dicates that the colonial powers - that is, Britain
and France - had no straightforward colonial policies for the dissolution of their respective
empires before the end of the Second World War.[2]
Most of the informed studies of the period are particularly illuminating on the impact of the de-
pression of the 1930s and the protectionist economic strategies which were pursued by these imperial
powers. From this particular period onwards the
colonial empires became even more significant to
the metropolitan economies of the colonial powers.[3]
Evidently, the continuation of such linkages was
more than desirable; they were seen to be essential
by the central countries. Britain and France
wanted to continue monopolizing the markets and
resources available in their respective colonies.

        In contradistinction to this imperial per-
spective was the American predilection for the
elimination of colonialism and, moreover, the
liquidation of the Imperial Preferences concluded
in 1933.[4] This view was popularly held by the
Roosevelt administration in the early 1940s.[5]
President Roosevelt also believed that the continued existence of the empires would be a possible cause of future world wars. Thus he tried
to bring pressure to bear upon the imperial powers
to decolonize.[6] It would appear, however, that
Roosevelt was more interested in opening up the
empires to American capital than in advancing
order and development. This basic interest even
found expression in the pages of the famous
Atlantic Charter, concluded and signed by the
American President Roosevelt and the British Prime
Minister Winston Churchill.[7]

        Among the ideals of the Atlantic Charter
was the principle which called for "the respect
of the rights of all people to choose the form of

government under which they will live." Paradoxically, however, the Americans had hoped to use
this clause to pressurize Britain into decolonizing
the empire; hence the diametrically-opposed inter-
pretation of it by the signatories of the Charter.
Whereas the Americans entertained the view that
this principle applied to all humanity,[8] the view
in London was far from the above, just as London
is far from Washington. For the British, the
official perspective was that the principles of
the Charter applied only to European nations who
had been disorganized by the war and not to the
colonial peoples outside of Europe.[9] This view
was made clear by Churchill in person on two occasions. In October 1941 he maintained in the
House of Commons that:

> The Joint Declaration does not qualify
> in any way the various statements of
> policy which have been made from time
> to time about the development of con-
> stitutional governments in Burma, India
> or other parts of the British Empire.[10]

In November 1942, Churchill further clarified the
above policy posture at the Guildhall in London
in the following words:

> Let me however, make this clear in
> case there should be any mistake in
> any quarter. We mean to hold what
> we own. I have not become the King's
> First Minister in order to preside
> over the liquidation of the British
> Empire.[11]

Roger Louis contends that parliament strongly
supported Winston Churchill's view and resolved
that Britain would hold fast to her colonial
responsibilities.[12]

This view from Downing Street did not
impress U.S. State Department officials, who
desired to see the colonial empires set on the

road to independence or self-government along with the eventual abolition of all trade discriminatory measures. In a word, the United States anti-colonial policy was not so much motivated by genuine democratic principles as by her broader economic determinants. The need for areas of capital expansion, consumer markets and sources of raw materials was the prime motto behind her anti-colonial policy, and officials of the U.S. State and Treasury Departments were more than determined to see it succeed.[13] As a result, a number of strategies were used to pressurize and blackmail the colonial powers, particularly Britain, into decolonizing the empire and cooperating in the establishment of a multilateral global regime.

To achieve the above objectives, a two-pronged strategy was formulated. The first strategy had to do with the policies and structures which the U.S. wanted Britain to abandon. These included the abolition of preferential tariffs concluded in 1933, and the liquidation of the system of dollar pooling among the Sterling Area countries.[14] All the countries in the Sterling Area had acted in unison to reduce their dollar expenditures by discriminating against U.S. goods.

The second strategy involved adroit diplomatic manipulation of Britain into accepting the construction of a multilateral world economy.[15] In the early years of the war (1941), the U.S. Treasury attempted to maneuver Britain into commitments to end all trade discrimination against the U.S. as a quid pro quo for lend-lease aid to the Commonwealth amounting to thirty billion pounds sterling (£30 billion), of which twenty seven billion pounds sterling (£27 billion) was to go to Britain.[16] Unfortunately, the latter strategy did not succeed because Britain strongly resisted any commitments which proved inconsistent with the system of Imperial Preferences. Thus the most Britain could do at the time to accept participation in discussions of a more liberal world economy.[17] Britain also resisted U.S. demands that she should formulate specific timetables for setting the empire on the road to self-government.[18]

However, the British government could not remain forever impervious to U.S. demands to devolve political power to the colonies. Somehow, the British government had to accommodate American anti-colonial sentiments. A number of reasons go a long way to explain the imperative of such an accommodationist policy towards the U.S. Besides lend-lease, which the State Department used as a lever in diplomatic contacts with Britain, there was the impact of the war which was gnawing badly at the Anglo-French economies.[19]

By 1943 this problem was causing serious concern to the officials of the foreign office. Louis notes that Gladwyn Jebb and Cadogan came to grips with the reality of forging common ground with the Americans in order to secure further financial aid in the future. This required breaking the intransigence of the Colonial Office. Subsequently, as a result of U.S. anti-colonial sentiments, backed by lend-lease arrangements, pressure was brought to bear upon the Colonial Office to introduce a progressive colonial policy for decolonization. Ronald Robinson captures this particular turning point well:

> Nothing strengthened the case for colonial reform in Whitehall so much as this American scare for the British Empire now hung to a large extent on the whim of the United States of America.[20]

Apparently, as a consequence of the above developments, the Secretary of State for Colonies, Colonel Oliver Stanley, issued a general policy statement in 1943 that some African colonies would achieve "self-government as soon as possible", probably after sixty to eighty years.[21] This statement was soon followed by Williams' plan for colonial self-government.[22] The Plan was, however, general and non-commital.

A related development was the introduction
of the Colonial Development and Welfare Act, approved by parliament in 1945.  Through this Act,
Stanley managed to squeeze £ 120 million from the
Chancellor of the Exchequer for post-war colonial
development.[23]  Paradoxically, however, Stanley's
1943 policy statement and Williams' Plan for colonial self-government did not create a positive impression on U.S. State Department officials about
the commitment of Britain to lead the empire to
self-government.[24]  As noted above, neither the
colonial secretary's policy statement nor Williams'
plan were very specific.

As also indicated above, U.S. policy embraced both the French and British empires,though
attention was concentrated on the latter.  The
belief entertained by State Department officials
was that if Britain could be convinced to set her
colonies on the road to political independence and
to transform the Commonwealth into an "Open Door
Economy"  then it would be much easier to draw
other colonial powers into the same system of a
liberal world economy.[25]  This explains why, up to
1944, the French government still considered its
overseas colonies to be integral parts or consti-
tuents of the Republic.

This official French perspective was given
expression at the Brazzaville Conference held in
early 1944.[26]  The conference concentrated on what
was thought the "only possible path of future
political development for the African populations
- that is, the integration of the colonial peoples
within the French Community".  One of the influential French delegates inspired the Conference participants to have

...the will to take into our hands
and above all, without sharing anything whatsoever with any anonymous
institution the immense, but chal-
lenging responsibilities we have
vis-a-vis those who live under the
Flag. In colonial France, there are
no people to liberate, no racial
discrimination to abolish. The overseas populations do not want any
kind of independence other than of
France.[27]

Thus any possibility of decolonizing the
French empire was shelved. As L. H. Gann and
Peter Duignan concluded, "the eventual constitu-
ional development, even in the far-off future,
for self-government in the colonies is out of
question".[28] The other reason why U.S. State
Department officials did not bother much with
France was probably due to the fact that France
had been defeated in the war. They assumed,there-
fore, that she would be easier to manipulate once
Britain was won over.

b) After the war: retreat from decolonization

However, by 1944, the apparently vigorous
American pressure on Britain to decolonize its
empire had shifted towards supporting its preservation. Moreover, U.S. rhetorical support for
nationalism in the colonies had receded to the lowest ebb.[29] A number of reasons account for this
policy restraint.

First, the apparent change in American anti-
colonial policy appears to have been a response to
changes in the global balance of power. The end
of the Second World War witnessed the emergence of
the Soviet Union at a socialist superpower in
Eastern Europe, opposed to the capitalist system.
Coupled with the latter was the spread of communism
into countries flanking the Soviet Union. In addition to the above, was the dissemination of social-

ist propaganda against capitalism in the Western
metropolis as well as the colonial empires.[30]   In
a word, a wartime ally had turned into an arch-
enemy.  This development was seen to pose grave
danger for the very survival of the capitalist
system so dear to the Americans.  Reflecting on
this change in the superpower configuration, David
Horowitz has aptly observed that;

> While the First World War was climaxed
> by a union of victorious powers who
> organized and presided over a post-
> war settlement, the close of the Second
> World War witnessed a dramatic and un-
> precedented reversal of alliances in
> the West, with the former enemies be-
> coming intimate allies.[31]

Thus the U. S. thought it had to protect the Western world from the threat of communism.

    And second by 1944 it had become evident
that the U. S. would emerge as the other super-
power in the post-war world.  She had not suffered
the devastating consequences of the war; rather,
she had achieved further industrialization during
the war-time period and her economy was booming.[32]
As a result, she could use other measures to influence both economic and political changes in the
post-war world.  After all, Britain had been crip-
pled as a super-power by the same event,and thus
she could be easily manipulated through financial
arrangements.

    Most of the American designs were achieved
through the conclusion of the Bretton Woods agreement towards the end of 1944, though Britain only
signed it towards the end of 1945.[33]   The other
constraining factor had to do with the American
desire to occupy the Pacific Islands for strategic
considerations.  This serves to explain America's
tolerance for a return to the status quo in the Far
East.  Thus British authority was restored in Burma
and Malaya and the French re-occupied Indo-China.[34]

Ironically, following the end of the war,
Britain, unlike the Americans, was more determined
than ever to decolonize its empire.  Developments
during and after the war partly explain this quite
radical change in colonial policy.  Louis points
out that by 1945 Britain's power was greatly undermined by two developments:  notably, the development of air technology and the invention of atomic
weapons.[35]  Coupled with these developments was
the emergence and intensification of nationalism
in Asia, Greece and Turkey, and the possibility of
it spilling over into Africa.  This watershed
period of the 1940s marked the final decline of
British power and did not escape the observant eye
of Clement Attlee:

> ...the British Empire was the creation
> of sea power.  Quite apart from the
> advent of atomic bomb which affected
> all considerations of strategic area,
> the British Commonwealth and the empire
> is not a unit that can be defended
> by itself...  With the advent of air
> warfare, the conditions which made it
> possible to defend a string of posses-
> sions scattered over five continents
> by means of a fleet based on island
> fortresses have gone.[36]

The above quotation indicates that Britain was no
longer the master of the world and could no longer
afford to protect her empire given the new equation
in the balance of power.

Another development which prevented Britain
from influencing European diplomacy and post-war
settlement was the position of the British economy
at the end of the war.[37]  By 1945, the British
economy was almost completely shattered.  A commen-
tator with a keen eye on its precarious position
noted:

We emerge from the struggle with a
distorted economy:   with an enormous
burden of external debt and a balance
of payment problem such as we have
never before had to face.  The system
of international economic collaboration to be established now must pro-
foundly affect our ability to play
any useful part  in the affairs of
the post-war world and may even involve our standards of life.  We must
determine our course of policy not in
relation to this particular plan or
that, but upon a review of the situation as a whole.[38]

Richard Gardner in his informed study of "Anglo-
American Collaboration in the Reconstruction of
Multilateral Trade" points out that by the end of
the war Britain had lost £7,300 million from her
total national wealth of £30,000 million.  In
addition, British exports had dropped to a third
of their pre-war level.  Moreover, Britain's
balance of payments deficit had reached a record
of £545 million, and a dollar deficit of U.S.
$2,646 million.[39]

In contradistinction to Britain's gloomy
picture was the rosy position of the U.S. economy
at the end of the war.  By 1945 the U. S. had
achieved massive industrial expansion and its
national output had more than doubled.  U. S.
military strength had also greatly improved. These
disequilibria in the economies of the industrialized capitalist world in favour of the U.S. meant
that she had to assume the leadership, economically,
militarily and politically over Britain and other
imperial states.  Samir Amin could not have been
more correct when he observed:

> The Second World War not only altered
> the relations of strength among the
> great powers as the First World War
> had done, but also set up a new fun-
> damental hierarchy in which the U.S.
> henceforth played a part out of all
> proportion to that played by other
> great powers of the West.[40]

So the weakened position of the British economy
and changes in the super-power configuration more
than anything else determined the direction and
impetus of imperial policies for decolonization.

The influence of the United States on
Britain became even more pronounced when Britain
had to depend on U.S. aid to resuscitate its shattered economy. France, Portugal and Belgium were
also brought into the nexus of U.S. policy through
the Marshall Plan for the Reconstruction of Europe.[41]
It should be pointed out that the smaller colonial
powers were not initially the major targets of U.S.
policy. As indicated above, the belief entertained
by the State Department was that those countries
would easily follow the direction of the major
powers, especially Britain.[42]

c)  U.K.-U.S. asymmetry and ambivalence

Following the end of the war, the Labour
Party in Britain was swept into power at the 1945
polls and decided to secure financial aid from the
United States.[43] The Labour government sought a
substantial loan in the form of grants-in-aid or
at best an interest-free loan amounting to U.S.
$6 billion. In the negotiations that ensued from
September to December 1945 it became evident to
the British delegates led by John Maynard Keynes
that U.S. negotiators under Fred Vinson were not
prepared either to grant Britain such a substantial loan in the form of grants-in-aid let alone
an interest-free loan. The U. S. team argued that
Congress would not listen to the idea of an interest-

free loan, let alone a grant-in-aid.[44]

      Nevertheless, the American negotiators seized upon this loan as a diplomatic lever to get Britain to open the empire for free trade. Moreover, the best the Americans could do was to give Britain a loan reduced to U.S. $3.75 billion at 2 per cent interest, on condition that Britain i) accepted the principles of the Bretton Woods system[45] and ii) introduced progressive changes in its colonial policy. Gardner observed that the above American stance had a strong backing of American businesses and public opinion, both of whom desired the elimination of the Imperial Preferences established in 1933. A concerned correspondent wrote to one of the U.S. negotiators:

> If you succeed in doing away with
> Empire Preferences and opening up
> the Empire to U.S. commerce, it may
> well be that we can afford to pay a
> couple of billion dollars for the
> privilege.[46]

A report prepared by a special committee of the U.S. House of Representatives emphasized that:

> A prerequisite to the granting of a
> large scale loan to England would be
> the removal of discriminatory treat-
> ment of quotas, exchange controls
> and tarrif preferences.[47]

      Britain, badly in need of financial assistance, was more than vulnerable to such U.S. pressure. Subsequently, in December 1945, the Financial Agreement was signed, embracing almost all the principles of the Bretton Woods system, which literally introduced an "Open Door Economic System" into the so-called "British" empire.

      The completion of the Bretton Woods system with Britain's admission marked the emergence of Pax Americana and signalled simultaneously the

beginning of the end of colonial empire(s). Thus
from 1946 onwards the colonial powers, particularly
Britain and France, were busy propounding policies
to devolve political power to their colonies.[48]
Coupled with the above development, was the emergence of nationalism, which in many ways acted as
a catalyst to this emerging trend and thus short -
ened the official perspective on the process of
decolonization. In anticipation of nationalist
uprising, Britain decided to hurry along policy
formulations for decolonization.

The reality of the situation, however, was
that the British economy, and indeed the French
one too, could not afford to meet the expense of
suppressing African nationalism. Britain actually
had had to capitulate to the nationalists in
Greece and Turkey in 1947.[49] As a result, from
the 1950s to the 1970s, many parts of the colonial
empires gained self-government, or "independence",
although the economic linkages with the metropoles
were continued albeit in different degrees: the
former French colonies tended to be more dominated
by France compared with the British ones. The end
result in both cases however, was the creation of
neo-colonial states whose economies and cultures
were and still are dominated by the metropoles or
at least are conditioned to serve the economic
interests of international capital.

The significance of the Bretton Woods
system (1945-1973) on the political economies of
the colonial powers and the contribution of
nationalist forces to the direction of post-war
colonial policies have been dealt with at length
by other scholars and thus should not detain us
here. However, because of their contribution to
the theme of this chapter, it is necessary to
briefly capture their essence separately.

d)   The Bretton Woods system

As indicated, the signing of the Bretton
Woods system marked the emergence of Pax Americana

at the global level. The U.S. dominated the policy
formulations under Bretton Woods and tended to
divert the system's purpose from that originally
intended to a liberalizing mission.[50] The very
introduction of a multilateral regime undermined
the major purpose of colonial possessions; that is,
exclusive bilateral monopolies of the colonial
powers. The days of imperial monopolies were thus
swept away and in their place a multilateral regime
was introduced for the world system. Ironically,
this was made possible by a proponderance of U.S.
influence in the political economies of the Western
world.

        In the major institutions of Bretton Woods
- which were and still are not characterized by
one country - one vote structures - U.S. voting
strength uses and still is proportionately higher
than that of other members.[51] At their inception,
the distribution of votes in the I.M.F. and the
World Bank was as follows: U.S.A. 27.83%, U.K.
13.33%, China 5.79%, France 5.54% and lastly India
with 4.28%. This preponderance of American votes
gave it a diplomatic arsenal not only to influence the discussions of the Fund and Bank but
thereby also to determine the direction of the
cpaitalist economic system as a whole. To this
extent, colonial empires were to be brought to an
end and thus open the way for the expansion of
American capital in particular or international
capital in general. In summing up this new U.S.
dominance in the political economy of the Western
World, W. M. Scammell wrote:

        In the years which were to follow the
        United States was to remain a pacemaker
        in international monetary affairs. In
        the Bretton Woods system,through the
        I.M.F., in the stabilization and recon-
        struction problems of the immediate post-
        war period, through the European Re-
        covery Programme, in the tariff bar-
        gaining of G.A.T.T. and the Kennedy
        Round, and in the extension of the

I.M.F. at the 1967 conference at Rio
de Janeiro, the United States has been
a central and leading participant.[52]

Operationally, however, the Bretton Woods
system was in abeyance from 1945-1959. It could
not start working until full convertibility of the
major currencies (sterling, the deutsch-mark, the
franc and the U.S. dollar) was achieved. This was
realized in December 1958 and the U.S. dollar from
then until 1971 became the key currency in international transactions. The decade of the 1960s
thus provided a testing ground for the operation
of the new international financial system dominated
by the United States. Although the system seemed
to work up to the late 1960s or early 1970s, it
was being challenged by a number of developments,
such as:

i)   the devaluation of the pound sterling (a
second key currency) in November 1967;

ii)  lack of confidence in both sterling and
dollars after 1967 (there was a propensity on the
part of the major holders of international balances
to seek security outside these key currencies);

iii) huge U.S. trading deficits which indicated an
overvaluation of the dollar, leading major trading
countries to disengage from the system and float
their currencies;

iv)  an unsustainable drain on the U.S. gold reserves from encashment of surplus dollar balances
abroad;

v)   a widening gap between real and monetary
prices which made the gold exchange standard im-
practicable; and

vi)  U.S. domination being challenged by the emergence of the EEC grouping of the nine (now ten)
states as well as by the expansion of the Japanese
economy; Pax Americana was now operating in an

anarchic international financial arrangement.[53]
However, up to the present the system has seemed
to have operated in anarchy. But it does continue
to exist and the leading industrial powers, which
continue to dominate the I.M.F. and the World Bank,
are apparently still benefitting from the system.

In conclusion, it is important to note that
the U.S., through the Bretton Woods system and bilateral financial aid, manipulated the former colonial powers into i) devolving political power to
the colonies, however nominal, and ii) opening up
the Commonwealth and the other empires to a multilateral economy. It has been argued that although
the Bretton Woods system has been challenged by
other developments, it still lingers on and is
still dominated by the United States.

e)   Nationalism

In considering the contribution of nationalist forces to the process of decolonization,
emphasis will be limited to the general currents
of the mainstream rather than to any specifics.
It is hoped that such an approach will be broad
enough to encompass the wide diversity of the
nationalist activities in the various colonies.
In summarizing the movement and impact of the
mainstream of the Third World nationalism or revolution, I will quote in extenso from Kenneth Koma's
celebrated Pamphlet No. 1.

What then was the character and impact of
the Third World nationalism or revolution? The
initial and basic factor in the development of
nationalism in the colonies in general was without
doubt:

i)   the oppressive and exploitative colonial
situation.[54] This system was first ruptured by
the October Revolution which was such a major
breach in the capitalist system of world domination. Indeed the declaration of the Communist
Worker Parties issued in 1960 was most pertinent

when it observed that:

> --the October Socialist revolution
> aroused the East and drew the colonial
> peoples into the common current of the
> world-wide revolution. This develop-
> ment was greatly facilitated by the
> Soviet Union's victory in the Second
> World War, the establishment of the
> people's democracy in a number of
> European and Asian countries, the
> triumph of Socialist Revolution in
> China and the formation of the Social-
> ist System.[55]

ii) The slogan of the right of nations to self-
determination, a slogan first launched by the
Bolsheviks, the tactics and strategy for waging
a successful struggle against oppression and the
general influence and results of the Socialist
revolution as it affected the peoples of the East,
gave all the oppressive colonial peoples of Asia,
Africa and Latin America inspiration and determination to overthrow colonialism.

iii) The heroic struggle of the Chinese people,
the wars in Indo-China etc., could not but con-
comitantly accelerate the tempo and intensity of
the struggle against colonial domination in Asia,
Africa and Latin America. The colonial peoples
who participated in the Second World War learnt
the strategies and tactics used by the people of
Indo-China, Burma and Malaya in their wars of
independence. Subsequently, the Algerians took
up arms against the French soon after the end of
the War. The resultant protracted struggle of the
Algerians facilitated the freedom of Tunisia,
Morocco and francophone West Africa, thereby pre-
cipitating an official re-evaluation. In consequence the ill-fated French Community came into
being with a multiplicity of puppet republics.
France could not afford to suppress nationalist
forces on four fronts simultaneously; that is, in
Morocco, Algeria, Tunisia and West Africa.

iv)  Nationalist activities in Ghana and Nigeria
which precipitated independence and later those in
Guinea-Conakry  made almost impossible the continued existence of the French Community.  The independence of Ghana deserves special emphasis. After
achieving independence, Ghana became the cornerstone of the African revolution and the hub of the
Pan-African movement; thus the struggle for independence continued throughout Africa.  And,

v)  The peasant uprising in Kenya under the leadership of Dedan Kimati, an ex-serviceman in Asia,
dealt a blow to white domination in East Africa
and quickened the independence of Tanzania and
Kenya.  The independence of East Africa inspired
the peoples of Malawi, Zambia and Zimbabwe to
resist the imperialist-imposed federation.[56]

    It should be pointed out however, that
nationalists in the various colonies did not simply
import the dynamics of the mainstream.  For
struggle to be effective, it was essential to make
it indigenous; that is the struggle had to draw its
motive force from the concrete local situation and
only inspiration from the general currents of the
mainstream of the Third World revolution.  Thus
the decade of the 1960s witnessed the achievement
of self-government in the majority of the colonies,
save Angola, Mozambique and Zimbabwe which had to
liberate themselves later through the revolutionary
process.

    The delay of independence in the above
three states was due to a number of factors.  Key
among these factors was the interests of international capital.  In Angola, the Cabinda oil enclave was the major attraction and, of course,
cheap labour was central in both Angola and Mozambique.  With regards to Zimbabwe the situation was
the same:  its fertile land, favourable climate
and strategic chrome as well as other minerals
made Britain in particular and international
capital at large suppress nationalist activities
until the people effectively took up arms to pros-

ecute a revolutionary war of liberation. Angola
and Mozambique achieved independence in 1975 and
1974 respectively and Zimbabwe came last in 1980.
The struggle continues in Namibia.

f)    Conclusion

It may now be appropriate to examine the
results of the decolonization process in the Third
World in general in order to ascertain whether the
masses received their own indigenous version of
independence or whether a foreign variant of independence was imposed by the colonial powers in
collaboration with the local bourgeoisie:   the
limits of decolonization.

In most countries, decolonization resulted
in the creation of neo-colonial states which were
integrated into the global capitalist economic
system.[57]   The economies of Third World states continue to be dominated by the metropoles.   Another
observable symptom of this center-periphery paradox
manifests itself in unequal exchange between the
primary commodities of the Third World and the manufactured products of the industrialized countries.
These inequalities at the international level are
also reflected in disparity in the distribution of
wealth in the Third World.   The result has been the
intensification of class differentiation.[58]   In a
word, independence for the majority of the people
was in practice a great deal different from the content of the slogans which had mobilized the peasants
and workers and inspired sacrifices in the hope of
a better future.

Up to the present, most    Third World
political leaders have not made any meaningful
efforts to restructure their political economies.
This apparent reluctance to undertake measures
aimed at restructuring their economies may be due
to the fact that they are powerless within the
global economy.   Or it may well be that they share
with international capital some of the benefits
derived from a dependency relationship, albeit

asymmetrically.

The reality of the situation, however, is
that the political decolonization of the Third
World states and further integration into the
global economy has deepened these states' impover-
ishment. Attempts through global economic negotiations to remedy this situation as indicated,
have been going on from 1964 (UNCTAD 1) or even
earlier. But these do not seem to be yielding the
desired results, at least not from the Third World
point of view. The industralized countries have
not been, and still are not, prepared to effect any
changes in the international economic system. As
pointed out, such changes may jeopardize the
latters' continuing lucrative positions within the
global economy. Indeed, the achievements of these
international negotiations, insofar as terms of
trade with the Third World are concerned, cast a
rather gloomy picture, though they will ensure the
supply of primary commodities to the global economic system. Given this asymmetrical equation,
which in many ways is detrimental to the Third
World economies, the only viable solution appears
to be disengagement from the capitalist system[59]
accompanied by an ideological reorientation of
society and the development of interdependent self-
reliant economies in the Third World, especially
in Africa.

63

Notes

1. Immanuel Wallerstein, "The three stages of African involvement in the world economy" in Peter C. Gutkind and Immanuel Wallerstein (eds.) The Political Economy of Contemporary Africa (Beverly Hills:  Sage Publications, 1976) 48.

2. Henri Grimal, Decolonization:  the British, Dutch and Belgium Empires 1919-1963 (London:  Routledge and Kegan Paul, 1978) 291.  Also see Andrew Cohen, British Policy in Changing Africa (London:  Routledge and Kegan Paul, 1959) 27.

3. Ronald Robinson, "Sir Andrew Cohen:  the pro-consuls of African nationalism" in L. H. Gann and Peter Duignan (eds) African Proconsuls (New York:  Free Press, 1978) 355.

4. Roger Louis, Imperialism at Bay, 1941-1943: the United States and the decolonization of the British Empire (Oxford:  Clarendon, 1977) 243.

5. ibid 1 and 7.

6. ibid 9.

7. ibid 5.

8. ibid

9. ibid

10. ibid 123.

11. ibid 200.

12. ibid 201.

13. W. M. Scammell, International Monetary Policy: Bretton Woods and After (New York: Wiley, 1975) 10.

14.  Fred L. Block, The Origins of the International
     Economic Disorder (Berkeley:  University of
     California Press, 1977) 57.

15.  ibid 58.

16.  Richard N. Gardner, The Sterling-Dollar Dip-
     lomacy (Oxford:  Clarendon, 1956) 170.

17.  Block, The Origins of the International Eco-
     nomic Disorder, 57.

18.  Louis, Imperialism at Bay, 9.

19.  Gardner, The Sterling-Dollar Diplomacy, 178
     and 309.

20.  Robinson, "Sir Andrew Cohen," 356.

21.  Hansard, Colonel Oliver Stanley, 13 July 1943.

22.  C.O. 5541/132727; O.R.G. Williams, Memo,
     July 1943.

23.  George Padmore, Africa:  Britain's Third
     Empire (New York: Negroe Universities Press,
     1969) 157.

24.  Louis, Imperialism at Bay, 393.

25.  Block, The Origins of the International
     Economic Disorder, 59.

26.  Grimal, Decolonization, 125.

27.  ibid.

28.  Quoted in ibid 126; also see L.H. Gann and
     Peter Duignan (eds) Colonialism in Africa,
     Volume 2 (Cambridge:  University Press, 1970)
     253.

29.  Louis, Imperialism at Bay, 555.

30. David Horowitz, _Imperialism and Revolution_ (London: Allen Lane, 1969) 181.

31. _ibid_.

32. Gardner, _The Sterling-Dollar Diplomacy_, 178.

33. _ibid_ 199.

34. Louis, _Imperialism at Bay_, 555.

35. _ibid_ 549.

36. _ibid_.

37. _The Times_ (London), 5 July 1945.

38. _ibid_.

39. Gardner, _The Sterling-Dollar Diplomacy_ 178.

40. Samir Amin, _Accumulation on a World Scale: a critique of the theory of underdevelopment, Volumes 1 and 2_ (New York: Monthly Review, 1974) 104.

41. This started in 1948 as a grouping of European countries in receipt of Marshall Aid, or the European Payments Union formed in 1950.

42. Gardner, _The Sterling-Dollar Diplomacy_, 18-20 and 40-47. Also see Block, _The Origins of the International Economic Disorder_, 56.

43. Gardner, _The Sterling-Dollar Diplomacy_, 189.

44. _ibid_ 188.

45. _ibid_ 191.

46. Quoted in _ibid_ 197.

47. _ibid_ 198.

48. Ivor Thomas, Minute, November 1946. Quoted in Robinson, "Sir Andrew Cohen," 357.

49. Gardner, The Sterling-Dollar Diplomacy, 344.

50. Scammell, International Monetary Policy, 115.

51. ibid.

52. ibid 11.

53. ibid 237.

54. Frantz Fanon, The Wretched of the Earth (New York: Grove Press, 1968) 252.

55. Quoted in Kenneth Koma, Pamphlet No. 1 (Mahalapye, 1976) 10.

56. ibid 9-12.

57. Amin, Accumulation on a World Scale, 262.

58. Andre Gunder Frank, Capitalism and Under-development in Latin America (New York: Monthly Review, 1967) 258.

59. A number of studies have been done on global economic forums. In most of them the con-clusions indicate that to date nothing has been achieved and neither is there a pos-sibility that those global forums (UNCTAD, NIEO and North-South Dialogues, etc.) will bring any meaningful changes in the present arrangement of the global economy. These studies include the following: Samir Amin, "UNCTAD IV and the New International Economic Order", Africa Development 1 (1), 1976, 5-20; David H. Pollock, "Pearson and UNCTAD: a com-parison," International Development Review (1970/4) 14-21; Sidney Dell, "Retrospect and Prospect" in Annual Review of the United Nations Affairs, 1964-1965(New York: Oceana,

1966) 52-85; and D. Wadada Nabudere, Essays on the Theory and Practice of Imperialism (London: Onyx Press, 1979) 157-180.

Chapter Four

## The Role of International Trade
## in the Afican Political Economy

Amechi Okolo

This chapter starts with a brief review of
the African political economy which is held not to
be a less developed continent (LDC) or a developed
one, as most orthodox political economists want us
to believe, but an "underdeveloped and underdeveloping" world ghetto. It tries to sketch the
development of capitalism stressing the inherent
nature of its exploitation. However, exploitation
per se is not the cause of African underdevelopment but the cause is, rather, exportation and
transfer of the exploited surplus value from Africa
to the West. And international trade, by means of
unequal exchange and hidden transfers, is the essential mechanism for the siphoning away of African
surplus value to develop the West.

In essence, both the development of the
West and the underdevelopment of Africa constitute
the two sides of the development and dynamics of
capitalism. As the umbilical cord linking the two
economies, international trade facilitates one
(the West) to develop while the other (Africa)
stagnates and underdevelops.

The most striking feature of the contemporary African political economy is its abject
poverty. The continent is notoriously poor with
its members numbered amongst the lowest ranks
internationally along the conventional indices of
"development". In Africa many people are liter-
ally dying of starvation and wretchedness, many
cannot afford cloth for their bodies, disease is
rampant and death rates are the highest in the
world.[1]

> Among our century's most urgent problems
> is the wholly unacceptable poverty that
> blights the lives of some 2,000 million
> people in the more than 100 countries of
> the developing countries. Of these 2,000
> million, 800 million are caught in what
> can be termed absolute poverty -- a
> condition of life so limited as to pre-
> vent the realization of the potential of
> the genes with which they are born; a
> condition of life so degrading as to be
> an insult to human dignity.

In short, Africa is a huge world ghetto, a symbol
of destitution, hopelessness and deprivation which
constantly beckons for help. It is the continent
where death from all sorts of human and natural
hazards stares one in the face and many people are
virtually on the brink of extinction.[2]

Moreover, despite the present level of
wretchedness, the dimensions of human misery are
multiplying in Africa geometrically. Africa is
a disorganized society. She is not the "developing" continent that most popular literature would
want us to believe, but rather an "underdeveloped
and underdeveloping" slum where the harsh realities
of human existence are most evident.[3] All the
countries of Africa have been categorised into the
Third World group (with the significant exception
of South Africa) based on their level of development. But recently it has become necessary and
fashionable to subdivide them into Fourth and
possibly Fifth Worlds based on their degrees of
wretchedness and proximity to extinction.[4]

Yet Africa is by no means a poor continent;
in fact she is one of the richest continents on
earth. Her soil is extremely rich but the products
from below and above her surface have enriched
other parts of the globe rather than her own
peoples. Africa has an impressive range of resources of most of the world's major minerals.

Her iron ore reserves are about twice those of
the United States and two-thirds those of the
Soviet Union based on an estimated two billion
metric tons. Her petroleum reserves are perhaps
unequalled anywhere and she pumps virtually all of
them to the West. Take the Nigerian case as an
example. Of the 2.5 billion barrels of Nigerian
oil produced in 1976, 2.1 billion barrels were
shipped to the West; and she exports the second
largest amount of foreign oil to the U.S. next to
Saudi Arabia.[5]

In some instances Africa is the only known
source of certain vital strategic minerals like
chrome and uranium for the West.[6] Her arable and
pasture lands surpass those of the United States
and the Soviet Union. She has over forty percent
of the world's oceanic and hydroelectric power
potential. And as solar energy emerges to become
the next vital source of energy, Africa's share of
global energy potential will become even greater.
At present she supplies the West with oil to fuel
its industralised economy and in the future Africa
- the tropical continent in the "colonial sun" -
will be the main source of solar energy.

So Africa's poverty is not natural or inherent; instead, we are dealing with man-made
poverty. She has all that it takes to be a great
continent. She has the resources and the manpower
of about 280 million people; yet most of her
resources -- human and material -- have been
devoted to the development of the West to her own
detriment and underdevelopment. Linked to this
increase in poverty as the striking feature of
Africa's political economy is its extrovertedness.

An extroverted economy is one that exists
primarily to service a foreign economy.[7] All the
important sectors of such an economy exist to
service foreign interests. The African continent
as a whole is organised to produce for export
and whatever sparse rewards it receives from this
production for export is again spent on foreign

imports. Both the mechanisms of production for
export and consumption of imports -- that is,
international trade -- constitute a vital key to
the understanding of African poverty. The logic
of capitalism with its mechanisms of international
trade has resulted in the "development of underdevelopment" in Africa, to use Andre Gunder Frank's
phrase.[8]

Before the Western incursion and the continent's integration into the world economy,
Africans were in a comparable stage of social and
economic formation equal to, if not higher than,
that of the West. Long before the first contact
with Europeans, by about 1100 AD, Africans had produced renowned philosphers,artists,and scientists.
At the end of the first millennium African astron-
omers and geologists were already probing into
the secrets of the celestial bodies and the causes
of earthquakes while Europeans were still wondering
at these phenomena with amazement. Africa produced
the great University of Sankore which was a world
center of learning and the legendary town of Timbucto
which was a world center of commerce long before
Venice ever rose to fame. In the medical field,
the first successful eye surgery operation for
blindness was performed in Africa about the year
1100 AD.[9] Archeological excavations have confirmed
the existence of sophisticated bronze and iron castings long before the Europeans came into Africa.
In fact some Africa iron castings predated Western
civilization. According to West Africa, in some
iron workings recently discovered at Abuja in
Nigeria, "about a dozen furnances were found which
are dated to about 400 BC giving a lengthy lineage
to Nigeria's iron and steel industry."[10]

Many great empires were flourishing in
Africa when Europe was still a collection of small
feudal units.[11] Above all, John Jackson contends
that Africans built the first great civilization
and were the first to cross the Atlantic. According to him they were the first to reach and "dis-
cover" America even before Columbus' arrival.[12]

And Bittinger has compiled an impressive list of
some important philosophers and rulers produced
by Africa such as Ibn Batuta (1303 AD) and Sonni
Ali (1450 AD).[13]

However, the big question is what happened?
Why and how did such a reversal occur that Africa
-- the original home of man, craft and civilization
-- would become in the twentieth century the bastion
of stagnation, poverty and underdevelopment?  The
question of how the African indigene was initiated
into the world system is of great importance to
contemporary scholarship.  But presently I am concerned with how this dependence is being maintained.

Inequality and exploitation have existed
throughout human history.  A few groups of people
have always been able to acquire more than their
share of a people's wealth and hence lord it over
them politically and culturally.  So society has
always been divided into the "exploiters" and the
"exploited" and the struggle between them has been
the essential force of world history.  In fact,
as Marx sees it, "the history of all hitherto
existing societies is the history of class struggles."
So Marx sees exploitation and class struggles as
not only inherent in history but as the very factors
that <u>constitute</u> history.[14]  So we accept that man
has always exploited man and that "whoever says
organization says oligarchy."[15]

Oligarchy means exploitation.  It means the
exploitation of the majority by a few.  It means
that one class, usually small in number, exploits
another class -- the larger part of society.  Oligarchy and social formations involve political
exploitation as well as economic exploitation.
With the crystalization of social formations into
nation-states, intra-national exploitation was
transformed into inter-national exploitation.  One
state was able to exploit the labour and natural
resources of another state.  Although development
and underdevelopment deal with the comparative

political economy of nation-states, I am concerned here primarily with the latter type of exploitation; that is, the exploitation of one nation by another -- a process that happens essentially through the mechanisms of international trade. This process is offered as the major cause and explanation of contemporary African under-development.

The primary feature of exploitation through international trade is "Unequal Exchange "[16] in the trade between the industrial nations and under-developed nations. Unequal exchange obtains when products involving the same amount of labour are rewarded unequally. The subsequent transfer of the surplus to another state causes one to stagnate while the other prospers. This means that products coming from Third World nations embody "hidden transfers" of surplus value to the West which causes the unequal development of the two groups.[17]

So in trading with the West, Africa helped to develop Europe in the same proportion as Europe helped to underdevelop Africa. There is necessarily an inverse relationship between the development of one and the underdevelopment of the other. The uniqueness of labor power in contradistinction to other exchange commodities in a capitalist context exists because it is the only commodity which is capable of producing a value greater than its worth. In other words, labor power alone can produce its value plus something extra. This extra is the source of profit and this is what the capitalists keep in their companies and countries.

This uneven appropriation of the surplus value of labor power is the source of exploitation everywhere -- in the industrial world as well as in the developing nations. However when dealing with international trade -- that is, with cross-national trade -- a new dimension is added. Within the boundaries of a state, the bourgeoisie appropriates this surplus value from the workers and hence exploits them. But this surplus remains within the nation so that, through a series of multiplier effects and leakages from the bourgeois class, some of the accumulated wealth eventually trickles down to the people, even if in unacceptable quantities.

This trickle down happens in a number of ways. The government usually gets hold of a sizable amount and spends it on infrastructure-- roads, public buildings, education, health care, etc. -- and on the provision of other social services and amenities. The cases of highly-developed social services in Europe,[18] and the government's involvement in very sophisticated inter-state highways in the United States are examples of this. Or some super-capitalists (usually called the millionaires or billionaires depending on their degree of success in exploiting the workers) will set up all sorts of charitable organizations and foundations to help the people.[19] All these are attempts to redistribute national wealth. Though they may constitute reluctant concessions in response to worker agitation by the national bourgeoisie, nevertheless they help to increase general societal wealth. Such charitable and philanthropic activities help to improve the workers' welfare and thus moderate the perceptions of exploitation.

The important point for this analysis, though, is that most of these forms of bourgeois "socialism"[20] would and could not have been possible if the accumulated wealth had not remained within the country even if it remained with the bourgeoisie at the "top" of the national ladder. Hence the importance of international trade in the study of development and underdevelopment is that it helps us to focus not on how each national bourgeoisie exploits the working class of another state -- in short how one "nation" exploits another. Exploitation as a system of production and distribution goes on in every society; but in some societies the accumulated wealth stays within the society while

in others it is transferred out, usually involun-
tarily.  Where it remains within the boundaries
of the state, attempts are made, however, imperfect
they might be, to redistribute it, thus improving
the societal welfare by increasing national wealth
and contributing to national development.  In
societies where the accumulated wealth is transferred outside the state, internal redistribution
is impossible and exploitation becomes routine,
leading to the full force of deprivation and underdevelopment.

Figure 1 should help to clarify this point
further.  In essence, development and underdevelopment can be studied on two conceptual levels with
international trade being the umbilical cord which
ties the two types of economies together.  On the
effect of trade Marx said:

> If the free traders cannot understand how
> one nation can grow rich at the expense
> of another, we need not wonder, since
> these same gentlemen also refuse to under-
> stand how within one country one class
> can enrich itself at the expense of
> another.[21]

Figure 1

Effect of International Trade on

National Economics and Welfare

$$\boxed{\text{I.E.}} + \boxed{\text{N.N.E.}} = \boxed{\text{N.D.}} + \boxed{\text{M.I.D.}} \quad \text{Rich State}$$

$$\boxed{\text{I.E.}} + \boxed{\text{N.E.}} = \boxed{\text{N.U.}} + \boxed{\text{I.D.}} \quad \text{Poor State}$$

Key

| | | |
|---|---|---|
| I.E. | = | Individual Exploitation |
| N.N.E. | = | Non-National Exploitation |
| N.E. | = | National Exploitation |
| N.D. | = | National Development |
| M.I.D. | = | Mediated Individual Exploitation |
| N.U. | = | National Underdevelopment |
| I.D. | = | Individual Deprivation |

Underdevelopment can be understood, then, in terms of degree of exploitation and from the vantage point of what happens to the accumulated wealth resulting from the exploitation. Only a unity of individual exploitation plus national exploitation can bring about national underdevelopment. This approach makes sense because historically the mere presence of national exploitation (N.E.) did not by itself bring about national underdevelopment. A nation could be

"undeveloped" in contradistinction to being
"underdeveloped". An undeveloped state occurs
when the nation is unable to optimize the use of
its human and natural resources. Therefore, it
should be noted that the bulk of Africa was undeveloped before the march of capitalism on the
continent. Also Europe was undeveloped before
the industrial revolution. Before the Caucasian
invasion of the North American continent, that
area was also undeveloped.

From undevelopment, Western Europe and
North America moved towards development, except
for the few Indian reservations scattered across
the United States. This means that the West was
never underdeveloping. And comparing the Western
state at that period to the situation of the
African nations today overlooks the historical
context of the Western nations at their undeveloped
stage when there was no "developed" nation. The
West was undeveloped at an historical epoch before
the industrial revolution turned the wheels of
progress. At the undeveloped stage the vast riches
of the soil and sub-soil remained untapped and man
was able to wring a subsistence existence directly
out of nature. Society at large was in a state of
"infancy" to use Hegel's phrase.[22]

But underdevelopment is a different thing
which is unique to the modern world system. It
has no historical antecedent and it requires three
critical components to actualize, namely:

(i) Use of automated and sophisticated machinery
to extract the greatest possible resources from
nature;

(ii) Expansion of the productive potential of
labour power to its maximum limit; and

(iii) Above all, the extracted resources and surplus value from the above must be removed from
their areas of origin to serve a "foreign" economy.

It is the unity of the above three components -- automated and greatest extraction of
natural resources; exhaustion of labour power in
an attempt to get maximum productive potential
from it; and the transfer of resources and surplus
value to another economy -- that gives rise to the
phenomenon of underdevelopment. If any of the
three components is absent, the process will not
be one of underdevelopment. It will be something
else, and it will no longer be centered in Africa
-- a totally disorganized continent with no focus
or cohesion.

Hence underdevelopment started when the
industrial revolution released enormous potential
for man to exploit and employ the resources of
nature. For those societies which can exploit
natural resources "better" than others, development is assured. Individual wealth is thereby
increased and by arithmetical addition plus interaction multiplier effects national wealth is also
increased.

And the society is collectively developed
to the degree to which it can conjure up the
forces of nature to serve it. In this regard the
Soviet Union commands tremendous power over its
natural resources. It has been able to perform
as great national feats as that of the most advanced capitalist state: the United States. The
Soviet Union ponders the celestial bodies with as
much success as the United States[23] and commands
an equal amount of political clout in the international arena yet Soviet citizens are materially
deprived relative to those of the United States.
In fact Soviet "exploitation" of its workers is
legendary.[24] It started with Lenin and intensified during Stalin's era with agricultural
collectivization and forced labor camps,[25] when
virtually everything that the worker produced was
removed from him leaving him at the level of mere
subsistence.

Today the situation is a little different. The workers are still being exploited but the Soviet state which directly controls the accumulated capital mediates the individual worker's exploitation by a massive infusion of assorted kinds of social services. These ameliorate the effects of individual exploitation just as in the United States and Europe. There is, though, a difference between the two, with which this chapter cannot deal. In the Soviet Union the comprehensiveness and scope of the social services are of such immensity as to cancel out nearly totally individual exploitation while in the West the mediation is quite limited relatively. However, both of these types of society have one thing in common which is notoriously absent in Africa -- each maintains substantial control over its economy while Africa does not. Hence the relevance of the first part of Figure 1:

$$(I.E.) + (N.N.E.) = (N.D.) + (M.I.D.)$$

This formulation suggests that when individual exploitation (IE) merges with non-national exploitation (NNE), the result is a mediated individual deprivation (MID) with national development (ND). Contemporary Africa presents a totally different picture. Apart from the usual capitalist drive for more profit, a number of factors have contributed to the unusually high degree of exploitation of the African worker. In Africa the natural tendency of the capitalist drive for profit was reinforced by the Western racial bias towards black inferiority. Capitalism introduced racism in Africa and, in turn, racism sustained and reinforced the capitalist super-exploitation of the Africa worker.[26] The long Western heritage of slavery in Britain and North America had treated the black race as inferior to whites and consequently deserving of wages, if any at all, far below those of white workers. After all, these capitalists had been used to having free black labour in slavery so the extension of semi-slavery

wages to Africa after the abolition of slavery itself was conceived as a magnanimous act for which
the Africans should be grateful.[27]

Also colonialism entailed not only foreign
rule but foreign dictatorship. It meant the
summary execution of political and military authority by a foreign power. Dictatorship everywhere
meant the destruction of all social intermediaries
and a direct imposition of state power over the
people.[28]

In Africa it was no different; it was only
more vicious and more efficient in application.
Above all, colonialism means the imposition of a
caste-type system on the natives. It is a caste-
type system because social prestige and rank, and
accompanying rewards, are meted out on the basis
of race -- whites get the best of everything while
blacks scramble at the base of the social ladder
for mere existence. Colonialism also entails a
racist political economy because life possibilities
like job opportunities, financial remuneration and
political and general advancement are racially
determined. Robert Schrum calls the United States
a racist economy because the economy discriminates
against blacks and other non-Caucasian minorities[29]
but the situation was worse in colonial states.

Consequently the African worker did not
even have the opportunity to organize into unions
and apply some of the techniques of labor bargaining so useful to the workers of the West. The
labor aristocracy in the United States (eg. the
AFL-CIO, Teamsters, UAW, etc.) maintains a political
clout which neither the government nor the industrialists can ignore except at their own peril.
John Kenneth Galbraith contends that, in the face
of monopoly power of large corporations, American
labor developed its own countervailing power to
bargain for differentially lower prices and higher
wages. These "new restraints" in the form of large
unions and buyers' monopolies have replaced the

classical competitive model so that "private
economic power is held in check by the countervailing power of those who are subject to it."
According to Galbraith,

> The economic power that the worker faced
> in the sale of his labor -- the compe-
> tition of many sellers dealing with few
> buyers -- made it necessary that he
> organize for his own protection... And
> it is not an accident that large auto-
> mobile, steel, electrical, rubber, farm-
> machinery companies bargain with power-
> ful unions. Not only has the strength
> of the corporations in these industries
> made it necessary for workers to develop
> the protection of countervailing power;
> it has provided unions with the oppor-
> tunity for getting something more as well.
> If successful they could share in the
> fruits of the corporation's market power.[30]

In Britain the labor movement, the Trade
Union Congress (TUC), even has a party -- the
Labour Party -- which alternates government power
with the Conservative Party, the party of British
industrialists and aristocrats.[31]  No wonder that
Samuel Beer would state that British politics has
entered an era of "collectivism", an end of
politics when issues and policies are "managed by
a collectivist consensus" amongst the cabinet,
the bureaucracy and labor.[32]

The above relationship including labor
organizations helps to contain some of the
capitalist drive for over-exploitation within the
metropole while in Africa the labor class is
usually small, scattered and politically insignif-
icant. It can neither organize for political
power on its own nor can it "deliver the vote"
since it is usually split and rendered impotent by
a matrix of cross-cutting cleavages.[33]  For these
reasons African workers get wages that are too low

to comprehend even given the capitalist record.
For example the Nigerian coalminer received "one
pence for jobs on the surface" in the sixties.
This meant that a counterpart in the West, for
example in the United States, got in one hour what
the Nigerian coalminer got in a complete six-day
week. To illustrate the completeness of the
exploitation of the African worker, Farrell Lines,
an American shipping company, in 1955 paid five-
sixths of the wages spent on loading cargoes to
the Americans and one-sixth to the African dock
workers.[34] The American longshoremen received
five-sixths of the wages yet the same amount and
weight of merchandise was loaded in America and
unloaded in Africa. Western economists are not
slow in trying to explain why it is that due to
higher productivity and other factors of the
American dockworkers via-a-vis the African dockworkers, the former are entitled to higher wages.
But the issue is simple and straightforward: when
the Americans loaded a certain tonage of goods
into a ship and got five-sixths of the wages, and
the Africans unloaded the same tonage and got one-
sixth of the wages, any attempt to explain it
apart from crass exploitation is pure and simple
"ideologized economics."

Also it has been possible to pay the
African worker low wages -- even below the subsistence level -- because unlike his counterpart
in Europe, the African worker still maintained
connections with the village and the land. Indeed,
given inadequate wages, most have had to supplement
their wage labor in the towns with subsistence
farming in the villages where they grow many of
their needs themselves. All these factors contribute to the higher level of the exploitation of
the African worker relative to the Western worker.
In addition, the uniqueness of African exploitation
rests not so much on exploitation per se but on the
fact that the surplus is transferred outside the
country so that no leaks get back to the indigenous
people in any shape or form. The exploitation of

the individual is transformed into national exploitation. When both merge the result is complete individual deprivation and national underdevelopment, hence the second part of Figure 1:

$$(I.E.) \quad + \quad (N.E.) \quad = \quad (N.U.) \quad + \quad (I.D.)$$

African underdevelopment is, then, a consequence of the world-wide expansion of capitalism and the integration of Africa into this international system.

The cardinal role of international trade as the primary means by which African wealth is transferred to further develop the already "developed" West should be well understood. Without the international exchange of goods and services, the wealth generated by a society should accumulate and remain within it. Eventually some wealth might trickle down to the society so contributing to over-all national development and social welfare.

Historically, the major concerns of international economics have been

(i) the relationship between international trade and the productive capacity of a nation; that is, what gains should be derived from the division of labor, specialization and exchange; and

(ii) the balance of payments problem; that is, the relationship between domestic demand and the terms of trade.

The basic justification for international trade is essentially the same as the one for domestic trade -- the certain propensity in human nature to "truck, barter, and exchange,"[35] -- which in turn gives rise to a division of labor occasioning a general increase in the national wealth. In trading every individual or nation concentrates on producing things it can produce best whilst trading to obtain those things it cannot produce efficiently.

In so doing the general wealth of nations should
increase. This is known as the theory of "comparative advantage" which was developed by Smith
in 1776 and refined by Ricardo in 1817.[36]

Smith's proposition was a defense of free
trade. It was ringing attack against government
intervention in international trade, in which he
argued that all nations would be better off if
government allowed the free flow of trade. In
spite of the many centuries which have passed since
such laissez-faire theories were first enunicated
it is remarkable that the notion of "comparative
advantage" has remained at the cornerstone of
international trade theory. In spite of the many
attacks and reformulations over the years, the
basic tenets of the theory are still considered
valid today.[37] Basically it is assumed:

(i)    that there are gains from international
trade which accrue to the trading nations; and

(ii)    that the specialization of labor further
increases this gain.[38]

This has remained a cardinal truth passed
from generation to generation of economists -- that
nations do "gain" from trade. From this perspective, the worst that could happen to a nation
which engages in international trade is that its
gains might not be as great as those of others but
in theory it can never lose -- "never that it may
become poorer than it was before".[39] There can
only be differences in the "size of gains" which
accrue to the respective nations.[40] Heller identifies two factors which will influence the size
of such gains as:

(i)    the size of the foreign trade sector; and

(ii) the elasticity of substitution.[41]

The first proposition assumes, according to him that "the larger the relative size of the foreign trade sector, the larger the relative gains to be realized by engaging in international trade".[42] Elasticity is the responsiveness of demand to changes in price. It is measured by the percentage change in the quantity of goods demanded over the percentage change in the price of the goods as follows:

Elasticity = $\dfrac{\text{\% Change in Quantity Demanded}}{\text{\% Change in Price of Goods}}$

In traditional economics, when the rate is greater than one, it is called elastic demand; when it is less than one, it is inelastic demand; and when it is equal to one it is unity.[43] The size of gains is supposed to be affected by the direction and magnitude of this equation. On this proposition Heller declared that:

> If it is possible to substitute domestic
> commodities for foreign ones with great
> ease; the gains to be realised from
> being able to obtain the foreign goods
> will be modest. On the other hand, if
> it is not easy to substitute domestic
> for foreign goods, the gains from trade
> will be larger.[44]

Two important propositions emerge from this:

(i) that nations which engage more in foreign trade relative to their gross national products should gain more; and

(ii) that the increasing rarity of a nation's products should be concomitant with increasing gains from the trade which accrue to the nation.

However, in the case of Africa, these propositions are negated: they tend to operate in the opposite direction and to contribute to the

growing underdevelopment of the continent. In
Africa the nations with a larger foreign trade
sector relative to gross national product are the
ones which suffer most and are most exploited
through trade. However, they suffer more precisely for the very reasons that orthodox international economics predicted increasing welfare.
This is due to "an increasing rarity of their
trade products" which in economic parlance means
"comparative advantage".

Third World nations with important rare
resources benefit least from such advantages because:

(i)     they become targets of major international
rivalries;

(ii)    they are cornered into becoming mono-crop
economies; that is, economies that depend on one
product; and

(iii)   they typically get far less income for their
products because a few multinational corporations
usually control their production and marketing.

All these factors reduce the chances of the
African nations benefiting from either the rarity
or the large reserves of their products. In many
cases, the nations seem to be particularly unfortunate because nature endowed them with large reserves
of important rare products. For instance, Namibia's
independence has been stalled because South Africa
and the West want "access" to her important uranium
reserves while the Congo debacle and her continued
poverty is because of her rich copper reserves.

Classical economists, wedded to the theory
of comparative advantage, have, in fact, predicted
what should constitute a booming era for the Third
World nations. For this theory holds that specialization and a division of labor and exchange will
increase national welfare; that is, they will move

the society to a higher indifference curve.[45]
They are able to do this because each nation will
be able to specialize in producing and marketing
these products which it is naturally better endowed
to produce.  The rarer the product, that is, the
more unique the product or the greater the inability of other nations to produce it, the greater the
benefits accruing to the one nation or group of
nations which produce it.

However, in practice, African nations lose
from their trade with the West because of the
absence of certain assumptions of the theory of
comparative advantage:

(i)  The first condition for the realization of
the benefits of international trade/comparative
advantage is the existence of free trade.  The
theory assumes that there will be free flow of
goods across national boundaries.  And

(ii) the second condition is the existence of
politico-social parity; that is, trading nations
should not only be in a comparative stage of socio-
economics formations but they should be militarily
paripassu with one another or, at least, as near
to it as possible.  In short, trading partners
should exhibit a "rough equivalence".  This is
because in the final analysis it is the "international weight" or the "political energy" of a
nation that determines how much she will be made
to buy and sell for the goods and services she
produces for and receives from other nations.

Hence if the theory of international trade
was purely an "economic theory," the terms of
trade[46] should move against the industrial nations
in favor of the developing nations.  This was
exactly the theoretical stance which international
trade theory had posited over the years from J.S.
Mill through Smith and Ricardo to even Marx and
contemporary "political economists."  On this John
Stuart Mill said,

> The exchange values of manufactured articles, compared with the products of agriculture and mines have a certain decided tendency to fall.[47]

And Robert Torrens echoes the same when he wrote that,

> The value of raw material is, in the progress of society, perpetually increasing with respect to manufactured goods or to express the same thing in a different form, the value of manufactured goods is perpetually diminishing with respect to raw produce.[48]

Alfred Marshal was perhaps more emphatic. He foresaw a day when the new nations would possess "an unassailable monopoly"[49] in the field of international bargaining due to their abundance of primary products.

At this point the operations of OPEC come to mind. The question then becomes whether OPEC has "proved" Marshal and other orthodox economists to be right? I do not think so. On the contrary, I think that the operations of OPEC only confirm the point I have been emphasizing -- that it is not the products per se which determine their prices in cross-national markets but rather the political power which the supplier(s) can wield within the international system. According to Mana Al-Otaiba

> Oil prices had for twenty-four years remained well below the level that could have been fetched if the forces of supply and demand had been allowed to interact freely. They did not rise between 1947 and 1971 and moreover OPEC itself was created in 1960 in order to prevent further price reductions after two drastic cuts in the 1950s. In the twenty-four year period, however, the price of industrial goods and food-stuffs increased by 300 percent.[50]

Hence OPEC was created because,

> The same largest seven or eight
> petroleum companies control, in their
> own different ways, the greater part
> of production in all the major exporting
> countries. It is obvious, however,
> that this great concentration of power
> in the hands of a small group of large
> international companies is greater than
> it should be.[51]

The major task of OPEC, then, has been to "weaken
the dominance of major petroleum monopolies."
The organization's success or failure has been
determined by how far it has punctured the power
of these monopolies.

So political power has always been needed
to redress and/or moderate the prices of international goods. And despite the running consensus
amongst orthodox economists that the price of
primary products should overtake that of manufactured goods, the terms of trade have usually been
consistently against Third World nations. This
means that the prices of their exports have been
decreasing either relatively or absolutely. The
effect of this has been that the Third World
countries have been made to export a greater
quantity of their products and hence a greater
quantity of their labor power for a constant or
shrinking quantity of foreign imports.

When the net barter terms of trade turn
against the Third World nations, two things happen,
both of which adversely affect their national
development. First, as already indicated, adverse
terms of trade mean that African nations are
exporting greater amounts of national labor and
resources for fewer amounts of foreign labor; that
is, they are exporting increasing amounts of their
surplus labor in the form of "hidden transfers".
And second, because of the institutional constraints on and the constant supply structure of

most of their exports, they are unable to take
advantage of the supposed increase in demand for
their products to export more. Consequently what
has happened over time is that they just export
at lower prices while importing at higher prices
and so become worse-off.

In the face of present day realities, where
the African nations are suffering deteriorating
terms of trade and general worsening in their
situation,[52] apologists are now finding excuses
why the products of the Third World nations are
underpriced. Ironically they try to do this while
remaining within the orthodoxy of comparative
advantage in international trade. They argue that
the African nations are underpriced in world market because they export essentially primary products
while Western nations export mainly manufactured
goods which incorporate a high degree of value
added quality. Even some dependence theorists
accept the notion that it is the inherently greater
value of manufactured goods from the developed
nations which accounts for their higher prices in
international trade.[53]

Such an argument is metaphysical, with
ideology clothed in the euphemism of scientific
objectivity and neutrality. Arghiri Emmanuel, to
the contrary, calls it an "optical illusion" which
results from the mistaken identification of the
exports of rich nations with the exports of manufactured goods and the exports of the poor nations
with the exports of primary products.[54] And with
such an equation of Western exports with manufactured goods and Third World exports with primary
goods, economists, then, have the bases for
rationalization based on (unequal) comparative
advantage.

The fact is that the terms of trade have
been deteriorating not against products per se --
primary or manufactured -- but against countries.
This is particularly important because the present

tendency in the debate seems to have ignored the
fact that it is African "nations" which have been
suffering from the worsening conditions of trade.
The terms of trade have been deteriorating against
Third World states in favor of European and North
American countries.

For example, until recently when coal was
the chief export of Britain, it was considered a
"manufactured" product which commanded a high
price in the world market; yet coal was no more
"primary" or "manufactured" than Zambian copper
or Third World oil whose prices did not rise
between 1947 and 1971.[55]  Palm oil from West
Africa is as much "manufactured" as soap and
margarine or whisky or wines from Europe.  Cotton,
coffee, cocoa and ground nuts usually undergo
extensive machine treatment before being exported,
perhaps as much as United States' wheat or
Canadian or Swedish timber.  Bananas and spices
from Third World nations are produced with as
much sophistication as meat and dairy products
from the West.[56]

India at the time of its contact with
Britain was already an accomplished textile and
cotton producer whose products Britain was importing at a depressed price.  But over the years,
Britain appropriated textile technology from
India, turned textiles into the pillar of her
industrial revolution and started exporting
textiles at prices sufficient to maintain the
higher living standards of her own workers.  Within the past decade, textile production has again
begun to revert to Third World nations where
workers hardly obtain starvation wages.[57]  In some
parts of the United States textile industry have
since moved to the Third World areas from where
they produce textiles, with the same machinery
and sophistication, for export back to America
and other industrialised areas.  Yet these Third
World workers barely scrape a living from their
wages for producing the same products which only
a few years ago left the American workers in

relatively comfortable circumstances.

The interesting thing about it is that
economists are never short of "theories" to explain
the wage disparities. Now they have distinguished
between "light" and "heavy" industries.[58] According to them, light industries bear lower remuneration to workers while heavy industries generally
attract higher wages because of the tasks involved.
But anyone who is familiar with American or other
Western industries will know that it takes as much
"energy" and "expertise" to work in the production
line of either a food processing industry or an
automobile factory. In fact, as if to make the
point that the distinction serves no useful purpose as a factor in determining wages, one Detroit
auto production worker has been going to work
dressed in complete white suit with white shoes,
tie, etc.. His clothes were never soiled and his
co-workers confirm that his productivity has not
been affected.[59]

Zenith Corporation, following the examples
of other United States electronic and television
industries, "moved" its production plants to the
Third World areas in the fall of 1977. The workers there, who will produce the same RCA, Zenith
and other color television sets to which Americans
are used, will still be "primary" producers good
only for subsistence wages even though they will
be producing the same things with the same sophistication as their counterparts in the United States
and Europe. United States Steel is also contem-
plating moving some of its factories to Latin
America. I have no doubt that the Latin American
workers will receive a meagre fraction of American
steel workers' wages while I do not doubt that the
quality of steel produced in both locations (United
States and Latin America) will approach parity.
It will be interesting to watch economists
"theorize" on this coming trend of "deindustrial-
ization" in the north and "industrialization" in
the south. The fact is that as long as they shy

away from considering the "international weight"
and "political energy" of the nations involved as
the vital factor in determining prices and wages
they will continue to be wrong.

Perhaps the commonest and most popular
argument for the sub-human wages in Africa is that
its standard of living is low while the standard
is much higher in the West. This is a remarkable
piece of "biblical" reasoning based on the saying:
"he who has least, that much will be taken away
from him and given to he who has more."[60] The
truth is that the high living standard was made
possible by the exploitation of the African
nations. To use their inverted low living
standard as an arguement against them is like
spanking a child and punishing him further for
crying.

Petroleum, uranium, chrome, tin, copper,
diamonds and other minerals from Africa require
as much sophistication and machinery to drill and
dig as steel or any other Western industry. Yet
when the products come from Africa, they are underpriced because they are classified as "primary"
products. When they come from the West, they command high prices because they are considered "manufactured" with high technology content.

But the exports of the developing areas
are not comprised primarily of primary agricultural
products which come from the "primitive" sectors
of low productivity. Rather they come from the
"modern" sectors. For example, in 1966 the total
exports from Third World were of the order of $35
billion, out of which the ultra-modern capitalist
sector -- oil, mining and modern plantations like
United Fruit in Central America or Unilever in
Africa and Asia -- contributed over $26 billion,
or seventy-five percent of the total. Samir Amin
calculates that if these same products were provided by the advanced nations the worth would have
been to the tune of $34 billion. Hence the

"transfer of value from the periphery to the center under this heading alone would amount, at a modest estimate, to $8 billion."[61]

So the question is not "primary" versus "manufactured" products but "Western" versus "African" exports. And the important, consistent and meaningful distinction between the two sets of products is the socio-political-cum-military power base of the products. Those that originate in the West and are supported by superior politico-military machinery fare better in the world market while those supported by the weak sycophantic political systems of the Third World are always underpriced. Hence there seems to be a curse upon certain nations such that whatever they produce will sell at a lower price in the world market while others, even if they export Coca-Cola or Kentucky Fried Chicken, sell at a higher price. In short, some nations are structurally constrained to export an ever-increasing amount of their national wealth and labor for an ever-shrinking amount of foreign wealth and labor. Consequently, certain nations are continually being underdeveloped while others develop progressively.

Referring to the Portuguese commercial achievements over the Asians in the sixteenth century, Immanuel Wallerstein reports that

> The ouster of Moslem traders, which comes first in time was "by brute force and not by peaceful competition." It was primarily due to politico-naval superiority.[62]

This was because the Portuguese were

> Not merchants--private entrepreneurs--but a formidable naval power, acting, in the name of a foreign state, on behalf of its merchants and itself. This meant that trade relations--indeed prices--were fixed by treaties recognized under international law.[63]

In essence capitalist development and
expansion has been possible by the existence of
strong states which supported their merchants with
enough political power and military force (if need
be) to get the best possible terms of trade. Hence
trade has been profitable to a nation to the extent that it wielded politico-military power. In
spite of the overwhelming evidence of the use of
political power to set the prices and conditions of
goods which cross national boundaries, conventional
international trade theory still fails to account
for the political power side of international trade
and pricing. It remains wedded to the concept of
comparative adventage which has historically played
little or no role in determining the price of goods
that cross national boundaries.

This chapter has tried to do three things.
First, to sketch the development of capitalism
stressing its inherent logic and dynamic which
necessarily led to imperialism and colonialism.
The logic of capitalism diminishes the rate of
profit. To limit this, capitalists have expanded
into Third World areas both for cheap labor and
for raw materials. Second, to establish that
African underdevelopment is as a result of the
capitalist development of the West. The development of the West and the underdevelopment of Africa
constitute the two sides of a single phenomenon --
what Wallerstein calls the development of the
"modern world-system."[64] And third, finally,it is
contended that international trade is the primary
mechanism by which African wealth has been used to
develop the West. Surplus value produced in Africa
has been transferred to the West (now that outright
brigandage and robbery are no longer used) in the
form of "hidden transfers" and "unequal exchange."

The basic tenets of the theory of international trade are largely irrelevant and inapplicable to the trade between Africa and the West
because the necessary condition to realize the advantages of international trade which is free cannot be assumed to be operative. Most African

states were colonized and by institutional legal-
cum-military restraints were forbidden to trade
with anyone else except with their colonial master.
So the extent of their freedom to choose both trade
partners and the products to be developed compares
well with the freedom given to a condemned man to
choose whether he wishes to be hanged or to be
electrocuted. I submit that neither case amounts
to much of a choice.

Products to be traded were thus decided by
the colonial masters according to their needs and
requirements with little regard to real potential
and needs of the producing nations. The high trade
partner concentration of the colonies makes them
vulnerable to the exigencies of particular foreign
demands. Also the colonies were barred at particular periods from producing certain types of
products. For example, Nigeria was once barred
from developing groundnut processing plants and
the growing of potatoes was barred before and
after the second world war in Ghana.

All these artificial limits reinforce the
contention that the theory and the assumptions of
international trade are largely inapplicable to contemporary North-South trade. Further, they were
developed by classical political economists from
their observations of European development. They
have been echoed, reformulated and amended over the
years by Western political economists still largely
based on Western experience. Any remaining truths
in them (and they are really tenuous) are relevant
only for the Western industrialized nations which
are in a comparative stage of socio-economic-cum-
political development. But for the African nations,
the theory and its assumptions collapse as sheer
ideology. The need for an international trade
theory which recognizes the economic-socio-politico-
cum-military powerlessness of the African nations
is long overdue.

Notes

1. Robert McNamara _Assault on Poverty_ (Washington: IBRD, 1975). According to McNamara,

> . . . over the past 25 years (1950-1975), average per capita income in Less Developed Countries rose by 3%. But in Sub-Saharan Africa, the annual growth was 2%, lifting GNP per capita from $175 in 1950 to $285 in 1975 . . .
>
> Within that region the poorest nations lagged still further behind averaging 1.5%, and that average still breaks down more gloomingly to rates of 2.6% from 1950-60, 1.8% from 1960-70 and 1.1% from 1970-75. 1,200 million do not have access to safe drinking water, 700 million are seriously malnourished, 550 million are unable to read or write, 250 million living in urban areas do not have adequate shelter . . . These are not simply large numbers, they are individual human beings." (_West Africa_, 10 October 1977).

2. McNamara _Assault on Poverty_.

3. The industrial nations have added nearly $2 billion to their reserves, which now approximate $52 billion. At the same time, the reserves of the Less Developed group have not only stopped rising but have declined some $200 million. To analysts such as Britain's Barbara Ward the significance of such statistics is clear: the economic gap is rapidly widening "between a white, complacent, highly bourgeois, very wealthy, very small North Atlantic elite and everybody else, and this is not a very comfortable heritage to leave

to one's children." See Kwame Nkrumah <u>Neo-Colonialism: the last stage of imperialism</u> (New York: International, 1965) xviii.

And see in McNamara <u>Assault on Poverty</u>:

> For the vast majority of mankind the most urgent problem is not war, or communism, or the cost of living or taxation: it is hunger. Over 1,500,000 people, something like two-thirds of thc world's population, are living in conditions of acute hunger, defined in terms of identifiable nutritional disease. This hunger is at the same time the effect and the cause of the poverty, squalor and misery in which they live.

4. Jozsef Bognar <u>Economic Policy and Planning in Developing Countries</u> (Budapest: Akademiai Kiado, 1975) 35-37.

5. See <u>West Africa</u>, September 1977.

6. Raymond F. Miksell <u>Nonfuel Minerals: U.S. investment policies abroad</u> (Beverly Hills: Sage, 1975) <u>passim</u>.

7. Samir Amin <u>Unequal Development</u> (New York: Monthly Review, 1976) 191-197 and 203-210.

8. Andre Gunder Frank "The Development of Underdevelopment" in Charles K. Kilby (ed) <u>The Political Economy of Development and Underdevelopment</u> (New York: Random House, 1973) 94-104.

9. See E. B. DuBois <u>The World and Africa</u> (New York: International, 1972) 320-327.

10. <u>West Africa</u>, 16 January 1978, 79.

11. There were great empires like the Songhai

Empire, the Melles Kingdom, the Kingdom of
Benin, the Ghana Kingdom, et al. See Chan-
cellor Williams The Destruction of Black
Civilization: great issues of a race (Dubuque,
Iowa: Kendal Hunt, 1971) and Nwafor Orizu,
Without Bitterness (New York: Creative Age,
1944).

12. John J. Jackson An Introduction to African
    Civilizations (New York: Negro University
    Press, 1969).

13. D. S. Bittinger Soudan's Second Sunup (New
    York: Elgin, 1939) 55.

14. Karl Marx Communist Manifesto passim.

15. All systems of government including democracy
    are permeated with oligarchy: oligarchy pre-
    sents itself with democracy. Organization is
    the weapon of the weak against the strong,
    but it is the source from which conservative
    currents flow over the plain of democracy.
    Even in socialism the masses must be content
    to constitute the pedestal of an oligarchy.
    They trade masters for masters, probably in
    the hope that the new master might be better.
    For more on the "Iron Law of Oligarchy" see
    Robert Michels Political Parties: a sociological
    study of oligarchical tendencies of modern
    democracy (Glencoe, Ill.: Free Press, 1949),
    Gaetano Mosca The Ruling Class (New York:
    McGraw-Hill, 1939), and Vilfredo Pareto The
    Mind and Society (New York: Harcourt Brace,
    1935).

16. Arghiri Emmanuel Unequal Exchange: a study of
    the imperialism of trade (New York: Monthly
    Review, 1972).

17. Amin Unequal Development 144.

18. During my research for part of this study in
    London in June 1977, I fell sick and went to
    see Dr. Freeman in Stockwell. The consulta-

tion, medication and treatment cost 20 pence,
about 30 U.S. cents.

19. For a list of U.S. charitable organizations,
    see The Foundation Directory (New York:
    Foundation Center, 1977).

20. Marx called all these sorts of charitable and
    philanthropic organizations "Petty-Bourgeois
    Socialism." See D. A. Drennen (ed) Karl Marx,
    178.

21. Karl Marx The Poverty of Philosophy (New York:
    International, 1963) 223.

22. G. W. F. Hegel The Philosophy of History (New
    York: Dover, 1956).

23. For more comparisons in the socio-military con-
    ditions between the United States and the
    Soviet Union see Newsweek, 3 and 10 October
    1977.

24. Philip Selznick The Organizational Weapon: a
    study of Bolshevik strategy and tactics (New
    York: McGraw-Hill, 1952) and Marshal Shulman
    Stalin's Foreign Policy Reappraised (Cam-
    bridge, Mass.: Harvard University Press,
    1963).

25. Alexander Solzhenitsyn One Day in the Life of
    Ivan Denisovich (New York: Praeger, 1963).

26. Eric Williams Capitalism and Slavery (New
    York: Capricorn, 1966).

27. Amechi Okolo "The Historical and Theoretical
    Stance of Dependency and Underdevelopment"
    Korean Journal of International Affairs,
    January-February 1981.

28. C. J. Freidrich and Z. K. Brzezinski Total-
    itarian Dictatorship and Autocracy (New
    York: Praeger 1966) 15-30.

29. Robert Schrum "Jimmy gets job, forgets jobs"
    New Times, 20 February 1966, 6.

30. John Kenneth Gailbraith American Capitalism
    (Boston: Houghton Mifflin, 1956) 115.

31. Samuel Beer The British Political System
    (New York: Random House, 1974) 125-126 and
    186-187.

32. Ibid. 66-68, 137-140 and 166-169.

33. Robert Melson "Ideology and Inconsistency:
    the cross-pressured Nigerian worker"
    American Political Science Review 65(1),
    March 1971, 161-171.

34. Walter Rodney How Europe Underdeveloped
    Africa (Dar-es-Salaam: Tanzania Publishing
    House, 1972) 163.

35. Adam Smith The Wealth of Nations (London:
    Dent, 1964-66), 14-15.

36. R. G. Kipsey and P. O. Steiner Economics
    (New York: Harper and Row, 1972) 678.

37. Ibid. 679.

38. H. R. Heller International Monetary Economics
    (Englewood Cliffs: Prentice-Hall, 1974) 4.

39. Emmanuel Unequal Exchange xx.

40. Ibid. xii.

41. Heller International Monetary Economics
    chapter 1.

42. Ibid. 8.

43. Taylor A New Dictionary 85.

44. Heller International Monetary Economics 9.

45.  <u>Ibid</u>. 4.

46.  Terms of trade compare a country's imports
     and exports in terms of their prices. Thus
     if the price of imports rises relative to the
     price of exports, the terms of trade are said
     to be less favorable and if export prices rise
     faster than import prices then the terms of
     trade are said to be more favorable. For
     more detailed treatment of terms of trade in-
     cluding the various types see Heller <u>Inter-
     national Monetary Economics</u> 117-120.

47.  J. S. Mill <u>The Principles of Political
     Economy</u> (London: Longmans, 1929) 254.

48.  Robert Torrens <u>Essay on the Production of
     Wealth</u> (London: Longman, 1821).

49.  Alfred Marshal <u>Money, Credit and Commerce</u>
     (London: Macmillan, 1923), 53.

50.  Mana Saeed Al-Otaiba <u>OPEC and the Petroleum
     Industry</u> (New York: John Wiley, 1975) iii.

51.  <u>Ibid</u>. 1.

52.  See <u>West Africa</u>, 10 October 1977.

53.  Johan Galtung "A structural theory of imper-
     ialism" <u>Journal of Peace Research</u> 2, 1971.

54.  Emmanuel <u>Unequal Exchange</u> xxx.

55.  Al-Otaiba <u>OPEC and the Petroleum Industry</u>
     chapter 1.

56.  U.S. Senate <u>Report on the Agrarian Reform
     Program of Developing Countries</u> (Washington:
     U.S. Senate, 1960).

57.  Emmanuel <u>Unequal Exchange</u> passim.

58.  Hagen <u>The Economics</u> 142.

59. "Mr. Clean" N.B.C. telecast, 18 November 1977, Narrator: John Chancellor.

60. Amin Unequal Development 143.

61. For more on legal constraints on development of products and trade in the colonies see Nkrumah Neo-Colonialism, Rodney How Europe Underdeveloped Africa, and Earl Ofari The Myth of Black Capitalism (London: Modern Reader, 1970).

62. Immanuel Wallerstein The Modern World System: capitalist agriculture and the origins of the European world economy in the sixteenth century (New York: Academic Press, 1974) 217.

63. Ibid.

64. Ibid.

Chapter Five

Africa in the World System: Towards
More Uneven Development?

Timothy M. Shaw

"Ex Africa semper aliquid novi"
 - Pliny the Elder Natural History Book Eight

"What comes out of Africa is neither new
nor exciting, nor seeming likely to be such,
but what is old, predictable and boring.
The liberating nationalism of twenty and
thirty years ago was nearly always a joy-
ful lift to the spirit... the formative
experience of Africa's under-30s one of
deepening crisis apparently beyond cure
by any familiar remedy; whether...in a
painfully large and spreading gap between
the few rich and many poor, or in political systems which falter or collapse, or
in the broadening shadow of interstate
rivalry and conflict. More and more often,
from all I hear, there is a new consciousness of choice: that Africa must revo-
lutionise itself and soon; or go, and
sooner, entirely to the devil."
 - Basil Davidson "Beyond the flags and
   anthems" New Statesman 24, March 1978,
   391-392.

"To know the future we must look into the
past and the present"
 - A.M. Babu "Postscript" to Walter Rodney
   How Europe Underdeveloped Africa (Dar es
   Salaam: Tanzania Publishing House, 1972)
   316.

The continent of Africa is poised half way
between  the achievement or recapture of formal
"independence" in the early 1960s and the year 2000.
The first twenty-year period has been characterized
by a rediscovery of Africa's identity and by a realization of the continent's unpromising inheritance;
the second twenty-year period is likely to be characterized by a reconsideration of established
development strategies, as Basil Davidson's opening
quote suggests, as well as a recognition that
divergent responses pose difficulties for the continent as a whole.[1]  In short, the rest of this
century may be a period of insecurity and instability and of decay and disintegration at
national, regional and continental levels.[2]

However, out of this process of reflection,
reevaluation and reorganization -- a second African
revolution -- may emerge a transformed continent,
one no longer constrained by a pervasive inheritance of dependence and underdevelopment.  But this
transition will be protracted and painful, resisted
by established interests both within and outside
Africa.  Without such a transformation, however,
the future may be even less promising, as projections indicate a growing gap between demand and
supply.  Forecasts and foresight require, therefore,
that Africa reconsider its past inheritance and
performance both to avoid difficulties expected in
the mid-term future and to transcend the dilemmas
anticipated in the second set of social trans-
formations.  In sum, Africa's next twenty-year
period may involve more contradictions, conflicts
and changes than the first post-independence era,
so adding support to Pliny's own observation about
the continent.

This chapter proceeds, then, from a review
of Africa's past -- its historical incorporation
into the world system -- to an overview of Africa's
present -- its current position in the world system
-- and onto a preview of Africa's future -- its
projected and possible places in the evolving world

system.  So the analysis is based on the assumption of A.M. Babu's own quotation:  that the
continent's future is a function of its past and
present.[3]

i)  <u>An inheritance of incorporation and inequality</u>

        The present and potential of the continent
is, then, related to its history of integration
into the world system and the reaction of its
leaders to this inheritance.[4]  In general, at least
until the second half of the 1970s, the new "political class" in Africa did not question the prevailing ideology of "development".  As Davidson
suggests in his own opening citation, the excite-
ment and anticipation of the post-war nationalist
period had by the 1960s given ground to a rather
orthodox and unimaginative response in which
clinging to power became the criterion of success
rather than the overthrow of the residual colonial
legacy.  In short, the immediate post-independence
period was characterized by caution and conservatism
rather than by creativity.  Such a mood reflected
a prevalent strand throughout much of Africa's
history in which collaboration has been the motif
rather than confrontation.

        This rather dominant mode of reaction to
changes in the global division of labor has its
origins in Africa's initial involvement in extra-
continental affairs.  For Africa was "discovered"
in response to a changing mode of production in
the center of the capitalist world:  through incorporation it came to provide raw materials, markets
and labor to fuel the industrial revolution in
Europe.  Its function was determined exogenously;
its mode of production was determined externally;
and the rate and direction of its "dependent development" were determined by foreign forces.[5]

        But whilst the dominant pressure was exter-
nal, some internal interests were able to benefit
from international developments.  And the introduction of new forms of economic activity led to

opportunities for accumulation and differentiation;
external exchange exacerbated internal inequalities.
International incorporation produced exploitation,
but this exploitation was not only between center
and periphery states.  Some social groups within
the periphery stood to gain as well.  Colonialism
generated not undevelopment:  a process of differentiation within the colonies as well as between
them and the metropole.[6]

The established African mode of production
took time to absorb the manifold changes in technology, demand and communication brought into the
continent through contact with the industrial
revolution in Europe.  But over time the peasant
mode of production has come to coexist with the
plantation and extractive modes (and in the future
with an industrial mode too?).  And yet the process
of adaptation was always tardy, leading to further
vulnerability.  Africa was hit hard by the depres-
sion of the 1930s and by the recession of the 1970s.
As Davidson notes:  "Up to 1939, the important
point of change since 1890 was not the First World
War.  It was the great slump which began in Europe
and America in 1929 and hit the colonies of Africa
a year or so later."[7]  Likewise, since 1939 the
major period of structural transition has been the
"stagflation" of the mid-1970s rather than the era
of nationalism of the 1950s.

This vulnerability to foreign forces is
reflective of the continuity of dependence; of the
responsiveness of Africa's political economy to
external demands rather than to internal needs.
Such an inheritance is a primary determinant of
Africa's future prospects and constraints.  This
focus is similar to that proposed by Steven Langdon and Lynn Mytelka:

the external pressures and ties created
for periphery African societies by the
expansion and adjustment of the capitalist
world economy.  These pressures and ties...
have generated certain socio-institutional

effects that influence contemporary
change. Furthermore, such ties in the
contemporary context influence both internal class structure and class consciousness within Africa. And finally,
such external realities constitute a
continuing constraint on rapid transition to new internal structures, even
in cases where regimes emerge with some
independence from transnational integration and some commitment to escape from
historical legacies.[8]

Dependence and incorporation go some way, then, to
explain the lack of choice and the absence of
development in Africa.[9] Langdon and Mytelka argue
themselves that "the structural change and capital
accumulation taking place in interelationship with
these strong external links have led and are leading to increasing segmentation and inequality in
many African countries, to growing employment
problems, and to ongoing poverty for most
Africans."[10] As noted below, these characteristics contain the seeds of revolutionary potential. But the process of transnational integration amongst classes as well as countries provides
the means of local order and oppression as well as
the causes of change. Moreover, African leaders
and populations tend to be preoccupied with the
imperative of survival and with past rather than
future disturbances.

The success of the nationalist movement
can be explained, then, in terms of shifts in the
world system rather than in terms of the intrinsic
merit or forcefulness of its claims. The demise
of the colonial powers after World War II --
brought about not so much by war-weariness as by
technological change -- led to new forms of center-
periphery relationship that could accommodate
readily many of the demands of the nationalist
leadership. As Davidson comments on the late
1950s and early 1960s: "This period of 'decolonization' thus became the decade of US ideological

hegemony. Transnational capitalism had evolved
its own techniques of indirect rule; and the
European model acquired, as it were, a large
American extension."[11]

Likewise, the present period is characterized by upheaval in the global order, with particular implications for Africa. American dominance
is presently being undermined by several forces,
notably "inter-imperial rivalries" (mainly emanat-
ing from Japan and the EEC) and the emergence of a
select group of "Newly Industralizing Countries"
or "Newly Influential Countries" (NICs).[12] The
shift away from bipolarity to multipolarity has
profound implications for African unity and development and, combined with the issues of resource
depletion and environmental pollution, is leading
to new inequalities both between and within the
states of the continent.

Such changes in the world system, along
with the apparent limits to strategies of import-
substitution and regional integration, have generated a reassessment of the achievements of the
first nationalist period. In particular, the
elusiveness of development has led to a more
fundamental reconsideration of Africa's inheritance of incorporation within the international
political economy. As Davidson comments himself,
this review has become a feature of the second
decade of independence, particularly the second-
half of the seventies, when the limited achievements of the nationalist movement became more
apparent:

> The kind of thinking that emerged in the
> 1960s was not yet capable in a systematic
> way of questioning the accepted structures
> of the nation-state in Africa, nor was
> there, at least until after 1965, any
> sufficiently pressing reason for doing so;
> that would be the task of the 1970s.[13]

ii)  From the 1970s to the 1980s:  revision and
     response

     The second-half of the 1970s takes on,then,
many of the characteristics of an historic conjuncture in which external and internal forces
produce a fundamental reassessment of Africa's
place in the world system.  The intensifying
energy crisis and resource shortages,[14] increasing
levels of inflation and indebtedness, and rising
concern over population and pollution, combined
with liberation in lusophone Africa, have compelled
a reevaluation of Africa's development constraints
and potential.  The continent has grown tired of
"paying the price for independence on the imported
model"[15] and instead has begun to search for an
alternative to further incorporation and dependence.

     This search has been intensified and ac-
celerated because of future forecasts as well as
past disappointments.  The consensus emerging from
a set of projections of the mid-term future envisages a continent beset by high rates of population, inflation, indebtedness and assistance,
leading to low rates of increase in gross and _per
capita_ products.[16]

     The implications of such trends, indicative
of Africa's continuing underdevelopment, are, and
will continue to be, profound in terms of continental order.  Contemporary crises and conflicts
at the level of superstructure are intrinsically
related to contradictions at the level of sub-
structure.  According to Davidson, such tensions
exist both in history as well as in the future,
and both in superstructure as well as in sub-
structure.  The post-independence period has led,
then, to

     the working out of confrontation between
     the colonial heritage and the pre-colonial
     heritage, now that the second is free to
     challenge the first; and along with that,

the resultant development of ideas concerned with searching for a different
model. These are the fields of theory
and practice within which this history
plays out its ongoing and decisive
themes into the 1980s and beyond.[17]

The tension between inheritance and future, between
tradition and innovation has been heightened not
only by the search for a new, appropriate model
for national and continental political economy but
also by the intensification of intra- and inter-
state conflicts.

iii)  Contemporary patterns of cooperation, con-
      flict and contradiction

Africa has been rarely united in its
response to external incorporation or intervention.
Indeed, in both pre- and post-colonial periods it
has been vulnerable to such foreign interests
because of linkages between its own social formations and external structures which undermine
continental cohesion. The brief era of nationalist unity was the exception rather than the norm,
brought about by an historic conjuncture -- World
War II, commodities boom, decline of the colonial
powers etc. Moreover, unity existed at the level
of super- rather than sub-structure.

"Independence" did not transform the
political economies of Africa; the modes and relations of production have remained remarkably
stable despite frequent shifts in some countries
in the arena of politics. The contradiction
between formal independence and real dependence --
between the attributes rather than the substance
of "independence" -- has grown over the past two
decades and is now a central issue at the levels
of both super- and sub-structure.

At the level of superstructure, the "gap"
between formal national sovereignty and real

national dependence has led to various forms of
xenophobia and dictatorship. At the level of sub-
structure, the "gap" has led to various forms of
nationalization and protectionism. But just as an
"authoritarian response" in politics is essentially
superficial, so a nationalist response in economics
is incomplete without being part of a comprehensive
plan for industrialization, self-reliance and
socialism.[18] The latter issue -- of type of development strategy -- is addressed in the next section;
the former issue -- of politics -- is tackled here
first.

African regimes have attempted to treat
their political problems by a range of measures
generally categorized as departicipation, central-
ization and control. Many contradictions within
the substructure and between it and the superstructure may have been ameliorated by such
"political engineering" from the mid-1960s to the
mid-1970s but they have been neither resolved nor
transformed into a new synthesis. Indeed, Colin
Legum argues that the "gap" between state and
nation in Africa (with very few countries being
nation-states), combined with various forms of
"pluralism", constitutes an inflammable situation:

All those factors suggest that Africa
is at a most difficult and volatile
stage of development. During the 1980s
quarrels within one country or between
hostile neighboring countries are likely
to erupt into violent conflicts...the
efforts of the Organisation of African
Unity notwithstanding. Such conflicts
will affect not only the localities or
countries directly involved, but in many
cases also will provoke foreign intervention. This is not to say that Africa
will be the passive victim of international power politics. On the contrary, African factions will actively
seek foreign military and economic
assistance to bolster fragile positions
....[19]

Legum envisages increased territorial, regional and
expernal conflict over communal, national and external interests occuring in several parts of the
continent:  southern Africa, Nigeria, Zaire/Angola,
the Horn, East Africa, the Sudan and the Maghreb.[20]
He is particularly concerned with the international
dimensions of civil wars, expansionist nationalism,
and transnational military interventions as forms
of crisis.  And he identifies five continuing
issues that will "keep Africa high on the agenda
of international decision-making in the 1980s":
ocean politics, racial confrontation in southern
Africa, Afro-Arab politics, Sino-Soviet rivalry
and the North-South dialogue over NIEO.[21]  In short,
Legum sees the twin constellations of global insecurity and continental instability leading towards a period of continuing conflict in which
coalitions form over particular issues to secure
external support and involvement, thus opening the
continent up to further foreign involvement.

A complex and comprehensive set of transnational coalitions has arisen, then, over contemporary conflicts in Africa:  African and non-
African states, international and transnational
organizations, liberation movements and support
groups active in a wide range of issues, not just
southern Africa.[22]  So, over the Horn, Chad,
Sahara, Shaba and Uganda, intra- and extra-African
coalitions were created to advance opposing interests on both the battlefield and the conference
floor.[23]  And Egyptian and Moroccan, Libyan and
Tanzanian troops have got involved in a range of
activities outside their own borders as have Cuban
and French soldiers, East German and American
pilots.[24]  Given structural as well as strategic
links amongst African and non-African ruling
classes it is naive of The Times, reflecting a
wide-spread Western concern about Soviet involvement, to call for a "Monroe Doctrine for Africa."[25]
Western intervention may be more established and
substructural than that from the East, which tends
to be rather vulgar and involve overt coercive

instruments; but both forms are related to Africa's place in the world system and to the vulnerability and instability that underdevelopment brings.

So Africa once again became the subject of international diplomacy in the late 1970s as it was in the early 1960s. Indeed, the decade from 1965 to 1975 may be seen increasingly as an interregnum between more normal periods of external attention and intervention: the Congo crisis of the early 1960s became the Shaba crisis of the late 1970s. In reality, Africa has always been incorporated into the world system but the ties that were structural and covert for awhile are once again controversial and overt. Yet whereas the continent could shield behind the mask of nonalignment and collective foreign policy in a bipolar international system and in the early years of the OAU,[26] such a strategy is more tenuous now that multipolarity has replaced bipolarity and the OAU is visibly divided.[27] Moreover, faith in development and resources has been superseded by fears of underdevelopment and shortages since the oil crisis of the mid-1970s.[28] Changes in the global and continental orders have revealed Africa's essential vulnerability and contemporary events have reinforced this at the level of superstructure and diplomacy.[29]

As Legum has noted, there are continuities as well as changes in Africa's world position, even at this level of diplomacy:

Looking back to the Berlin Treaty of 1884 and the carving out of separate spheres of influence by the colonial powers, Africans began to speak uneasily in 1977 about "a new scramble" for the continent...the colonial memory persists, reinforcing the association of foreign power rivalries in Africa with the subjugation of the continent ...But in the 1970s, the foreign powers had to take the interests of competing

African states and groups fully into
account in order to hope to promote
their own national interests.  Only
by offering themselves as allies to
particular interest groups could they
expect to expand their influence on
the continent.[30]

Africans were never passive bystanders in continental or global affairs; even in pre-colonial
and colonial times they affected outcomes by
adopting alternative strategies of conflict or
cooperation.  But in the late 1970s, given the
emergence of multipolarity extra-regionally and
new inequalities both within and between the
African states themselves, novel patterns of complex coalitions began to emerge over continental
issues, as already noted.  The substructural vulnerability of the continent was thus revealed and
reinforced by superstructural associations.  As
Legum remarks,

> The new phenonemon, then, was the
> externalization of inter-African con-
> flicts, brought about by militarily
> and economically weaker local forces
> engaging the support of foreign
> powers.  When interests coincided,
> alliances became possible.  So far
> from being helpless victims - as in
> the past - Africans themselves had to
> accept full responsibility for the
> greater involvement of both western
> and communist countries in the con-
> tinent's affairs.[31]

"Intervention" was no longer a simple function of
external interests; rather "externalization" was
a function of the occasional coincidence of intra-
with extra- African interests.  Moreover, such
coalitions were not just bilateral -- African
state with foreign power -- but were typically
multilateral -- several African states in a group
in association with one or more foreign powers[32]

--and mixed actor -- involving African and non-African non-governmental interests, whether they be parties, corporations, religious organizations, trade unions or international institutions. Given the rise of such complex coalitions of forces, considerable diplomatic time was paid to assembling and maintaining them on particular issues.

Because the Western association with Africa is more established and substructural it has been less visible and controversial than Eastern involvement in the continent's conflicts. Moreover, in the post-Vietnam era of a "new isolationism" in the United States and "inter-imperial rivalries" between it and the EEC and Japan, the West was in the mid-1970s initially less prepared for a renewed and overt intervention. However, by the end of the decade

> Developments in Africa - and in the
> capitals of the great powers - made
> that continent an important testing
> ground for the foreign policies of
> the Western nations and the Soviet
> Union...While clearly still the
> dominant foreign influence in Africa,
> the Western countries were thrown on
> the defensive and groped for new ways
> of protecting their interests there.
> In the open diplomatic confrontation
> with the Soviet Union and Cuba, the
> West came off worst in the Horn of
> Africa but continued to manoeuver
> actively in southern Africa. In
> neither area were the western powers
> able to discourage the Soviet Union
> and Cuba from intervening militarily
> in the continent's internal affairs.[33]

African disunity and divergence both facilitated and exacerbated external involvement. And the related inequalities are likely to increase exponentially given continued foreign attention to the continent.

However, post-colonial conflicts and pre-colonial exchanges also combine to point the continent in the direction of reassessment. Any improvement in Africa's development prospects, either now or by the end of the century, requires a revision of its place in the world system. As Davidson says,

> Africa today is the product not only of
> its pre-colonial history, or more recently
> of the history of the colonial period,
> but also of a direct trading relation-
> ship with the mercantile and early
> capitalist systems of Europe which began
> before 1500... On this view of histor-
> ical processes, beginning to be quite
> widely held by the 1970s, the twentieth
> century acquires a still more dramatic
> and decisive interest. For this emerges
> as the century in which the Africans
> not only come out of their isolation and
> begin to measure where they stand, but
> learn to analyse their limits and capac-
> ities within the wider scene of the world
> itself and embark on new destinations.[34]

iv)   Independence, interdependence and dependence:
      Africa in the 1980s

Africa's recapture of its formal inde-pendence through the activities of the nationalist movement did not by itself change the continent's place in the world system in terms of either super- or sub-structural relationships. It did, however, open up new options, which some states have begun to identify and adopt, particularly at the level of superstructure. And it did gen-erate a "wind of change" in analysis as well as in practice. For before 1960 liberal and radical scholars and leaders could all agree on the imperative of "freedom"; indeed the nationalist period was characterized by a remarkable degree of cohesion because of the commonly recognized goal of independence.

Unity has been increasingly elusive since then, however, precisely because new options are now available that undermine the ready cooperation of those days. As Davidson laments, the "liberating nationalism" has been replaced by awareness of a "deepening crisis." Not only has the mood changed; but there is renewed disagreement over how to deal with dependence, underdevelopment and inequalities. This disagreement is especially pronounced over questions of sub- rather than super-structure.

The orthodox prescription for Africa's political economies remains further externally-oriented growth, along with foreign investment, technology and assistance; that is, more "interdependence." On the other hand, an emerging radical response advocates greater autonomy and self-reliance as the way towards development; that is, more "disengagement." The former strategy of interdependence is the dominant mode preferred by liberal interests in the north as well as by ruling classes in the south. The latter strategy of self-reliance is a radical response to the elusiveness of development and to the presistence of dependence; it is advocated by alternative interests in both north and south. It puts the satisfaction of Basic Human Needs in Africa above production for the "international" (i.e. advanced industrial states) market.[35]

This is the "new consciousness of choice" to which Davidson refers in his opening quotation. It constitutes a belated response to the elusiveness of development despite formal freedom; it also involves a belated attempt to close the "gap" between political and economic independence.[36] For despite some shifts in its political and economic systems since independence, Africa has remained thus far an essentially cautious continent. Guy Arnold has commented on this somewhat surprising yet well-established characteristic, given the vibrancy of its nationalist period and the intensity of its present problems:

> As a continent, despite the pace of change over the past two decades, Africa is conservative; it is a minority of countries that have achieved any real moves away from the elitist pro-Western styles of running affairs that were inherited from the colonialists - and this remains true even when one- party states have replaced multi-party systems or the army has replaced the politicians.[37]

But whilst political form does not correlate very highly with economic strategy -- that is, whilst there is no simple relationship between super- and sub-structure -- there has been a growing trend apparent in the late-1970s towards more self-reliant political economies. This trend is by no means unilineal -- there has been decay and regression as well as development and progression -- yet the minority is no longer so small and embattled as it was in the early 1970s. Indeed, voting in the OAU and alignments over African crises as well as more substantial forms of inter-action point to the emergence of a radical coali-tion on the continent.[38]

Characteristic of the reappraisal of development strategies in Africa is, then, the growing adoption of radical rhetoric and, at times, radical remedies. By 1977, Legum argues that there were

> ten African countries which formally adhere to the Marxist system - Mozam-bique, Angola, Guinea-Bissau, Cape Verde, Sao Tome e Principe, Madagascar, Congo, Benin, Ethiopia and Somalia. However, there are considerable differ-ences in the systems established in

these ten countries, with only the
first three conforming to the classical
Marxist pattern.[39]

Nevertheless, about 20% of the states of Africa
are now in some sense "socialist", the result of
colonial contradictions in the Portuguese empire
and of social contradictions elsewhere.

If popular struggles -- against racism
and colonialism in southern Africa and against
reaction and conservatism elsewhere on the continent -- have produced this cluster of more progressive and innovative regimes, other forces have
produced more capitalist or more centralist
variants. The majority of regimes in Africa remain "state capitalist" or "state socialist"; in
both types the state apparatus is a dominant
feature.[40] In the former more capitalist system,
the state exists to facilitate an unequal division
of labor in which national as well as transnational
bourgeois interests can accumulate surplus;whereas
in the latter more socialist system, the state
exists to promote a more equal division of labor
in which a variety of class interests benefit,
although the "political class" does tend to enjoy
more privileges than the peasants and the workers.
In the third, minority grouping of states -- the
more orthodox "socialist" variety -- the state is
less central and other institutions -- party committees, branches and cells, cooperatives, unions,
and self-help groups, etc. -- insist on more
popular decision-making and distribution.[41]

This third group constitutes the most
dramatic response to date to the unsatisfactory
performance of the "imported model" as identified
by Davidson:

A first category now consisted of a few
regimes with relatively strong economies.
Their ruling groups could still add
wealth and status to themselves, and,
by continuing to grow, hope to become a

middle class capable of building an
indigenous capitalism... A second
category was numerous. These were
regimes with relatively weak economies
in most or all of which the parlia-
mentary model had decayed into an
autocracy, but where, because of
economic weakness, ruling groups had
no thought of being able to grow
into dominant middle classes. Often
relying on foreign partners for their
survival, these were bureaucratic
dictatorships of a peculiarly crude
type... A third category, few in
number, was also composed of regimes
with weak economies... These were
the regimes that had turned away from
the given model and its decadent
derivatives, and were ready to experiment with democratic politics.[42]

   This later group of more self-reliant and
socialist political economies may represent the
wave of the future, as a response both to the
limitations of the "imported model" and to the
prospect of withdrawal by the major capitalist
powers from at least the extremities of their
global reach. Ecological and economic pressures
in the mid-term may force the capitalist countries
and corporations to concentrate their attentions
on the few, relatively successful semi-industrial
states in the semi-periphery, essentially the
state capitalist group, leaving the state socialist
and socialist varieties to their own devices.
This reorganization on a global scale -- particularly the association between interests in the
center with those in the semi-periphery to the
exclusion of the rest of the periphery[43]-- may
serve to accelerate a trend, which Davidson sees
emerging in the 1980s, away from state capitalism
and towards some sort of socialism: "The development of programs for constructive change aimed
at building indigenous models; and some of these,
in the perspective of the 1980s, were manifestly

within an entirely new field of independent
thought, having discarded the various simulacra
of other people's systems along with the rest of
the decorative verbiage of the 1960s."[44]

If Pan Africanism and nonalignment were
the watchwords of Africa's collective foreign
policy during its first two decades of independence then self-reliance is likely to be the
motif of the next twenty years. Given Africa's
inheritance of dependence and underdevelopment,
some form and degree of disengagement are increasingly recognized to be the sine quo non of
development. However, although self-reliance is
an increasingly popular policy, it is still
elusive and often ambiguous; continued incorporation within the world system remains the
characteristic motif of the continent. Yet the
meagre benefits of such association with external
interests in post- as well as pre-colonial periods,
and the projected problems of further external
exchange, have generated a new skepticism amongst
both analysts and planners.

The majority of African states and peoples
have not benefitted significantly, if at all, from
decolonizaton and independence. With most indigenous regimes following orthodox development
policies the results have been disappointing.
Therefore, the continent, half-way between independence and the year 2000, confronts a very
difficult pair of decades, particularly so given
the moves towards recession and protectionism in
the industrialized states.

The emerging response to such difficulties
and contradictions and to (under)development with
(inter)dependence is to advocate some form of
disengagement and self-reliance. Adebayo Adedeji
and the ECA reflect this new perspective:  "It is
therefore imperative that African states should
reformulate their policies and economic strategies
and instruments with a view to promoting national

and collective self-reliance."[45]  Self-reliance
means not more of the same -- ie. more foreign
finance, technology, skills, and exchange -- but
rather a fundamental reassessment of all external
linkages.  Instead of the criteria for development being externally- or internally-defined
they would be based on internal needs (not wants).
Such a break, or decoupling, would be designed to
maximize internal exchange and national autonomy
and overcome externally-oriented growth and local
disarticulation.  It would also improve the prospects of avoiding the potential problems posed
by projections for the continent based on present
trends.

Adoption of self-reliance would advance
African development in at least three ways. First,
it would improve the rate and quality of development at the national level.  Second, it would enhance autonomy and unity at the continental level.
And third, by reviving African institutions and
images it would advance the continent's interests
at the global level.  It would, therefore, reduce
the tendency to fragmentation of the national and
continental political economies and support
Africa's collective demands for a New International
Economic Order.[46]

So collective self-reliance could serve
to minimize the dangers of a few semi-peripheral
countries emerging on the continent to replace
indigenous continental institutions as the focus
of linkages between global and national regimes.
But given the demise of Pan-Africanism, the
essential, intermediate, continental level of
agreement is likely to prove the most problematic.
As Adedeji himself remarks:

>     Regionally, there is an urgent need for
>     concentrating on achieving an increasing
>     measure of collective self-reliance
>     among African states...Indeed, economic
>     cooperation among African states is a

_sine qua non_ for the achievement of
national socio-economic goals, and
not an 'extra' to be given thought to
after the process of development is
well advanced. African states have
also to learn very soon how to insulate
economic cooperation institutions and
arrangements from the vagaries of
political differences.[47]

It is the intensification of such inequalities and differences -- based increasingly
on substructural rather than superstructural
factors -- that poses a challenge to African
solidarity as well as to its self-reliance. The
emergence of a group of more socialist regimes
with the "second wave" of decolonization (especially in southern Africa) and revolution (especially in middle Africa) undermines the easy
consensus that characterized continental politics
in the mid- to late-1960s.[48] As already noted,
there is now a strong and growing faction in the
OAU that defines development and foreign policy
in more materialist terms based on somewhat
dialectical assumptions.[49] This faction is not
readily persuaded by the rhetoric of Pan Africanism
and good neighborliness. And it conceives of
self-reliance as an adjunct to socialism rather
than as an aspect of embourgeoisement. Such
alternative definitions and regional levels may
come to pose problems for Africa in planning and
projecting, let alone seizing the future. And
the decision about whether to stay with or to
abandon the imported model is increasingly informed by future forecasts as well as by past
failures.

v) The mid-term future: alternative scenarios
   and strategies
_____

Forecasts for Africa's next twenty years,
based on established trends, are not promising.

Indeed, the next two decades are likely to be
much more difficult than the last two, involving
further underdevelopment, inequalities and exogenous determinants.[50]  However, whilst the projections are quite pessimistic the outlook may,
by contrast, be considerably more optimistic.
For the very contradictions generated by the
elusiveness of development in Africa may generate
their own dialectic and synthesis.  The second
African revolution is likely to be more fundamental then the first; the second wave is likely
to be the more powerful.

     Any transformation of the continent's
political economy over the next couple of decades
may lead to alternative scenarios and strategies
in which endogamous development comes to replace
exogenous underdevelopment.  Africa has no future
-- or certainly not much of one -- under the old
orthodoxy; but under a new regime its potential
could be considerable.[51]  Hence the current debate
over alternative responses to Africa's inheritance
of dependent and uneven development.

     On the one hand, then, a consensus exists
about the generally unpromising projections for
Africa's mid-term future based on established
trends:  high rates of population growth, low
levels of economic growth and problems with in-
frastructure, environment, debt, food and
resources all add up to a difficult period to
the year 2000.  On the other hand, however, there
is a spreading and lively debate over how to
respond to these difficulties and how to avoid
an unpromising future.

     Although there is a growing appreciation
in Africa that inequalities are increasing and
that development remains elusive, nevertheless
something of a lacuna still exists over how to
respond to such unfavorable trends.  And the
absence of a collective response exposes the
continent to continued buffeting by divisive

external forces and pressures. These tend to
exacerbate inequalities at the levels of both
relationship and policy. The rise of subimperial
states and residual fidelity towards established
development theories are indicative of the continuing salience of extra-continental influences.
And it is these very established factors -- at
both national and continental levels -- that self-
reliance is intended to resist by redefining
development policies and practices.

Moreover, the exacerbation of inequalities
both within and between states, as already
suggested, may generate its own dialectic; namely
a series of increasingly revolutionary movements
and events within the periphery, leading towards
the establishment of new regimes characterized
by greater degrees of socialism and self-reliance.[52]
In other words, if the Basic Human Needs (BHN) of
most of the people are not met either in the semi-
periphery or in the periphery then pressures will
build for fundamental change throughout the continent: for "real" as opposed to "formal" decolonization.

The prospect of more radical movements
emerging throughout Africa by the year 2000 is
enhanced by the distinctive patterns of decolonization presently apparent in the remaining unfree
territories concentrated in Southern Africa. The
mode of transition to independence in Mozambique,
Angola and Zimbabwe -- and perhaps yet in Namibia
-- stands in considerable contrast to that which
occured in most of the rest of Africa, and points
to another way: that of a non-capitalist path.[53]

Given the essentially capitalist character of the present world system, the adoption of
self-reliance means in effect following a semi-
or non-capitalist path.[54] The cases of Angola,
Mozambique, Namibia and Zimbabwe and, in time,
South Africa itself, may become not only significant and suggestive models for the rest of Africa.

These states also possess a range of resources --
political and administrative as well as economic
and infrastructural -- that will enable them to
contribute to increased intra-continental interaction and exchange as a way of facilitating and
advancing self-reliance elsewhere on the continent.
This group of countries may indeed emerge as a
non-capitalist semi-periphery, able to satisfy
BHN as well as possessing the power capability of
influencing neighboring states away from continued
dependence.  As Langdon and Mytelka argue themselves, change in southern Africa is crucial to
the theory and practice of socialism and self-
reliance throughout the continent:

> South-South trade in the African con-
> text could be especially useful on a
> continental basis.  But the prospect
> of such development depends heavily
> on successful overthrow of the white-
> run regimes in southern Africa.  The
> possibility of that taking place is
> likely to be a central focus on much
> international concern in Africa, on
> many levels, throughout the 1980s.
> Self-reliant black regimes in Namibia,
> Zimbabwe and South Africa would make
> an immense contribution to alternative
> development strategy for all Africa,
> but considerable conflict will occur
> before such regimes finally emerge.[55]

Paradoxically, therefore, the region of the
greatest degree of incorporation into the world
system because of its mineral-rich, settler-dom-
inated and strategically-important characteristics is likely to be the one that is crucial
to the successful disengagement of Africa from
the world system.  The current conflict in
southern Africa has, then, a long-term structural
as well as shorter-term symbolic significance.[56]
As Langdon and Mytelka conclude in their own preview of Africa in the global political economy,
the orientation and outcome of this regional

situation has both superstructural and substructural importance:

> Armed conflict in southern Africa, though, is likely to be no more than the most dramatic African form of confrontation between dependence and self-reliance in the 1980s. We expect the contradictions of periphery capitalism in Africa to become more acute in most countries on the continent in the next decade, and we expect the struggles for change in such countries to become more bitter as a result. We are confident, however, that out of such conflict can come more equitable and self-reliant development strategies that benefit the great majority of Africans.[57]

Notes

1. For an overview of these projections and
   policy responses see Timothy M. Shaw "Introduction: the political economy of Africa's
   futures" in his collection on Alternative
   Futures for Africa (Boulder: Westview, 1981)
   and "On projections, prescriptions and plans:
   towards an African future" Quarterly Journal
   of Administration 14(2), July 1980.

2. For alternative forecasts and scenarios of
   Africa's futures see Colin Legum et al. Africa
   in the 1980s: a continent in crisis (New York:
   McGraw-Hill for Council on Foreign Relations
   1980s Project, 1979); Helen Kitchen (ed)
   Africa: from mystery to maze (Lexington:
   Lexington Critical Choices for Americans
   Volume II, 1976); Jennifer Seymour Whitaker
   (ed) Africa and the United States: vital in-
   terests (New York: New York University Press
   for Council on Foreign Relations, 1978);
   "Special number on Africa in the year 2000"
   Issue 8(4), Winter 1978, 1-63, and Shaw (ed)
   Alternative Futures for Africa.

3. See also Raymond L. Hall "Towards the invention
   of an African future" and Paul Goulding and
   Timothy M. Shaw "Alternative scenarios for
   Africa" in Shaw (ed) Alternative Futures for
   Africa.

4. For applications of this historical approach
   see, inter alia, Immanuel Wallerstein "The
   three stages of African involvement in the
   world economy" in Peter C. W. Gutkind and
   Immanuel Wallerstein (eds) The Political
   Economy of Contemporary Africa (Beverly Hills:
   Sage, 1976) 30-57, and Timothy M. Shaw "The
   actors in African international politics" in
   Timothy M. Shaw and Kenneth A. Heard (eds)
   The Politics of Africa: dependence and development (London: Longman, 1979) 357-372.

5.  For such an overview see Steven Langdon and Lynn K. Mytelka "Africa in the changing world economy" in Legum et al. Africa in the 1980s and Samir Amin "Underdevelopment and dependence in Black Africa: origins and contemporary forms" Journal of Modern African Studies 10(4), December 1972, 503-524.

6.  See Timothy M. Shaw and M. Catherine Newbury "Dependence or interdependence? Africa in the global political economy" in Mark W. DcLancey (ed) Aspects of International Relations in Africa (Bloomington: Indiana University African Studies Programme, 1979) 39-89.

7.  Basil Davidson Africa in Modern History: the search for a new society (Harmondsworth: Pelican, 1978) 131.

8.  Langdon and Mytelka "Africa in the changing world economy" 127.

9.  See Timothy M. Shaw and Malcolm J. Grieve "Dependence or development: international and internal inequalities in Africa" Development and Change 8(3), July 1977, 377-408, "Inequalities and the state in Africa" Review of Black Political Economy 8(1), Fall 1977, 27-42, and "Dependence as an approach to understanding continuing inequalities in Africa" Journal of Developing Areas 13(3), April 1979, 229-246.

10. Langdon and Mytelka "Africa in the changing world economy" 127.

11. Davidson Africa in Modern History 210.

12. For an analysis of these see Timothy M. Shaw "Dependence to (Inter)Dependence: review of debate on the (New) International Economic Order" Alternatives 4(4), March 1979, 557-578, and "Towards an international political economy for the 1980s: from dependence to (inter)dependence" (Halifax: Centre for

Foreign Policy Studies, 1980).

13. Davidson _Africa in Modern History_ 287.

14. On the exploitation and depletion of Africa's
resources by extra-African interests see F.
Chidozie Ogene "The politics of scarcity:
African resources and international politics"
_Nigerian Institute of International Affairs_
(Lagos, n.d., Seminar Series Number 4).

15. Davidson _Africa in Modern History_ 294.

16. See Timothy M. Shaw and Don Munton "Africa's
futures: a comparison of forecasts" in Shaw
(ed) _Alternative Futures for Africa_.

17. Davidson _Africa in Modern History_ 295.

18. See Ann Seidman "Changing theories of political economy in Africa" in Christopher Fyfe
(ed) _African Studies Since 1945: a tribute to
Basil Davidson_ (London: Longman, 1976) 49-65.

19. Colin Legum "Communal conflict in international intervention in Africa" in Legum _et al_.
_Africa in the 1980s_ 23-24.

20. See _ibid_. 59-64.

21. _Ibid_. 49-55. See also I. William Zartman
"Social and political trends in Africa in the
1980s" in Legum _et al_. _Africa in the 1980s_
69-119 and "Conflict in Africa" (New York:
Council on Foreign Relations Study Group on
Conflict and Crisis in Africa, Background
Paper Number 5, June 1979).

22. On the latter case, however, consult Timothy
M. Shaw "Southern Africa: from detente to
deluge" _Year Book of World Affairs, 32_ (London:
Stevens and Boulder: Westview, 1978, for Institute of World Affairs) 117-138.

23. On the essential weakness and openness of the

continent to extra-continental interventions
see Anirudha Gupta "Africa in the 1980s"
India Quarterly 35(3), July-September 1979,
309-310 and 326.

24. See Timothy M. Shaw "Inequalities and conflicts in contemporary Africa" International
Perspectives, May/June 1978, 44-49, James O.
Goldsborough "Dateline Paris: Africa's police-
man" Foreign Policy 33, Winter 1978-9, 174-
190, and Raymond W. Copson "African international politics: underdevelopment and conflict in the seventies" Orbis 22(1) Spring
1978, 227-245.

25. See "Editorial: Monroe Doctrine for Africa?"
The Times 7 February 1978, 15.

26. See Timothy M. Shaw "The Organisation of
African Unity: prospects for the second
decade" International Perspectives September/
October 1973, 31-34, and "The political
economy of nonalignment: from dependence to
self-reliance" International and Indian
Political Science Associations Roundtable
on Nonalignment (Calcutta, November 1979).

27. On underdevelopment as a cause for such
extra-continental pressures and intra-
continental cleavages see Gupta "Africa in
the 1980s." See also Mihailo V. Slevovic
"As Africa enters the eighties" Review of
International Affairs 31(714), 5 January
1980, 38-41.

28. For overviews of these changes see Don Munton,
Timothy M. Shaw, Malcolm J. Grieve and Tom
Keating "Global problems for Canadians: forecasts and speculations" Behind the Headlines
37(6), 1981.

29. On the history, incidence and impact of resources and scarcities in Africa, with profound implications for its international
relations, see Ogene "The politics of
scarcity."

30.  Colin Legum "The year in perspective" in his
     collection <u>Africa Contemporary Record: annual
     survey and documents, Volume 10, 1977-78</u> (New
     York: Africana, 1979) xx.

31.  <u>Ibid</u>.

32.  For a useful conceptual framework in which to
     place such associations - based on Africa's
     unsatisfactory experience and performance
     since independence and on consequent increases
     in its dependence and vulnerability - see
     Gupta "Africa in the 1980s" 313-318.

33.  Colin Legum "The African crisis" in William
     P. Bundy (ed) <u>Foreign Affairs: America and
     the World 1978</u> (Elmsford: Pergamon, 1979).
     See also Tom J. Farer "Ethiopia: Soviet
     strategy and Western fears" <u>Africa Report</u>
     23(6), November-December 1978, 4-8, and
     Timothy M. Shaw "The international politics
     of Southern Africa: change or continuity?"
     <u>Issue</u> 7(1), Spring 1977, 19-26.

34.  Davidson <u>Africa in Modern History</u> 18 and 21.

35.  For overviews of this debate and its implica-
     tions see Malcolm J. Grieve and Timothy M.
     Shaw "Chronique Bibliographique - the polit-
     ical economy of Africa: internal and interna-
     tional inequalities" <u>Cultures et Developpe-
     ment</u> 10(4), 1978, 609-648, and "Dependence as
     an explanation of inequalities in Africa" in
     Larry Gould and Harry Targ (eds) <u>Global dom-
     inance and dependence: readings in theory and
     research</u> (forthcoming).

36.  On this attempt see Dharam Ghai (ed) <u>Economic
     Independence in Africa</u> (Nairobi: East African
     Literature Bureau, 1973).

37.  Guy Arnold "African politics" in Alan Rake
     (ed) <u>New African Yearbook 1978</u> (London:
     International Communications, 1978) 43.

38.  See Shaw and Newbury "Dependence or interde-

pendence? Africa in the global political
economy" and Copson "African international
politics: underdevelopment and conflict in
the seventies."

39.  Legum "The year in perspective" xxiii.

40.  As Richard Harris notes in his introductory
     essay on "The political economy of Africa -
     underdevelopment or revolution" the "state
     structure has served as the main instrument
     by which the African bourgeoisie have imposed
     their domination on the subordinate classes
     and secured their privileged position in the
     present neo-colonial system" [Richard Harris
     (ed) The Political Economy of Africa (Cam-
     bridge, Mass.: Schenkman, 1975)] 30.

41.  For an earlier presentation of this typology
     see Timothy M. Shaw "The political economy of
     African international relations" Issue 5(4),
     Winter 1975, 29-38.

42.  Davidson Africa in Modern History 329.

43.  On this trend see Timothy M. Shaw "Kenya and
     South Africa: 'subimperialist states'" Orbis
     21(2), Summer 1977, 375-394, and "Inequalities
     and interdependence in Africa and Latin
     America: subimperialism and semi-industrialism
     in the semi-periphery" Cultures et Developpe-
     ment 10(2), 1978, 231-263.

44.  Davidson Africa in Modern History 376.

45.  Adebayo Adedeji "Africa: the crisis of devel-
     opment and the challenge of a new economic
     order.  Address to the fourth meeting of the
     Conference of Ministers and thirteenth session
     of the Economic Commission for Africa, Kin-
     shasa, February-March 1977" (Addis Ababa: ECA,
     July 1977) 18.

46.  See Economic Commission for Africa "The
     African region and international negotiations"

(Addis Ababa, 1978. E/CN. 14/ECO/158).

47. Adedeji "Africa" 16. See also "ECA Review of
    Economic and Social Conditions in Africa in
    the light of development objectives, targets
    and strategies" in Shaw (ed) Alternative
    Futures for Africa Appendix One.

48. On alternative definitions and analyses of
    regionalism in Africa see Timothy M. Shaw
    "Towards a political economy of regional
    integration and inequality in Africa"
    Nigerian Journal of International Studies
    2(2), October 1978, and "Africa" in Werner
    Feld and Gavin Boyd (eds) Comparative Re-
    gional Systems (Elmsford, New York and Oxford:
    Pergamon, 1980) 355-397.

49. On this mode of analysis as well as prescrip-
    tion see Timothy M. Shaw "Review article.
    Foreign policy, political economy and the
    future: reflections on Africa in the world
    system" African Affairs 79(315), April 1980,
    260-268.

50. See Adedeji "Africa," Legum et al. Africa in
    the 1980s and Shaw (ed) Alternative Futures
    for Africa.

51. For an optimistic scenario see Albert
    Tevoedjre (Rapporteur) "Africa towards the
    year 2000" IFDA Dossier 7, May 1979; reprinted
    as Appendix Three in Shaw (ed) Alternative
    Futures for Africa.

52. As Richard Harris predicts in his essay on
    "The political economy of Africa: underdevel-
    opment or revolution"46-47:

>       In the meantime, the African situation
>       is likely to resemble increasingly the
>       Latin American pattern with coups and
>       counter-coups becoming commonplace, as
>       the different segments of the bourgeo-
>       isie take their turn at alternately
>       raiding the public treasury and trying

> to stop the deterioration of their
> position as a ruling class. In time,
> this pattern will serve to alienate
> all support for the bourgeoisie and
> preservation of the system will
> necessitate the direct intervention
> of the neo-colonialist powers to
> protect their interests. At this
> point, the contradictions in African
> society will be made clear for all
> to see and the present system of
> exploitative dependence and neo-
> colonialism will have no hope of
> continuing in the face of rising
> popular demands for an independent,
> united and socialist Africa.

53. See Mai Palmberg (ed) _Problems of Socialist Orientation in Africa_ (Stockholm: Almqvist and Wiksell and New York: Africana, 1978).

54. On the interplay between political economy and national ideology within the nonalignment movement and on the difficulties of being socialist or capitalist and yet outside of any bloc see papers presented at the "International Conference on Nonalignment" _Nigerian Institute for International Affairs_ Lagos, January 1980.

55. Langdon and Mytelka "Africa in the changing world economy" 211.

56. See Timothy M. Shaw "International organisations and the politics of Southern Africa: towards regional integration or liberation?" _Journal of Southern African Studies_ 3(1), 1976, 1-19, and "Southern Africa: from detente to deluge?"

57. Langdon and Mytelka "Africa in the changing world economy" 211.

PART TWO


Regional Level of Interaction

Chapter Six

## The Arab-Israeli Conflict and Afro-Arab Relations

Sola Ojo


In the past two decades, except for a brief
period between 1973 and 1978, the Arab-Israeli conflict has been the most crucial issue in Afro-
Arab relations. The situation can hardly have been
different. For the foreign policy objectives of
the Arab States since 1948 have largely revolved
around their opposition to the establishment and
subsequent expansion of the state of Israel. To
the Arabs, the issue of Israel was the bench-mark
against which all other foreign policy questions
tended to be tested.

The Arab-Israeli conflict has therefore
inevitably had a very great impact on Afro-Arab
cooperation, often deciding the extent to which
relations could be allowed to develop. It affected
relations between both groups in various international fora - in the United Nations Organisation
(UN), the non-aligned movement and the Organisation
of African Unity (OAU). Arab support for the decolonization of Southern Africa and the developmental efforts of Black OAU members were largely
made dependent on the degree of support the
Africans gave the Arabs in the latter's struggle
against Israel. The aim of this chapter is to
examine the impact the conflict has had on Black
African states' relations with the Arab World
since 1960, the year many African states became
formally independent actors on the international
scene.

The organisation of this chapter follows
the basic chronology of the Middle East crisis

itself: the first part covers the period from 1960 to the 1967 War; the second part deals with the period that ended with the Yom Kippur War of October 1973; the third part examines the period that followed Africa's near total rupture of diplomatic relations with Israel in 1973; and the fourth and final part describes the contemporary period following Egypt's peace accords with Israel.

i)   First Phase:  1960 - 1967

The primary objective of the Arabs in Africa has been to effect the diplomatic and economic isolation of Israel on the continent. They were not particularly pleased with the close ties that existed between Israel and Black Africa which had developed rapidly after Israel had re-evaluated her relations with the Third World countries following the Afro-Asian Conference held in Bandung in 1955.

The central Israeli goal in Africa was of course, primarily to break out of the diplomatic isolation into which the Arabs were trying to force her. Israel hoped that by frustrating the Arab boycott policy against her, the Arabs would be forced to negotiate peace. The Israelis also saw potential economic advantages accruing to them from close contacts with Africa.[1]

The period 1960-67 saw a very rapid growth in both official diplomatic and unofficial 'transnational' Afro-Israeli relations. With the spread of independence, Israeli diplomatic representation rose from 6 in 1960 to 23 in 1961. There was a corresponding growth in trade relations. From almost nothing in the 1950s, Israeli exports to Black Africa had by 1967 risen to US $20.4m while imports were worth US $23.8m.[2] Numerous cooperation agreements were signed with African states. By 1966, 21 such agreements had been concluded, usually during visits of high level Israeli or African officials to Africa or Israel respectively.

The most publicised aspect of Afro-Israeli
contacts was Israeli aid to African states. Though
the amount of money involved in the aid programme
was generally small, it nevertheless had a repu-
tation of being effective and easily obtainable.
Between 1960 and 1964 only $37.65m was involved.[3]
The Israeli aid programmes, consisted mainly of
technical assistance programmes, small-scale development projects, joint industrial ventures and
training of African students in Israeli institutions.[4]  Between 1958 and 1972 a total of 3,632
Israeli experts were sent to Africa and 9,182
African students were trained under cooperation
agreements.[5]

These close Afro-Israeli ties - both official and unofficial - had a very negative impact
on Afro-Arab relations.  The Arabs had tried to
discourage the Africans through a number of
measures which they adopted either collectively
through the Arab League or individually.[6]  Their
initial response to Israel's diplomatic and
economic offensive was negative:  they instituted
a total economic boycott of exports from certain
African countries.

Attempts were also made to exploit the
religious divisions within certain African states.
It is pertinent to note that a large number of
Black African states are either predominantly
Muslim or have a significant Muslim population;
religion can still be used as an effective political instrument in Africa.  The Arab-Israeli conflict was presented in such countries as a religious conflict between Muslim Arab and non-Muslim
Jews.  Israel was accused of distributing false
copies of the Koran in Africa.  The Islamic League
together with Al-Azhar University in Cairo resolved
to establish branches in all Islamic countries to
check "Zionist attempts to pervert the Koran."[8]
Muslim groups within African states were encouraged
to put pressure on the governments of their
countries to break diplomatic and other ties with

Israel.[9]  The Sixth World Islamic Conference of
December 1964 agreed that henceforth Islamic
preaching throughout the world would include
indoctrination on the "dangers of Israel."  It
further urged Muslim governments to take control
of all institutions run by missionaries since
they were accused of promoting Israel's interest.[10]

The use of Islam as a weapon in the fight
against Israel does not seem to have succeeded in
Black Africa during this early period.  Indeed
instead it had a generally negative impact on
Afro-Arab relations.  African leaders, including
those from predominantly Muslim countries were
generally unhappy at the attempt to inject
religion into the already turbulent internal
politics of their states by the Arabs.  It further
reinforced the long-standing suspicion held in
Black Africa of the Arabs and it encouraged many
African leaders to maintain some distance from the
Arabs.  During the period both Muslim and non-
Muslim states continued to maintain and in fact
strengthen political and economic ties with Israel.

The most one can claim for this Arab tactic
of politicising religion is that in certain
African states it acted as a constraint on going
the full hog with Israel.  In Nigeria for example,
it was the opposition of the Northern Muslim
elements that prevented the country from having
a mission in Israel.  Senegal - with almost 86%
of its population Muslim but with a long serving
Catholic President - is another country where
religion seemed to have had some impact. President
Senghor was always sensitive to the need to avoid
any action which might be misconstrued as directed
against the Muslim majority.  Although he was
personally quite friendly with Israeli leaders,
Senegal was one of the constant supporters of
the Arab States in the UN.[11]

The Middle East conflict affected Afro-Arab
relations at the UN, as the Africans were unpre-

pared to support anti-Israeli moves by the Arabs.
It sometimes led to very hot exchanges between
Arab and African delegates, particularly at the
beginning of the 1960's. For example Dr. Nkrumah's
contribution to the debates on the Middle East in
September 1960 provoked a very angry reaction
from the Saudi Arabian delegate. There were also
acrimonious exchanges between African and Arab
delegates during the UN debates on the subject in
1961.[12]

Afro-Arab disagreement over the conflict
also permeated pan-African conferences. The Arabs
had attempted to use these conferences to secure
an African endorsement of their position on the
conflict. They tried to have the matter included
on the agenda of these conferences. However,
nothing significantly positive was achieved. The
Second Conference of Independent African States
held in Addis Ababa in June 1960 merely expressed
concern over the non-implementation of the various
UN resolutions on the crisis. It was not until
1961 that a few African states endorsed the Arab
policy on the Middle East at the Casablanca Conference attended by Ghana, Guinea, Mali, Morocco,
Egypt and the Algerian Government-in-Exile. The
presence of the three Arab countries in the
Casablanca talks thus assured an Arab victory.
The conference did not only attribute the crisis
to Israel's denial of the legitimate rights of
the Palestinian Arabs, but it also identified
Israeli activities in Africa as neo-colonial.[13]
For Israel, the expansion of the diplomatic
struggle over the Arab-Israeli conflict to Africa
had thus backfired as her activities were now
regarded as neocolonial. This by implication
made Africa's role in the conflict a direct one.
Africa was therefore expected to take punitive
action against Israel including the immediate
termination of all contacts with her, both inter-
governmental and transnational.

On his return to Egypt from Casablanca,
President Nasser of Egypt told his National
Assembly that as a result of Casablanca, the
'Palestinian Problem had become an African
problem.'[14]  This was no doubt a premature claim,
and an exaggerated assessment of the results of
the Conference for three reasons.  Firstly, it
was attended by only three Black African states.
Secondly, although Mali, Guinea and Ghana were
signatories to the resolution, their close ties
with Israel were not affected by its passage.
President Nkrumah was reported not to have
approved the resolution, although this was denied
later.[15]  But whatever his position at Casablanca,
he, together with Haile Selassie of Ethiopia, Tito
of Yugoslavia, Makarios of Cyprus and Nehru of
India, vehemently opposed an Arab draft resolution
at the Belgrade Conference of the non-aligned
nations in September 1961.[16]  And thirdly, the
call on African states to oppose Israel was dismissed in many influential quarters in Africa.
Houphouet-Boigny of the Ivory Coast dismissed it
as "inopportune and unjustified."[17]

However, the Arabs did succeed in getting
many of the "peoples" conferences of the 1960s,
such as the All-African Peoples Conferences and
the Afro-Asia Solidarity Conferences, to adopt
their position against Israel.  But these conferences were far from representative of official
African opinion, as the participants were mostly
exiled politicians who were wanted for alleged
crimes by those in power.  This constituted a
paradox in, and a serious weakness of, the Arabs'
African policy.  They sought to enlist African
governments' support, yet they openly encouraged
and supported dissident elements against the same
governments whose friendship and support they
claimed to desire.  This is particularly odd,
given earlier Arab, especially Egyptian support
of African nationalism.

When the OAU was formed in 1963 its Arab

members saw in it a medium through which they
could put pressure on the African states to change
their Middle East policy.  It was thought that the
Africans would agree to censure Isreal rather than
risk an open confrontation with the Arabs which
could damage the Organisation's unity.  But this
hope was unfulfilled.  The Africans refused to
be drawn directly into the politics of the Middle
East.  They resisted all attempts to have the conflict included on the agenda of the OAU.  They
were not prepared to get the new Organisation involved in a conflict which they regarded as extra-
continental and which in any case, could divert
their collective attention from their own major
concerns; viz, decolonisation, national integration
and economic development.

Furthermore, the Africans did not hide the
high premium which they placed on the continuation
and development of their relations with Israel.
The Arabs could not force issues once the African
position was made known in no uncertain terms. To
have done so would probably have shown the Arabs
as putting Arab interests over and above OAU
priorities.  This would have created a lot of ill-
feeling at a time many Africans were even question-
ing the loyalty of the Arabs to Africa.[18]

Throughout this initial period, the African
stand remained pro-Israeli partly because of the
negative approach of Arab diplomacy[19] and partly
because of the positive benefits the Africans
derived from Afro-Israeli ties.  Israeli membership of the UN also played an important role in
influencing the African position on the Middle
East.  As late as 1969, the delegate of Zaire
opposed a pro-Arab draft resolution at the General
Assembly on the grounds that his country could not
accept a resolution which implied the disappearance
of a sovereign member of the UN.  The Liberian
delegate added that the draft resolution was
destructive of the principles "on which the UN
was founded."[20]  Throughout the period, the pre-

vailing environment in Africa was generally favourable to Israel. Africa accepted pro-Israeli
attitudes without question. It needed more than
another round of hostilities between Israel and
the Arabs and further Arab diplomatic pressures
before serious questions started to be asked about
Israel and the Middle East in Africa.

ii)   Second Phase:  1967-1973

Between 1963 and 1967, then, the African
states successfully resisted further Arab pressures to get the Middle East crisis to permeate
OAU politics; neither did they succumb to pressures outside the Organisation to reduce bilateral
ties between individual African states and Israel.
The situation changed in 1967 principally because
of the outbreak of the June War between the Arabs
and Israel. The War resulted in a massive military
defeat of the Arabs, with Israel occupying large
territories belonging to Egypt, Jordan and Syria.

Guinea broke ties with Israel because of
what it called Israeli 'aggression'. However,the
other African states refused to follow the example
of Guinea. The environment then was still generally
favourable towards Israel. Pro-Israeli attitudes
were generally accepted in Africa whereas in the
third phase in particular these attitudes were
reversed. So in the third phase there was a 'band-
wagon' effect whereas during the beginning of the
second phase no one else followed the Guinea
example in Africa.

The war led to the convening of a Special
Session of the UN General Assembly after discussions on it had become deadlocked at the Security
Council. Israel's continued fund of goodwill in
Africa was well demonstrated in the speeches and
voting record of the African delegates. For instance a Latin American draft resolution backed
by the United States found a relatively higher
degree of support among African delegates than a
pro-Arab draft sponsored by Yugoslavia and some

other non-aligned countries.[21]

However, partly because the OAU Summit of
that year came shortly after the abortive UN
debates and partly because of the passions these
debates had generated, it became inevitable for
the OAU Summit, which met in Kinshasa in
September 1967, to be preoccupied with the Arab-
Israeli conflict. This was despite the fact that
an earlier attempt by the Arabs to get an extra-
ordinary meeting of the Council of Ministers to
discuss the conflict had been frustrated by lack
of African support. The OAU Summit passed its
first resolution on the Middle East (in the form
of a Declaration) without formally debating the
issue.[22] An attempt to have it formally discussed
was defeated. In this Declaration, the African
Heads of State expressed concern at the deteriorating Middle East situation and sympathy for Egypt,
a member state. They decided to work within the
framework of the UN to secure Israeli troop withdrawal. The African decision to work within the
framework of the UN was in a way a polite rejec-
tion of the Arab call for militancy through the
OAU. If anything the Africans served notice that
they were not going to allow the Organisation to
take any independent initiative or action particularly if such moves were to threaten their
valued links with Israel.

From 1967 onwards, the Arab-Israeli conflict became a regular item on the agenda of OAU
Sessions. It often caused serious disagreements
among delegates at these meetings. For instance,
at the February 1968 Council of Ministers meeting,
the OAU adopted a resolution which called for an
"immediate and unconditional withdrawal" of
Israeli forces from Arab territories. This resolution was adopted by acclamation. However,
fifteen African states were reported to have expressed reservations, and the Madagascar government totally disassociated itself from the resolution apparently because of its one-sided nature.

The resolution had failed to touch upon any of the demands of the Israelis.[23] A draft resolution on the Middle East, essentially along the lines of the February 1968 Council of Ministers resolution, was the only one submitted by the Council which was rejected by the Heads of States at the subsequent OAU Summit in Algiers in September 1968. The interventionist role of the then-OAU Secretary General, Mr. Diallo Telli, in support of the Arabs often brought strong criticism against him and was a principal factor that cost him his job in 1972. His role also alienated many Black African states and was counterproductive, contributing to the defeat of the draft.

During this period, a majority of the African States were still opposed to any strong anti-Israeli resolution. By 1970, however, a number of them, particularly Burundi, Congo, Guinea, Nigeria and Tanzania had become more sympathetic towards the Arab position. The Africans were generally becoming impatient with the continued Israeli occupation of Arab territories.

This occupation became an embarrassment even for those states that did not have much sympathy for the Arabs as it was becoming increasingly ridiculous for the OAU not to take any practical steps to help a member state recover parts of its territories which were under foreign military occupation. Besides, the OAU did not want to be seen to be condoning territorial acquisition by force as a number of its members were themselves vulnerable to military occupation by South Africa. Moreover, the Arabs had begun to improve their tactics and had wasted no time in emphasizing the Charter obligation of all OAU states to defend Egypt against aggression. They also drew the Africans' attention to the possibility of South Africa forcibly occupying the territories of the 'Front Line States.'

The pressures were definitely mounting, and the African leaders did not want to wait until the situation had deteriorated to a point where they would be forced to choose between Israel and the Arabs. They therefore decided at the OAU Summit in 1971 to set up a 10-man Committee that would help promote a settlement of the crisis. The Committee was made up of Heads of State of Cameroon, Ethiopia, Ivory Coast, Kenya, Liberia, Mauritania,Nigeria,Senegal, Tanzania and Zaire. A Sub-Committee made up of the Heads of State of Cameroun, Nigeria, Senegal and Zaire was later appointed to make direct contact with Egyptian and Israeli leaders. This Sub-Committee visited the Middle East and made very far-reaching recommendations.[24] However, it was unable to bring the protagonists closer together.[25]

The failure of this OAU mission and the increasing suspicion that Israel was unwilling to evacuate occupied Arab territories hardened African attitudes against her. This became very evident in the stern tone of post-1971 OAU resolutions. The time also coincided with increased diplomatic pressure on the Africans. The Libyans and the Saudis were prominent in mounting this renewed diplomatic offensive. King Faisal of Saudi Arabia toured a number of African counties in November 1972 making promises of large scale development and financial assistance. Between 1970 and 1973 eight African Heads of States visited Tripoli, not to mention numerous visits there by lesser officials. These bilateral visits resulted in promises of aid as an incentive for a change in the states' Middle East policy.

The bilateral contacts and pressures in
some cases had the desired effect from the Arab
point of view. For example, in 1972 Congo,Chad,
and Uganda severed their diplomatic ties with
Israel ostensibly because of Israeli "intransigence." President Tombalbaye of Chad claimed
that his break of relations with Israel was intended to "remove all ambiguity over Africa's
solidarity with Arab nations."[26] But the real
motivation behind his action seems to have been
to dissuade the Arabs, particularly the Libyans
from aiding the rebellion against his regime and
to attract Arab financial aid to prop up his
drought-stricken economy. His break with Israel
was followed by the injection of Arab, especially
Libyan and Saudi aid into Chad.[27]

On the multilateral level, the beginning
of a decisive shift in African policy became
discernable. In 1972, the OAU Summit in Rabat
passed a resolution very critical of Israel.
This asked her to declare publicly her adherence
to the principles of non-annexation of territories
through the use of force.[28] However the resolution
fell short of the Arab demand for an African break
in diplomatic relations with Israel. This was a
source of disappointment for the Arabs. The depth
of the disappointment was revealed in an editoral
published by the Egyptian Gazette shortly after
the Summit. This editorial lamented that:

> Mere resolutions will not alleviate
> the sufferings of the Palestinian
> refugees or give the Arabs back their
> territories. Israel must be hit and
> hit hard so that it can see reason.[29]

The encouraging indicators, from the Arab
point of view, both on the bilateral and multilateral levels had a positive impact on Afro-
Arab relations, and no doubt encouraged further
anti-Israeli postures at both levels. For instance before the 10th OAU Summit in May 1973,

Burundi, Mali and Niger broke off relations with
Israel. Also in February 1973, the OAU Council
of Ministers pledged full support and solidarity
with the Arabs.

Encouraged by this trend, the Arabs, particularly the Libyans, sought to make the Middle
East crisis the central and overriding issue of
the 10th anniversary summit. But shortly before
this occasion, President Quaddafi of Libya precipitated a crisis by calling for the transfer
of the OAU headquarters from Addis Ababa on
account of Ethiopia's continued maintenance of
diplomatic relations with Israel. He further
urged pro-Arab African states to boycott the OAU
until African states had broken ties with Israel.[30]

The call was, however, ignored and the
Ministers, including the Libyans turned up in
Addis Ababa for a preparatory conference before
the Heads of State meeting. But the conference
soon became deadlocked over the Middle East crisis
as no agreement could be reached on a political
declaration to be submitted to the Heads of State.
The debates and exchanges at the meeting were both
hot and acrimonious.[31] The deadlock was not easily
broken even amongst the Heads of States. President
Bourguiba of Tunisia strongly supported the Libyan
call for the transfer of the OAU headquarters from
Addis Ababa. President Sadat of Egypt warned that
Arab support for the decolonization of Africa would
be dependent on Black Africa's showing a united
front for the Arab cause.[32]

The preparedness of some of the Arabs for
a show-down with the Africans at the OAU over the
Middle East crisis did not seem to have helped
advance their cuase. President of the Cameroons
whose government had consistently supported the
Arabs warned that the Palestinian people would
gain nothing from the attempt to provoke a "use-
less crisis" within the OAU.[33] In fact the two
principal demands of the Arabs - a resolution

calling for the total diplomatic isolation of
Israel and another which would have denounced
Israel as an 'agent of imperialism', and which
would have been the signal for more African
states to sever their relations with her - got
short shrift from the Africans.  More significantly,
the resolution adopted by the Assembly was less
critical of Israel than earlier ones.  It was
devoid of all the more extravagant condemnations
of earlier resolutions.[34]

However, the Arabs continued to mount pressure on individual African countries and through
the non-aligned movement.  Togo, for instance,
broke relations with Israel immediately after the
non-aligned Summit which met in Algiers in September 1973.  However, the conflict continued to
act as a divisive issue in Afro-Arab relations
until the October 1973 War.

iii)    Third Phase:  1973-1978

Relations between Africa and the Arab
World, however, took on a decisive turn with the
outbreak of new round of Arab-Israeli hostilities
in October 1973.  The tide of Arab diplomatic
pressure on Black Africa became irresistable as
a result of the War which led to further Israeli
occupaton of Egyptian territory.  The penetration
of Israeli forces across the West Bank of Suez
into the "African" territory of Egypt made the
Israeli position quite untenable in many African
capitals.  Previously many Africans had argued
that Sinai, which Israel occupied in 1967, was a
non-African territory, although it belonged to
Egypt.  Now continental integrity was clearly in
jeopardy.

Most African states broke diplomatic relations with Israel as a result of the 1973 War.  A
few like Chad, Nigeria and Uganda even offered
token help to assist the Arab war effort in the
defence of Arab and African territory.[35]  An

emergency session of the OAU Council of Ministers was convened in November 1973 at which Israeli activities were branded as 'evil acts of colonialism'. Her African policy and that of South Africa, Rhodesia and the colonial regimes in the former Portuguese territories now came to be viewed as coordinated attempts to "encroach and dominate the entire African continent."[36] Again at the June 1974 OAU Summit in Mogadishu, Somalia, the Organization listed conditions which it believed were necessary pre-conditions for a just and lasting peace in the Middle East. It is significant that neither the principle of recognition of the State of Israel, nor of her right to free navigation in the Straits of Tiran, nor any of the demands made by Israel, were included in this list. Rather the OAU demanded the acceptance by Israel of the principles of

(a)   a total withdrawal of Israeli forces from Arab territories occupied since June 1967

(b)   liberation of the Arab city of Jerusalem

(c)   the exercise of the Palestinian people's right to self-determination; and

(d)   the application of UN resolutions on the Middle East.[37]

The Summit further called on African states to give their total support to the PLO 'as the sole representative of the Palestinian people.'

The break in diplomatic relations with Israel by African states and the readiness of the OAU as a whole to pass very trenchant anti-Israeli resolutons did not mean, however, that the Middle East conflict ceased to be a divisive factor in Afro-Arab relations. Firstly, the

Africans were not prepared to support all Arab
positions all of the time. For instance, during
a stormy debate at the UN on the Middle East in
November 1974, Nigeria's Commissioner for Mines
and Power, Alhaji Ali Mongunu, told the General
Assembly that the reality of Israel's existence
as a sovereign state should be acknowledged and
that a realistic settlement in the area should
guarantee Israel's security within agreed borders.[38]

The Arab-Israeli conflict also generaged
a lot of ill-feeling between African and Arab
members of the OAU during both the Council of
Ministers and Heads of State conference in July-
August 1975. At both meetings the Arabs demanded
i) that the OAU should endorse the expulsion of
Israel from the UN and ii) that the OAU should
organise an African boycott of Israel in line with
the established Arab boycott policy. After hours
of acrimonious debate, the Council of Ministers
recommended suspension of Israel from the UN
rather than her expulsion.[39] Even then, delegates
from Ethiopia, Ghana, Ivory Coast and Zaire expressed strong reservations.

The call for an African boycott was totally
rejected. During the Heads of States meeting the
proposal for Israel's suspension sent up by the
Ministers took eight hours of stormy debate before
it was rejected. The vital suspension clause in
the resolution was watered down to a mere request
that the OAU members should reinforce pressures
against Israel "including the possibility" of
eventually depriving it of UN membership". President Mobutu of Zaire rejected totally both the
suspension and watered-down resolutions. Delegates from Ghana, Liberia, Senegal, and Sierra
Leone expressed strong reservations.[40] It is
also significant that, in 1975 too, 16 African
States refused to vote for the controversial UN
resolution equating Zionism with racism.[41] President Amin of Uganda's call at the UN for the
expulsion of Israel from the world body and the

extinction of the State of Israel was roundly condemned in Africa. Nigeria's Daily Sketch described
it as "pathetic" while the Daily Star said it was
"palpably unimaginative and smacks of sadism."[42]

Another related issue that marred Afro-Arab
relations during the period was the refusal of
many African states to allow the PLO to open
offices in their capitals. The Arab states collectively through the Arab League and also individually exerted a lot of pressure on the African
states to allow the PLO to open such offices. A
permanent presence of the PLO in African capitals
would not only have increased the international
prestige of the Organisation but would also have
inexorably drawn particular African states deeper
into the Arab-Israeli conflict. It would no
doubt be seen as a further action taken against
Israel. Palestine (ie. the PLO) was included by
the Arab League in every conceivable Arab delegation
that negotiated anything with the African states.
Special delegations were sent to some countries,
including Nigeria to convince their leaders of the
prime necessity of accepting a PLO presence.

Pressure was also put on the Africans to
extend to the PLO observer status in the OAU.[43]
From February 1974 the PLO started attending OAU
meetings as an observer. In the July-August 1975
summit, Yassir Arafat, the PLO leader, was given
Head of State treatment, an action which some
African leaders and liberation movements resented.
It is to be noted that the OAU was never accorded
any black African liberation movement leader
such a honour and privilege. Resolutions were
also passed by the OAU asking its members to allow
permanent representatives of the PLO in their
capitals.[44] But despite all these pressures, the
majority of the African states still refused to
allow the PLO to open offices in their capitals.

Moreover, the Africans resisted pressures
brought upon them through the various joint meet-

ings held with the Arabs during the period to get
them further involved in the Arab-Israeli conflict. For the vast majority of the African states
the Middle East conflict ceased to be a foreign
policy priority once they have broken formal
relations with Israel. Apart from the rituals of
passing very stringent anti-Israeli resolutions
at the OAU and non-aligned conferences, they were
not prepared to take any further action against
Israel other than diplomatic disapproval. Besides,
to the Africans, the other issues in Afro-Arab
relations - notably oil prices, the oil boycott
against racist regimes in Southern Africa, and
aid - overshadowed and definitely took precedence
over the conflict with Israel.

The refusal of the Arabs to meet major
African demands during this period hardened the
African determination not to go further along the
anti-Israeli road with the Arabs. In fact,
Africa's disappointment over the refusal of the
Arabs to offer both substantial financial aid and
lower oil prices made many leaders nostalgic
about previous Israeli aid. There was even
speculation in Africa that many states would
resume diplomatic relations with Israel in protest against perceived Arab lack of appreciation.
It was also alleged that the Africans refused to
issue any joint communique with the Arabs at the
end of their first joint Ministerial conference
held in Dakar in April 1976 because of the dis-
proportionate emphasis on the Middle East conflict
in the draft communique.[45]

It is also remarkable that some African
leaders, notably Presidents Senghor of Senegal
and Houphouet Boigny of Ivory Coast, made significant moves to bring the Israelis and the Arabs,
including the PLO, together for talks aimed at
finding a solution to the crisis.[46] Throughout
this period, and when compared with earlier periods,
Afro-Arab relations became strengthened primarily
because of the Black African states' severance of

diplomatic relations with Israel in 1973. However, the other unresolved issues in Afro-Arab relations continued to impose limits to the solidarity within and between both groups of states.

iv)    Fourth Phase:  1978-1980

The Arab-Israeli conflict remained largely quiescent as an issue in Afro-Arab relations until 1978. However, it resurfaced as an active political issue after President Sadat's peace initiatives in the Middle East. President Sadat had abandoned the war option in the resolution of the conflict with his dramatic visit to Jerusalem in November 1977. This initiative resulted in the Camp David accords between President Sadat, Prime Minister Menachin Begin and US President Jimmy Carter in September 1978, the signing of a peace treaty between Egypt and Israel in February 1979, and the formal establihsment of diplomatic relations with the bilateral exchange of ambassadors in February 1980. Predictably, many Arab states have been bitterly opposed to every stage of their bilateral peace moves. As a result, President Sadat has not only been castigated as a traitor, but Egypt has also been expelled from the Arab League. The League, apart from moving its headquarters from Cairo to Tunisia, has imposed diplomatic and economic sanctions against Egypt. All the 'rejectionist' Arab states have withdrawn their diplomats from Cairo as a result.

African conferences have been one of the fora which the Arabs have used to wage the anti-Sadat crusade since then. They wanted the OAU in particular to condemn roundly Sadat's peace moves as they had successfully used the Organisation to secure the diplomatic isolation of Israel. Perhaps, too, a condemnation of Egypt would have opened the door for the Organisation to take some punitive action against her. The 30th Session of the OAU Council of Ministers held in Libya in February 1978 was seized of the problem. The meeting opened with a fierce attack on Egypt by the

Libyan leader; this provoked a walk-out of the
Egyptian delegation.

There was some uneasiness in many African
quarters over Sadat's peace initiative. Some
African leaders were not fundamentally opposed to
it but they were unhappy with the way Sadat had
gone about it without consultation with the OAU
or some African leaders. Besides, many felt disappointed over his failure to link the Palestinian
issue with Southern Africa in the course of negotiations with Israel, as OAU resolutions had always done since 1973. They believed that Sadat
ought to have asked Israel to scale down its
economic and military links with South Africa.
Despite these reservations, however, most of them
were not prepared to support the rejectionist Arab
position on the issue.

The reasons for the African refusal to back
the rejectionist Arab states are obvious. First,
many of them believe the Treaty will eventually
lead to peace in the region. Second, the Africans
are not used to imposing sanctions on their "de-
viant" sister states. They were all aware that
many of them do pursue controversial policies; to
start imposing sanctions could lead to serious
troubles for the OAU and the stability of Africa
as a whole. And third, Africans were already
disillusioned with Arab "insensitivity" to African
problems and they therefore did not see why they
should get themselves involved in what they regard
as inter-Arab squabbles. After protracted debates,
the 30th Session of the Council of Ministers agreed
that direct negotiations and consultations with
"racist and Zionist regimes in Southern Africa
and occupied Palestine should not serve as a sub-
stitute for the legitimate armed struggle waged
by the oppressed people in Southern Africa and
Palestine."[47]

The issue again bedeviled OAU conferences
in 1979. Qaddafi refused to attend the summit in

Monrovia because of Sadat's presence there. And
when Sadat rose to address the meeting all the
Arab delegations, except that from the Sudan,
walked out of the conference. The Africans again
refused to endorse the Arab hard-line position on
the bilateral peace treaty.

Outside the OAU itself, disagreement over
the treaty has seriously affected Afro-Arab
relations. Many African States who were already
disillusioned with the Arabs on account of the
latters' insensitivities to African political and
economic interests and demands saw the peace
treaty as a good opportunity for re-establishing
diplomatic links with Israel. The Arabs reacted
argrily to the possibility of such a move. In a
note sent to the OAU at the end of 1979, Arab
Foreign Ministers threatened to cut off economic
aid to any African country that establishes diplomatic relations with Israel.[48] Disagreement
over the treaty has also prevented the holding of
the joint Ministerial Council of Arab and African
states scheduled to be held in Libya in July 1979.[49]
Such periodic Ministerial Council meetings were
one of the key elements in the decision taken to
foster closer Afro-Arab cooperation at the first
Afro-Arab Summit held in March 1977. In fact the
joint Ministerial Council was the highest "standing" organ set up to supervise the implementation
of the "Programme of Action" adopted at the Summit.

Afro-Arab cooperation has thus suffered a
terrible setback. According to the Cairo Agreement, another joint summit ought to have met around
March 1980. No meeting was held then and it does
not appear that there are any serious moves to convene one. However, it is doutful if any significant progress can be made without such joint ministerial and summit meetings on a regular basis.
Moreover the concerted efforts of the Arabs to get
Egypt expelled from the non-aligned movement during
the Sixth Summit of the non-aligned states held in
Cuba in September 1979 was thwarted by the Africans.

Rather than expelling Egypt, the conference adopted
a resolution setting up a committee to study Egypt's
suspension and report back in the light of developments in the Middle East to the movement's next
meeting of foreign ministers in 1981.[50] Even then,
Presidents Kaunda of Zambia and Samora Machel of
Mozambique explained that the Africans had agreed
to the resolution not so much because they wanted
Egypt suspended nor because they were opposed to
the peace moves in the Middle East but rather they
thought the threat of suspension would put pressure on Israel[51] to make necessary concessions in
the negotiation of Palestine autonomy which was
going on between Egypt and Israel. This amounts
to a complete opposite of Arab intentions. African
pressure also seems to have watered-down considerably the tone of the conference's condemnation
of Egypt in its final Declaration. For example,
the Declaration only noted 'with concern' that
after the Camp David accords, Israel had expanded
its settlements in the occupied territories. Most
of the harsh words in the Declaration were directed
against Israel and the United States rather than
against Egypt, still an OAU member.[52] In a way,
Afro-Arab relations have thus changed in a somewhat cyclical way with some of the pre-1973 characteristics now very much in evidence once more.

v)  Conclusion

From the above discussion it is quite evident that the Middle East crisis has been an important factor in Afro-Arab relations throughout
the period under review. It not only dictated
the extent to which Arab states would fraternise
with the Africans; but it also acted as a baro-
meter for measuring the overall state of Afro-
Arab relations.

Throughout the 1960s and the early 1970s,
it acted as a divisive factor in Afro-Arab relations. For a brief period after the Yom Kippur
War of 1973 the African states' break of relations

with Israel in support of the Arabs created a
myth of an emergent Afro-Arab "alliance". The
Africans thought that both the Arabs and Africans
once they have agreed to share political enemies
would come to share economic and other enemies.
However, this soon proved to be illusory, and
their disappointment over what they regarded as
the Arabs' refusal to accept African problems
as their own led to some soul-searching in Africa
over the demise of Afro-Israeli relations. Their
feelings were, however, largely contained at the
time and the OAU continued to maintain a semblance
of unity over the Arab-Israeli conflict. But this
was until President Sadat decided to make his own
peace with Israel. African states were generally
split along ideological lines on whether to oppose
or support the dominant anti-Sadat faction in the
Arab World. While many of the Africans disapproved
of the way Sadat went about his peace process, a
majority of them were nonetheless unprepared to
toe the rejectionist Arab line.

The final establishment of diplomatic
relations between Egypt and Israel has raised the
possibility of renewed diplomatic relations between Israel and the Black African states. It is
not yet known, however, what the OAU reaction
would be to the latest threat by the Arab Foreign
Ministers over the re-establishment of relations
with Israel. However, the OAU should not allow
itself to be intimidated. In fact, the cred-
ibility of the OAU as an autonomous African
regional body may very well hang on how it handles
this matter. It should feel free, despite rejectionist pressures, to discuss the 'new' Middle
East situation very objectively and to adopt a
position in its own interest whether or not this
coincides with Arab demands.

Africa's interests should be the major consideration rather than the threat of the withhold-
ing of a few million Arab petro-dollars which in
any case only filter in very reluctantly and

selectively. African leaders should end avoiding their responsibilities by publicly discussing the new situation that has arisen in the Middle East as a result of Sadat's initiative. However, whatever the Africans do, or refuse to do, in the short-term, the Arab-Israeli conflict will continue to be a major factor in Afro-Arab relations until a general and lasting peace is established in that troubled region of the Middle East.

If the current dialogue between Egypt and Israel eventually leads to a general peace, a big obstacle would then have been removed in the way of the further development of Afro-Arab relations. However, in a situation of 'no-peace and no-war', with the Arab world remaining hopelessly divided over peace initiatives, there would continue to be friction between the Arabs and Africans as the OAU is very unlikely to support the rejectionists' outright. The gains so far made in Afro-Arab cooperation may even be reversed if friction within the Arab ranks persists for too long. This friction may even lead to an open breach between the Africans and the Arabs if the situtation in the Middle East deteriorates into another round of open hostilities in which the rejectionists decide to treat both Egypt and Israel as equal enemies. For the future of Afro-Arab relations in general, as for the Middle East itself, much will depend on the appreciation by Egyptian and Israeli leaders of the heavy responsibilities which they carry in making a success of the current but seemingly protracted negotiation over Palestinian autonomy.

## Notes

1. For a detailed analysis of Israel's foreign
   policy goals in Africa, see Samuel Decalo,
   <u>Israel and Africa: the politics of cooperation. A study of foreign policy and technical assistance</u>, (Unpublished Ph. D. thesis,
   University of Pennsylvania, 1970) and Arnold
   Rivkin, "Israel and the Afro-Asian World",
   <u>Foreign Affairs</u>, 37(3), April 1959, 486-95.

2. Personal correspondence with Ministry of
   Foreign Affairs, Jerusalem, 1976.

3. <u>ibid</u>.

4. See Jehudi J. Kanerek, <u>Israeli Technical
   Assistance to African States</u> (Geneva, July
   1968).

5. Personal correspondence, <u>op. cit.</u>

6. Many resolutions and programmes of actions
   were adopted by the Arab League during the
   period aimed at discouraging Afro-Israeli
   close ties.

7. See for instance, A. B. Akinyemi, <u>Foreign
   Policy and Federalism: The Nigerian Experi-
   ence</u> (Ibadan: Ibadan University Press, 1974),
   103.

8. <u>Al-Akhbar</u> (Cairo) November 9, 1962.

9. See <u>West African Pilot</u> (Lagos) October 27, 1964.

10. <u>Africa Report</u> 10 (2),February 1965, 50-51.

11. For a more general discussion of the impact of
    Islam on African states' foreign policy, see
    Vernon Mckay "Islam and Relations Among New
    African States" in J. H. Proctor (ed) <u>Islam
    and International Relations</u> (London: Pall Mall,
    1965), 158-189.

12. See for instance United Nations General Assembly Official Records (UNGAOR) 15th Year, 869th Plenary Meeting, Sepbember 1960, 267-275. See also United Nations Document (UNDOC), A/SPC/L80, December 11, 1961.

13. African Conference of Casablanca 1961 (Rabat: Kingdom of Morocco, Ministry of Foreign Affairs, nd.).

14. African Conference of Casablanca, January 1961. Speech by President Nasser (January 23, 1961) at the National Assembly on the Results of the Casablanca Summit Conference (Cairo: Information Department, 1961), 13.

15. See Emanuel Lottem, "The Israeli Press and Israel's Relations with Africa", International Problems, 14 (3-4), Fall 1975, 10.

16. Middle East Record 1961 (Jerusalem: The Chiloah Centre for Middle Eastern and African Studies, Tel Aviv University, 1961) 192.

17. ibid 53.

18. At the founding conference of the OAU, some African leaders suggested the renunciation of the North African states' membership of the Arab League as a gesture of their commitment to African unity. See OAU Foreign Ministers Preparatory Conference Verbatim Report, Reel 3: 49.

19. For example, Arab 'negative diplomacy' led to the expulsion of Egyptian diplomats from Liberia in 1961 and Malawi in 1966. For details see West Africa, October 24, 1961, 144, and West Africa, March 4, 1966, 5. For a similar effect in Senegal in 1967, see W.A.E. Skurnik, The Foreign Policy of Senegal (Evanston: Northwestern University Press, 1972) 239.

20. UNGAOR, 24th Session of the Special Political Committee, 686th Meeting, December 5, 1961.

21. 17 African states voted for the Latin American draft as against 12 for the Yugoslav draft. See UNGAOR 5th Emergency Session, June-July 1967. A/L522 and A/L 523/Rev. 1.

22. OAU Doc. AHG/St. 2(iv), September 1967.

23. Keesings Contemporary Archives, October 26-November 2, 1968, 2291.

24. For full details of the Committee's report, see UNGAOR, Doc. 1/8566, A summary of its important provisions can also be found in UNGAOR, 26th Year, 2014 Plenary Meeting, December 11, 1971, 11-12.

25. For a detailed examination of OAU's effort, see Susan Aurelia Gitelson, "The OAU Mission and the Middle East Conflict", International Organization, 27(3), Summer 1973, 413-419.

26. Africa Confidential, 14(21), October 19, 1973, 4.

27. For example, less than a month after Chad broke relations with Israel Libya offered Chad about £40m sterling as aid. See Africa Research Bulletin (Political Series) (ARB), December 1972, 2684.

28. OAU Doc. AHG/Res. 67, 1972.

29. Egyptian Gazette, June 5, 1973.

30. The Observer (London) May 13, 1973.

31. New York Times, May 24, 1973.

32. OAU Doc. CON/AHG/SP 33 (x).

33. Foreign Report (London) May 16, 1973.

34. OAU Doc. AHC/Res. 70 (x), 1973.

35. The film which Nigeria offered Egypt on
    October 12, 1973 before Nigeria broke re-
    lations with Israel was said to have been
    rejected. See Salonga (Zaire) October 24,
    1973.

36. See OAU Doc. ECM/Res 19 (VIII) and ECM/St. 1
    (VIII).

37. ARB, June 1974, 3260.

38. West Africa, November 25, 1974, 1446.

39. ARB, July 1975, 3684.

40. ibid, August 1975, 3720-21.

41. UNGAOR, A/PU 2400, November 10, 1975.

42. ARB, October 1975, 3811.

43. Personal discussions with Mr. Jamal Sourani,
    Head, PLO Office in Cairo in January 1977.

44. OAU Doc. CM/Res. 393 (xxiv), February 1974.

45. Interview, Addis Ababa, February, 1977.

46. For details, see West Asia Diary, March 5-11,
    1977, 389 and June 25-July 1, 1977, 561.

47. ibid, April 16-22, 1978, 1012.

48. Sunday Sketch (Ibadan), December 30, 1979.

49. New Nigerian (Kaduna), July 17, 1979.

50. The Guardian (London) September 10, 1979.

51.  ibid.

52.  For full details of the Declaration, see
     Review of International Affairs (Belgrade)
     30 (707), September 1979, 27-30.

Chapter Seven

## The OAU and Continental Order

Amadu Sesay


The problem of order-social, economic and poltical - is a major one for the newly independent African states. How to treat this problem largely depends on clarifying the epistemological and definitional issues raised by the operative words "continental order". What do we mean by continental order in this context? For our purpose, continental order is taken to mean the relative absence of wars in Africa, whether they be civil or interstate wars, border disputes, territorial conflicts, guerrilla wars or insurrections.[1] In short, it implies a situation of political stability on the continent.

Continental order also refers to the collective efforts by African states through the umbrella of the Organisation of African Unity (OAU) to regulate and promote rapid economic development of the continent. We can thus distinguish three types of order: (i) political order, (ii) economic order, and (iii) military order. We can say that political and military order has prevailed when there is a relative absence of wars and other forms of instability on the continent. In the same vein, we can measure economic order using such indices as the number of institutions present on the continent, as well as the intensity of interaction among African states.

Whatever the case might be, and viewed from the above perspective, there is a clear linkage between order and peace. According to the Dictionary of the Social Sciences, "peace" in its very restrictive sense, means "the ending of hostilities as the Peace of Versailles" which brought to an end

the first world war.   In its more general usages,
however, peace refers to the activities of "certain
institutions which have successfully maintained
order[2] in the relations of two or more states in
general."[3]   Peace in this general sense, then,
refers mainly to the operations of international
and regional organisations whose major concerns
have been the prevention of war and the promotion
of the welfare of their members' citizenry.   The
United Nations (UN) and its predecessor, the League
of Nations, are examples of such world bodies
while the OAU, the Arab League and the Organisation
of American States (OAS) are examples of regional
institutions.

We can argue that, politically, the UN hopes
to maintain world order by trying not only to
eliminate conditions which give rise to wars and
conflicts, but also to regulate such wars and conflicts when they do occur.   These activities are
supported by the UN peace-keeping force which is
presently engaged in Lebanon.   On the other hand,
through its Economic and Social Council, the world
organisation tries to enhance and regulate international economic activities and achieve or restore
economic order in the world system.   Through such
institutions as UNCTAD and related conferences,the
UN tries to prevent a breakdown in world economic
order which might in turn lead to political chaos.
The end result, it is hoped, is relative peace,
stability and order in the world system.

The same could be said for the OAU which is,
as already pointed out, a regional institution.
There is hardly any doubt that one of the cogent
reasons for setting up the Organisation in 1963
was the urgent need to prevent disorder, conflict
and violence among the newly emergent African
states.[4]   The end product,it is hoped, would be
the preservation of order, peace and security of
African states.   Some sort of continental order
was imperative because of the newness of the
African states which had, and still "have little

power, less majesty and no resiliency..." Furthermore, as emergent societies, they are characterised
by rapid "social change and rapid mobilization of
groups into politics coupled with the slow development of political institutions"[5] to cope with the
changes. The increases in urbanisation and liter-
acy, which followed the withdrawal of the colonialists from Africa, have created pressure and strains
which could develop - and indeed have so developed
- into open violence and conflicts if left unreg-
ulated. This possibility was recognised in the
OAU Charter. For instance, members are urged to
settle their disputes peacefully through mediation,
conciliation and arbitration.[6] The rationale
behind this Charter provision was that given the
newness of independence and the arbitrary nature
of most African borders and boundaries, order and
peace could not be maintained on the continent if
African states resorted to force in their relations
with each other.

The order which was conceived at Addis Ababa
in 1963 was of a conservative and status quo-
oriented type. The founding fathers were eager to
protect and strengthen the fragile political order
and boundaries which they inherited from their
erstwhile colonial masters. For example, one of
the purposes of the OAU was "to defend their
sovereignty, their territorial integrity and independence". All members were accordingly declared
to be equal and sovereign. They were not to interfere in the internal affairs of other members and
each was to respect the other's territorial integrity.[7] The message was loud and clear; to live in
relative peace and have some stability in the
African system political boundaries should be
sacrosanct. They could only be modified, if at all,
with the consent of all the parties involved. Otherwise, the OAU would not give its blessing to such
revision. Ironically, and in their eagerness to
preserve the status quo, the founding fathers
ignored a cardinal principle which they had all
fought for in the run up to independence: self-

determination within independent African states.
Now no group of people has a right to separate
statehood in any independent member state no matter
how genuine their case might be. As suggested in
the course of this chapter this situation was to
contribute a great deal to the inability of the
Organisation to tackle some of the contemporary
issues confronting its members.

Two broad notions of order are discernible
from the Charter itself. First is political order.
This can be further subdivided into three cate-
gories: order within member states, inter-African
order and, finally, order involving the African
states on the one hand and the world's other actors
on the other; the latter essentially involves the
attempts by the OAU to reduce and to eliminate, if
possible, extra-continental influence especially
its military aspects. Second is economic and
social order. This refers mainly to the efforts
of the OAU since its inception, to improve what
might be called the Basic Human Needs (BHN) of the
continent's citizens. It was for that purpose
that the Specialised Commissions were set up under
Article 20 of the Charter. The over-all objective
was to accelerate the economic development and
industrialisation of the continent so as to narrow
the economic gap between the North and South. But
there was also a political case for promoting
economic development. If African states are unable
to feed their populations, as is true to some
extent at the moment, such a situation would lead
to political chaos and instability in the affected
areas. Such instability would in turn threaten
the peace and stability of the continent as a whole.
The above concerns and problems are reflected in
the organisation of this chapter. The first part
deals mainly with political order and in turn is
sub-divided into three sub-sections: (i) intra-
state order, (ii) inter-state order and (iii)
external intervention in Africa. The second part
deals with economic order, while the third and
final part examines some of the problems which

have hindered the activities of the OAU since its
inception seventeen years ago. We shall deal
briefly with specific case studies under each of
these types of order.

(i) Political Order

(a) Order within independent African states

The OAU has failed woefully to play an
effective role in either regulating or bringing to
a peaceful solution conflicts within member states.
"Internal" conflicts which result from personality-
cum-ideological or religious differences between
political leaders. The Organisation's failure has
been most glaring in cases where the integrity of
an independent state has been threatened as a
result of attempts by minorities to secede. This
is because, as we have pointed out, the OAU is
committed to the preservation of the status quo.
Thus, while it has given full and unreserved support
to colonial peoples in their struggle for independence from colonial metropoles, the same right has
been denied Africans in member states. In fact,
the OAU has condemned outright any notion of self-
determination for any groups in independent African
states. Such a situation is the result of fear
that the creation of new countries from independent
states would open a pandora's box. The legitima-
tizion of self-determination, it is argued, would
have a domino effect on the rest of Africa especially with regard to such giants as Ethiopia,
Nigeria,Sudan and Zaire. It is further argued that
the balkanisation of independent states would not
be conducive to African unity and order, two major
reasons for setting-up the OAU in the first place.

How valid are these perceptions and reasons?
Onyeonoro Kamanu, for instance, has argued somewhat convincingly against the domino effect of
self-determination.[8] As he has pointed out, one of
the major shortcomings of the domino theory is that
it assumes that all African states could be dis-

membered and still remain viable entities. But
that is stretching the point too far. While the
bigger African states definitely would remain
viable, the majority are already too small, even
by contemporary standards, to be independent states.
States like the Gambia, Lesotho and Sierra Leone
would surely not "survive" successful secessionist
movements.

But such a broad conclusion must be modified
if it is to be rendered unassailable. We assume,
of course, that irredentist claims would be based
on ethnic, religious and political grounds as much
as on economic viability. However, while economic
considerations were not paramount in the Southern
Sudanese struggle for independence, nor for that
matter for the Eritreans, it is nevertheless true
that both could become economically viable states.
While it is possible to envisage a situation whereby desparate groups would prefer to die in freedom
rather than "live" under the shadow of domination
by other groups within a viable state, so far, this
has not been the case. In fact, it is significant
to note that no irredentist claims have been made
within very small African states, only within the
larger ones.

As for the argument that the creation of
more states would impede Pan-African unity, this
is valid given the reluctance of the independent
states to part with their fragile sovereignty.
In the history of independent Africa so far only
one state has volunteered to relinquish its sovereignty in favour of Pan-Africanism-Ghana under
Nkrumah.[9] The others have jealously guarded their
independence and have resisted any move towards a
continental government. Kamanu's reasoning - that
the "break-up of such African giants as Nigeria
and Zaire, far from impeding the process of Pan-
African integration, might accelerate it by lessening the fear of domination entertained by the
smaller states, thereby predisposing them to
participate in common supranational arrangements"[10]

is therefore not born out by experience. The unity which was forged at Addis Ababa was a unity of sovereign nations. Consequently, no matter how weak or seemingly unviable an African state may be, it has got unreserved protection and guaranteed sovereignty under the OAU Charter and, indeed, under the UN Charter too.

The break-up of African giants would only promote Pan-African integration and supranationalism if unity were synonymous with continental government. But in such a situation there would conceivably be no more need for more states. And even if the need for states is felt, these would presumably also be created either to improve administrative efficiency or to meet the claims of significant minorities within the states concerned. This is the present situation within Nigeria. At the moment, however, the creation of more states from independent African states would be dysfunctional and retrogressive in terms of Pan-African unity. The new states would obviously be too jealous of their newly-won freedom to want to sacrifice it at once at the altar of union government in Africa.

As it is presently constituted, then, the OAU cannot effectively mediate in any conflict involving secessionist claims. This is essentially because of the principle of the territorial integrity of member states guaranteed under Article 3 of the Charter. This principle is so potent that in such cases as the Sudanese civil war and the current conflict in Eritrea the Organisation simply ignored such claims. In the latter conflict, in particular, the OAU has pretended that "all is well" within the country. In such a way, the conservative status quo has been maintained, albeit in a very uneasy way. A brief examination of the Organisation's role during the Nigeria-Biafra war further exposes its dilemma over wars of sucession.

When hostilities broke out in 1967 between
the Federal government and the former Eastern
region, rechristened "Biafra", the Federal authorities were quick to seek protection from the
Charter, and immediately declared the conflict to
be an "internal affair". It was consequently "not
within the competence" of the OAU to discuss. But,
nevertheless, as the fighting intensified the Organisation was forced to bring up the issue for discussion at its Kinshasa summit meeting in September
1967. A resolution was unanimously passed which
called for the setting up of an OAU Consultative
Committee on the Nigeria/Biafra war. However, the
Heads of State made it clear that they were solidly
in support of the maintenance of the status quo ante
in Nigeria. Hence, they re-affirmed their adherence
to the "principle of respect for the sovereignty
and territorial integrity of member states" and
condemned "secession in any member states"[11] irrespective of the "badness" or "goodness" of the
secessionists' argument for a separate nation.
Thus, even in the initial stages of conflict, the
Organisation had already sanctified the political
status quo in Nigeria. And by so doing, it also
ruled out any impartial or effective role for itself in efforts to secure a peaceful settlement of
the conflict. This impotence was reinforced when
the Consultative Mission was implored "to explore
the possibilities of placing the services of the
Assembly at the disposal of the Federal Government
of Nigeria." There was no mention of the Biafrans,
the other major parties to the conflict. Not only
that, the OAU also gave total support to General
Gowon's claim that the civil war was "purely an
internal affair of Nigeria and that no solution is
possible except within the context of the national
unity and territorial integrity of the Federation."[12]

Having declared itself openly for the Federal
side as early as 1967, it was little wonder that in
the course of the struggle, Biafra became disillusioned with the activities of the OAU which it
perceived as an "agent" of the Federal government.

Lagos authorities on the other hand saw the
Organisation as playing the role of an "errand
boy". For that was exactly what the Consultative
Mission set out to be. Thus, the "most valuable
contribution the mission can make" is to "call on
the rebel leaders to abandon secession."[13] The
mission in fact considered nothing more, apart from
calling upon the Biafrans to give up their struggle.
There was no attempt to investigate their grievances
to see what could be done to assuage the fears
which led to their secession. Emperor Haile
Selassie, the Mission's Chairman, made it known to
Gowon that the "national unity and territorial
integrity of member states is not negotiable. It
must be fully respected and preserved."[14] He concluded his speech on a personal note: he declared
his opposition to "any attempt at national fragmentation on religious and ethnic grounds", one
reason why "Ethiopia unreservedly supports Nigerian
national unity and territorial integrity."[15] Even
the choice of the Emperor as leader of the Mission
was a strategic mistake by the OAU. This was
because he was preoccupied himself with claims for
secession from Eritrea and for territorial ir-
redenta from Somalia. Given these claims on his
territory, it was natural for him to favour strongly
the territorial status quo throughout independent
Africa. Predictably, the Mission's communique came
out solidly in favour of maintaining Nigeria's
unity and Gowon "was in complete agreement with the
conclusions reached."[16] Nigeria's territorial
integrity was consequently preserved within the
conservative political order reflecting, in effect,
the main interests of the ruling elites. But the
Organisation's performance in other conflicts has
not been more successful either.

The Eritrean issue is a continuing one, yet
the OAU had not played any meaningful role in bringing about a peaceful settlement of the war. The
Ethiopian government has successfully prevented
the Organisation from discussing the situation
over the years by simply invoking the Charter in

support of its claim that the civil war is an internal affair. Suggestions that the Eritrean Liberation Front (ELF) would be given observer status at meetings were met with threats of Ethiopian withdrawal from the Organisation. This was what happened in 1975 at the Kampala summit when some Arab countries tried to put the issue on the agenda.[17] And at the Monrovia summit in 1979, "no one even glanced at Eritrea" throughout the week-long deliberations.[18]

In sum, the OAU has failed woefully to harmonise and regulate African affairs, one of the prime motives for setting it up in 1963. The poor performance and record of the Organisation is directly related to its commitment to the protection of a conservative political and territorial status quo amongst independent member states. As Bolaji Akinyemi has rightly observed, it would be hard for the Organisation to "harmonise and co-ordinate" the affairs of its members when it is barred from any disucssion of "internal factors in other countries which are detrimental to harmonisation."[19] But besides this, the OAU also lacks the resources to enforce order. Until an effective and lasting solution is found to this dilemma, the Organisation will be unable to establish or maintain order in the continent. A summary of the OAU's role in the management of conflicts in Africa since 1975 is found in Table 1.

Table 1

A Summary of African Conflicts* and the Role of the OAU

in Their Resolution or Management, 1975-80**

| Country/ Countries Involved | Conflict Type | Role of the OAU | Outcome as of June 1980 |
|---|---|---|---|
| Algeria/ Morocco 1975-1980 | Territorial/Liberation Movement. Algerian support for the Polisario and independence for Western Sahara. | Attempted mediation on several occasions. The last attempt was December 1979 in Monrovia when the ad hoc Committee on Western Sahara met. | Liberation war continues. Algeria continues to support Polisario. |
| Algeria/ Mauritania | Territorial/Liberation Movement. Algerian support for Polisario and independence for Western Sahara. | Attempted mediation on several occasions, but unsuccessful. | Resolved. Coup in Mauritania in 1978 brought pro-settlement government to power. It renounced claims to its own section of the territory in favour of independence in 1979. |

| | | | |
|---|---|---|---|
| Angola<br><br>1975–1976 | Civil war/external intervention. | Attempted mediation on several occasions, e.g. Nakuru in Kenya under chairmanship of Kenyatta. Emergency summit in 1976 deadlocked. OAU did not secure withdrawal of Cuban and South Africa forces from territory. | Resolved. Military victory by the M.P.L.A. under Neto and supported by Cuba and Soviet Union. |
| Angola/<br>South<br>Africa<br><br>1975–1980 | South African military intervention and subsequent military incursions in pursuit of SWAPO freedom fighters. | Limited to verbal condemnation and moral support for Angola and SWAPO. | Unresolved. Liberation war in Namibia continues. |
| Angola/<br>Zaire<br><br>1975–1978 | Subversion/<br>Intervention | Very minimal. | Conflict resolved bi-laterally tharough diplomatic channels. |
| Benin<br><br>1977 | External intervention/<br>mercenary invasion | OAU fact-finding mission to Benin | Resolved. Invasion beaten off by Benin army. |

| | | | |
|---|---|---|---|
| Benin/Togo 1976 | Border dispute. | None. | Resolved through bilateral diplomatic negotiations |
| Botswana/Rhodesia 1977-1979 | Border clashes/incursions. | Diplomatic condemnation and moral support. | Resolved. Rhodesian incursions ceased at Zimbabwean independence. |
| Chad (i) 1978-1979 | Civil war. | Limited to appeals for peace and end to hostilities. | Temporarily frozen through multilateral peace initiatives spearheaded by Nigeria. Nigeria sent peacekeeping force to enforce cease-fire. Government of National Unity formed. |
| Chad (ii) 1980 | Civil war. | Substantial. Peacekeeping force earmarked but not yet mobilised. | Unresolved. War continues. |

| | | | |
|---|---|---|---|
| Chad/Libya 1978–80 | Military intervention. Libyan support for rival nationalist faction led by Goukouni Weddeye. | OAU committee set up to mediate and ensure Libyans' withdrawal. | Resolved pro tem. Accusations continue of Libyan support for Goukouni by Hissene Habre. |
| Comoros 1977 | Power struggle/ external intervention, mercenary invasion. | None. | Resolved militarily. French mercenaries restored Ahmed Addulla to power. |
| Ethiopia/ Eritrea 1975–80 | War of secession. | None. | War in progress. |
| Ethiopia/ Somalia 1977 | Territorial irredentist, open war, and external intervention by Cubans and Russians on side of Ethiopia | OAU committee set up to mediate in 1973. Met in 1977 during conflict, but failed. | Resolved/quiescent. Ethiopian military victory. |

| Ethiopia/ Sudan 1977-1978 | Subversion, border clashes and refugee problems. | OAU 8-man mediation committee met in Freetown, successfully proposed a peace formula. | Resolved. |
|---|---|---|---|
| Ghana/Togo 1977 | Border clashes. | None | Resolved through bilateral diplomatic negotiations. |
| Kenya/ Somalia 1977 | Territorial irredentist. | Limited to appeals for respect for OAU charter provisions. | Quiescent. |
| Libya/Egypt 1977 | Border clashes. | None. | Quiescent. |
| Libya/ Tunisia 1976 and 1980 | Subversion/invasion. | None. | 1976 conflict resolved bilaterally. 1980 conflict quiescent after invasion resisted. |

| | | | |
|---|---|---|---|
| Mauritania/ Upper Volta 1975 | Boundary dispute. | None. | Resolved through bilateral mediation efforts of President Toure. |
| Mozambique/ Rhodesia 1975–1980 | Border incursions by Rhodesian soldiers in pursuit of freedom fighters. | Limited to diplomatic condemnation of Rhodesia and moral support for Mozambique. | Resolved through Zimbabwean independence. |
| Mozambique/ South Africa 1976–1979 | South African troop incursions. | Limited to moral support for Mozambique and diplomatic condemnation of South Africa. | Quiescent. |
| Nigeria/ Chad 1976–1980 | Border clashes, incursions by Chadian soldiers, dispute over fishing rights. | None. | Partial bilateral resolution in 1976, but clashes continue. |
| Uganda/ Tanzania (i) 1977–78 | Subversion, border clashes and ideological/personality conflict. | OAU mediation by Secretary-General, plus personal initiatives of other members. | Remained quiescent. |

| | | | |
|---|---|---|---|
| Uganda/ Tanzania (ii) 1978-1979 | Territorial dispute, border clashes, and intervention by Ugandan exiles and Tanzanian troops. | Substantial. Cease-fire appeals, commiteee of six to seek peaceful solution, and calls for mutual respect of territorial integrity. | Resolved militarily with Amin overthrown in April 1979. |
| Uganda/ Kenya 1976-1978 | Murder of Kenyan citizens border tensions, and refugees. | None. | Resolved bilaterally. |
| Zambia/ Rhodesia 1975-1980 | Rhodesian military incursions and raids on Nationalist camps. | Moral and diplomatic support for Zambia and condemnation of rebel government forces. | Resolved through Zimbabwe independence. |
| Zaire (Shaba i) 1977 | Subversion. Katangese exiles in Angola took over copper mines in Shaba province. | None. Invasion regarded as internal affair. | Resolved. Zairean military victory with the help of Moroccan, Eygptian, French and Belgian troops and U.S. logistical support. |

| Zaire (Shaba ii) 1978 | Katangese exiles again returned to Shaba province. | OAU Khartoum summit condemned external intervention in Africa, particularly the proposed Francophone "Pan-African" force. | Resolved. Zairean military victory with support of French and Belgian paratroopers. |

\* Conflicts are here defined to include civil wars, boundary and border disputes, personality and ideological conflicts, and external military interventions.

\*\* As of June 1980.

(b)   Inter-African conflicts

Inter-African conflicts for the purpose of this chapter refer mainly to border and territorial conflicts amongst African states; what might be called conflicts involving the integrity of the state and personal and ideological conflicts involving threats to the integrity of the regime in power.  Three cardinal principles were recognised to regulate inter-African affairs.  First, the inviolability of the inherited colonial-imposed borders which are in most cases erratic and ill-defined.  Second, non-interference in the internal affairs of member states.  And third, the settlement of inter-African disputes amicably through mediation, conciliation and arbitration - a provision which involves almost all the known modes of settling disputes short of outright military confrontation.

These principles of conflict resolution reflected the compromise which was struck at Addis Ababa in 1963.  The compromise between the radical and moderate factions of the Pan-African movement was, in effect, a victory for the numerically-superior moderates.  The end product was what Immanuel Wallerstein has called "unity as alliance" as opposed to "unity as a union."  The latter would have taken care once and for all of perennial problems over territoral claims by one African state against the other.  But because the Charter was a reflection of the status quo-oriented moderates' position, the Organisation has not been in a position to take mandatory decisions in regard to disputes among its members.  What is more instructive is the fact that even the Commission of Mediation, Conciliation and Arbitration, which was set up to handle inter-African disputes, remained unutilised for twelve years following its creation in 1964.  This is because, lacking in mandatory sanctions, the Commission had not been able to induce members to take their disputes to it for arbitration or mediation.  On the other hand,

African states are so jealous of their sovereignty
that they see it being eroded of that vital commodity by simply presenting themselves before the
Commission. The Heads of State assembly however,
got round the impasse by devising ad hoc means of
handling emergencies, such as the appointment of
commissions and committees to settle inter-African
conflicts.

These personal initiatives - or what we can
call "Presidential mediation" - have a number of
advantages over the Mediation Commission per se.
First of all, they predated the formation of the
Commission and were found to be more "effective"
in containing flare-ups. Besides, Presidents are
repositories of political influence and since conflicts are in most cases political, it appeared
logical and advantageous to utilise a political
rather than a legal forum, like the Commission.
In some cases, the Council of Ministers has also
been mandated to find peaceful solutions to border
and territorial disputes. As Table 1 shows, most
of the disputes between 1975-1980, and indeed
even those before that time,[20] have been largely
settled through the personal initiatives of
African leaders. That way, they have been able
to up hold the conservative status quo. In this
sense, one can conclude that the OAU as such has
failed in one of its main raisons d'etre: to
settle amicably all disputes among African states.

This failure is perhaps understandable given
the foregoing factors. Moreover, the Organisation
was unfortunate to have been confronted with a
series of boundary and territorial conflicts so
soon after its formation. These ranged from the
quarrels between Ghana and Upper Volta, Somalia
and Kenya and Somalia-Ethiopia, to the bloody
cross-border confrontation between Algeria and
Morocco, all in 1963-64. It was during the Algero-
Moroccan conflict that the Organisation virtually
passed the buck to the personal individual initiatives of African governments and heads of state.
Thus, following the personal intervention of the

Malian President Modibo Keita and Emperor Haile
Selassie of Ethiopia, a meeting of the disputants
- Hassan of Morocco and Ben Bella of Algeria -
was convened in Bamako in November 1963.  After
several days of negotiations, an accord was
reached - the now famous Bamako Accord.  Under
the terms of this agreement, a cease-fire was
agreed upon by Algeria and Morocco to be super-
vised by Malian and Ethiopian army officers.  It
was after this accord had been reached that the
OAU took over, apparently to give the agreement
its blessing and to "legitimise" it.  The Bamako
Accord succeeded in freezing the dispute for nine
years until it was finally resolved bilaterally
in 1972.[21]  King Hassan and President Boumedienne
told a crowded press conference during the Rabat
summit that year, that there was no territorial
dispute between their nations.  The "quality of
fraternal relations" between the two North African
neighbours was such that they had decided to "make
the border not an obstacle, but a place of inter-
penetration of feelings and interests." Accordingly, they decided to establish a "permanent peace
for the centuries to come."[22]  Such bilateral
settlements through "informal" as well as personal
interventions by other African "Chiefs" have
effectively replaced the OAU's own conflict management machinery.  The Organisation has had its
role reduced in most cases to merely rubber stamp-
ing the agreements reached through informal
channels.

But this is not to underplay the important
psychological effect which the OAU has had on
disputants.  For instance, during the Algeria-
Morroco war, there was no doubt that the existence
of the Organisation even at that early stage, was
a source of encouragement for the warring factions
to try and settle their conflict amicably.  The
OAU gave its blessings to the cease-fire agreement
thereby making it psychologically difficult for
the disputants to flout it with impunity.  Moreover, the "legitimisation" of unilateral, bilat-

eral or, indeed, multilateral initiatives by
African leaders also makes it difficult for the
contending states to ignore such diplomatic moves.
It arguably helps to "soften" positions thereby
making the conflict more amenable to peaceful
resolution. In such indirect ways, the Organisation has played regulatory and prophylactic
roles in intra-African conflicts.

In discussing the indirect role of the OAU
in crisis management on the continent, we should
perhaps add that the mere existence of the Organisation as a "club" of African Heads of State,
made it feasible for such leaders to meet regularly and know each other. In the process of
socialising together, African leaders have also
been offered an opportunity to identify and relate
with some of their colleagues, especially those
whose foreign and domestic policies exhibit more
or less similar patterns. African states have
been most willing to offer their diplomatic
services as mediators or conciliators to their
"friends" in times of trouble. Thus, the late
William Tolbert of Liberia successfully recon-
ciled Guinea-Ivory Coast on the one hand, and
Guinea-Senegal on the other, in 1975. The same
friendly disposition towards Nigeria and General
Gowon, led Tubman of Liberia to undertake a
number of diplomatic moves aimed at settling the
Nigeria-Biafra war in the late 1960s.

Many friendly African states are quite willing to devote a lot of time and sometimes even
resources to bring inter-African conflicts either
to a peaceful conclusion or to a quiescent stage
until a formula is found for a lasting solution.
This situation might explain the inability of the
OAU to develop its conflict-solving apparatus.
In the absence of such an apparatus and an African
Military High Command, there seems to be no alternative to ad hoc arrangements by the OAU and the
personal initiatives of African Heads of State.
The OAU is likely to continue to play a peripheral
role in    inter-African conflicts in the near

future.

(c)   External Military Intervention in Africa

The problem of extra-regional military intervention in the continent was dramatically displayed
in November 1970 when Portugal, with the assistance of some Guinean political exiles, invaded
Conakry and tried to overthrow the government of
President Sekou Toure.  However, before this
abortive invasion African leaders were already
alert to the dangers from possible armed attempts
by former colonial powers either to re-instate an
amenable African leader back in power or to overthrow one hostile to their interests and policies
in Africa.  The Belgian and American paratroop
drop in Stanleyville in the Congo (now Kinshasa
and Zaire respectively) was an earlier indication
of what to expect from extra-continental actors
when their interests are threatened.  This awareness by African's leaders that they presided over
weak states in a world which is still characterised by lack of a central political authority,and
whose members retained the prerogative to use
force as a last resort in their relations with
each other, was evident in the OAU's Charter.[23]
Under Article 11, the member states undertook to
"defend their sovereignty and territorial integrity and independence".  Besides the Charter provisions, the second annual summit in Accra 1965
emphasised the urgent need to eliminate as much
as possible future military expeditions to the
continent.  Members agreed "not to tolerate sub-
versive activity directed from outside Africa
against any member state."  They were "to oppose
collectively and firmly by any means at the disposal of Africa every form of subversion conceived,
organised or financed by foreign powers against
Africa, the OAU, or against its members individually."[24]

By 1965, therefore, the Organisation had
already come out with a clear-cut policy statement

on the issue of external military intervention.
The African High Command which was proposed at
Addis Ababa in 1963 by late President Nkrumah,
and the Defence Commission which was later set up
to look into the continent's strategic and defence
problems, reflected an appreciation of the vulnerability of member states to extra-regional military coercion.  Thus the Defence Commission and
the Accra resolution which we have already quoted
at length, should be seen in the light of the
attempts by the weak African states to strengthen
both their individual and collective defence capabilities.

     In trying to evaluate the Organisation's
responses towards extra-regional threats and
military actions, however, a number of important
factors have to be born in mind.  First, that
there is no unanimity among member states on the
question.  Second, that indeed several types of
external interventions could be distinguished.
And third, that the responses of members of the
OAU to the problem have by and large been dependent on the identites  of the victim as well as
the aggressor.  The latter phenomena are in turn
a reflection of different political, economic,
ideological, and idiosyncratic factors, external
and internal, to African states and the OAU.

     For our purpose, three types or modes of
intervention are identifiable.  The first category is what we call international socialist
military aid and/or intervention.  This is invariably from Soviet bloc countries and the
primary motive behind such assistance is to help
"progressive" forces on the continent to fulfill
specific aims and objectives.  In the majority of
cases, such objectives are also enshrined in the
OAU's Charter; for example, the liberation of
territories still under minority colonial regimes
in southern Africa.  We saw this type of intervention in Mozambique in the period before independence in Angola from 1975 to 1976 and in Zimbabwe

before the February 1980 elections; and we are
still witnessing this phenomenon in Namibia.
Another distinguishing factor in this type of
military intervention is that it has the tacit
approval of the OAU, although some states may
object to the identities of the intervenees.[25]

The second category of intervention is the
blatant and comtemptible interference in the
affairs of independent African states by former
colonial powers.  Their main purpose is to shore-
up regimes-and their ruling elites-which adopt
dependent political and economic policies favourable to the former metropole.  The colonial power
would try to topple any leader which it considered
antagonistic to its policies and interests in such
states.  The most notorious examples of this type
of intervention are provided by France in some of
her former dependencies.  For instance, Paris was
behind the coup which led to the ousting of David
Dacko, the first President of the Central African
Republic, and his replacement by General Bokassa
in 1965.  However, after the General's reign of
terror in that territory, France decided to pull
another coup in late 1979; Bokassa was quietly
replaced by Dacko from whom he had seized power
some fourteen years earlier.[26]

On paper at least, the OAU is totally opposed
to such blatant disregard for the sovereignty and
independence of its members.  The Charter spoke
very clearly against such gross interference in
the internal affairs of its members.  In practice,
however, opposition to French military activities
on the continent is far from being unanimous.
Fierce condemnation of Paris has come mainly from
the "progressive" states like Algeria, Libya,
Tanzania and Nigeria (especially during the
Mohamed-Obasanjo administration).  For the majority
of African countries, and particularly for former
French territories with the notable exception of
Guinea, reactions have either been subdued or
openly in support of French action.  This is

because many of the francophone states have French troops stationed on their soil. For example, while a handful of African states were busy condemning France's military intervention in Zaire (Shaba) to shore-up Mobutu's tottering regime, some 24 francophone African states were attending a Paris meeting called by President Giscard d'Estaing to set up a "Pan-African" peace-keeping force, headed by France. Ironically, but as expected, the Africans did not only express open support for the French idea but they were also actively looking for ways and means of expanding the metropolitian military presence in their own territories.[27] France has claimed that her military assistance has been requested by the African states themselves, especially those which are "weakly armed" and which are also "victims of external aggression."[28] Houphouet-Boigny of the Ivory Coast summed up the feelings of many former French territories: "we have no complexes at all about it, since the European members of NATO call on the United States in case of attack, and the Eastern European nations call on Russia."[29] Boigny's statement is noteworthy for two reasons. First, it was in line with the conservative notion of order within the continent. And second, it implied acceptance of the palpable balkanisation of Africa.

Our third and final category of external military intervention is that which is sponsored by colonial powers either individually or in collaboration with their western allies and disgruntled indigeneous political exiles. The objective of such incursions has been to topple African governments and leaders who are giving active support to liberation movements in the colonial territories. The most prominent example of this type was the abortive Portugese-led invasion of Guinea in 1970. But we also have instances like the series of South African raids into Angola and the Rhodesian incursions into Mozambique and Zambia during the Zimbabwean liberation war. Like the French type, this latter category has also been fiercely condemned by the

OAU.

For our case study on the Organisation's responses to externally-sponsored intervention, we have selected the Guinean invasion of 1970. This choice is influenced by a couple of factors. First, the invasion provided the first acid test of the Organisation's determination and ability to rid the continent of such military menace. Second, and perhaps more directly connected with the OAU, the intervention involved two related OAU principles: (i) opposition to aggression and (ii) opposition to colonialism.

It must be pointed out from the outset, that the OAU's response to the Guinea invasion was a poor testimony of its ability either to aid the victims of external military action or to stamp out such instances in the future. Firstly, there was no African High Command in 1970, so the Organisation had no troops at hand to despatch to Guinea to flush out the invading force. Secondly, even the Defence Commission could not meet on time to deliberate on the crisis. It was thus left to the Council of Ministers to work out a formula for the Organisation. A meeting of the Defence Commission finally did take place on 9 December, almost a fortnight after the attack on Conakry.[30] This time-lag was more than enough for Portugal to have consolidated its hold on Guinea if the invasion had been successful.

After several days debate, the Ministers could only pass a pious resolution which condemned in vigorous terms the "treacherous aggresson committed by Portugal against the Republic of Guinea. All mercenaries who invaded the Republic of Ginea as well as those forces which participated in planning the aggression", also came under strong verbal attack. Then, in a tone which must have disappointed Pan-Africanists, the Ministers "appealed" to the fascists in Portugal to make what they described as "adequate reparations" to Guinea so as "to enable it to face the consequences of aggression."[31]

But the resolution and its very strong language were merely symbolic. There was, for instance, no central agency to compel African states to give assistance to Guinea nor was there a central "relief fund" or agency to distribute relief material to the affected areas in Guinea. Moreover, the Ministers did not specify what sort of assistance they required from other member states. Was it humanitarian, economic and/or military assistance? The latter can be safely ruled out since the attack had already been re-pulsed by the Guinean army. Further, as already stated, there was no standing peace-keeping force under the command of the OAU and it would have been almost impossible to raise one at the time. So what the Council of Ministers had in mind was humanitarian-cum-economic assistance. Again, the question must be raised about how much help Africa could provide in the light of the poverty of most African states. Furthermore, how would the aid be transported to Guinea itself, even if it was available, in the absence of any substantial logis-tical capability in most African states?

The whole episode was a sad commentary on the lack of readiness of the OAU to tackle effec-tively the contemporary problems of its member-ship. It was a good reminder to all African states of the urgent need to reform and restruc-ture the whole OAU machinery to make it more responsive to the needs of the continent in such a very crucial area. What the Guinean invasion brought to light above all was the inability of the regional Organisation to effectively police its members against external penetration and military coercion. The OAU's protective umbrella has by and large been limited to making verbal statements condemning external intervention and passing resolutions which could not be effectively implemented.[32]

The foregoing discussion has exposed both the weakness and dilemma of the OAU over the question of extra-regional military action. African leaders have been very unwilling to surrender their so-called sovereignty either in part or in full, to a Pan-African military command structure. Such a refusal has in turn hindered the effectiveness of the OAU in maintaining order on the continent. Moreover, the monopoly which the OAU claims over the defence needs of the continent and its members has not been matched with action. Indeed, even the pronouncements of the Organisation on external military intervention sometimes contradict each other. For instance, while still condemning externally-sponsored aggresson in the continent, the Khartoum summit meeting in 1978 also protected the right of individual states to seek help, or to invite any friendly external power to their assistance if such a state feels its security and sovereignty are threatened. Such a proviso, paradoxically would only encourage and give legitimacy to the pleas for military assistance from France by the francophone states.

Countries which can solicit extra-regional military protection and assistance would obviously tend not be very enthusiastic about setting up a Pan-African defence force. Thus, while the OAU still maintains that the responsibility for continental defense will always "fall incontestably on Africans alone", the same Africans are also urged to "seek assistance from any state when its (their) security and independence were threatened." More significantly, the Council of Ministers' summit put the whole issue of an African High Command on ice. Its formation, it emphasised, "must be seen in the light of those countries that threaten Africa and the cause of liberating Africa from colonial rule."

With the independence of most African states, one is bound to ask whether Africans would ever

agree to the formation of an African High Command
(AHC). A committee was set up by the Ministers
"to study the Pan-African defence force in its
theoretical and scientific aspects."[33]   To all
intents and purposes, therefore, this directive
finally put the last nail into the coffin of the
AHC structure.  The idea has been buried until
some future date when the continent would be
ready both politically and psychologically to
face the AHC issue again with all its ramifications.

(ii)    Continental Economic Order

        The OAU was set up in 1963 for three broad
but inter-related purposes.  First, to bring the
emerging states closer together politically.
Second, to devise ways and means of speeding-up
the economic development of the continent through
concerted action and the pooling of economic
strategies and resources.  Finally, third, to
offer diplomatic, moral and political protection
to the newly-independent and weak political
structures inherited from the colonialists.  However, for most of its seventeen years' existence,
the Organisation has devoted its time and energy
almost exclusively to superstructural issues like
decolonisation, political instability and territorial and boundary conflicts.  Little attention has been paid to substructural matters like
the economic and social development of the continent and its citizens in spite of the presence
of Specialised Commissions responsible for economic and cultural matters.

        There are several reasons for this situation.
First, there can be no progress on economic cooperation without a stable political base from
which to operate.  Second, the nature of African
political regimes makes inter-African economic cooperation rather difficult to achieve; this is
because of the existence of a comprador class
which shares interlocking and dependent economic
and social interests with the erstwhile metropole.

Finally, third, there are great variations amongst
the political structures within African states.
The 50-odd members of the OAU have governmental
systems which range from plural multiparty democratic systems in Nigeria and the Gambia, through
military dictatorships in Uganda and Zaire to the
single-party one-man dictatorships in Ivory Coast,
Sierra Leone, and a host of others.  Such political
heterogeneity, coupled with idiosyncratic and personality factors in each of these states, has
made cooperation even at the regional level very
difficult.  Thus, the East African Community broke
down mainly because of ideological and personality
differences between Tanzania and her two neighbours,
Kenya and Uganda.

While political differences continued to
hold back continental and regional economic integration schemes, the predictions for the continent
got gloomier and darker every year.[34]  For example,
according to the World Bank's World Development
Report, 1977, "the continent's economy is projected to grow less rapidly than that of any other
region; at a rate of about 4 per cent per annum
between 1980 and 1990... the gross domestic
product (GDP) per capita may rise by just over 1
per cent over the decade."  Because of the rapid
increase in the number of mouths to feed in the
continent most of its citizens will be worse-off
in 1990 than now.  African leaders have become
aware of these adverse economic trends in the
continent:  "there is a growing appreciation in
Africa that inequalities are increasing and that
development remains elusive; nevertheless,  "something of a lacuna still exists over how to respond
to such unfavourable trends".[35]  One may add also
that the responses which have been made so far,
have merely accelerated the incorporation of the
continent into the global system that is partly
responsible for its deprivation.[36]  The consequences for African states have been imported
inflation, balance of payments problems, domestic
unrest and, of course, the continent's extreme

susceptibility to external pressures,both diplomatic and economic.

A number of measures have been initiated by
the OAU to try and arrest these unfavourable
economic trends. Under the auspices of the Economic Commission for Africa (ECA), a series of
conferences have been held to discuss Africa's
precarious position vis-a-vis other regions of
the globe.[37] However, none of these have been
devoted entirely to economic issues, and none were
laid down a blue-print for the irreversible economic and social development of African countries
in the future. In the main the Organisation's
role in economic and social issues has been
advisory; that is, it has acted as a link between
its members and the rest of the world economic
system.

Several conferences were called in the 1970s
to forge an "African" position in negotiations
with the industrialised North. In 1971 a meeting
of African Trade and Industry Ministers drew what
later became known as the "Addis Ababa Declaration."
Ostensibly a charter on the industrial development
strategies of its entire membership, its most
notable feature was a resolution stating "Africa's
position" on the then forthcoming conference of
the United Nations Industrial and Development
Organisation (UNIDO). In it, African countries
were advised to take all necessary steps to ensure
the "lowest foreign participation" in each development project undertaken in their territories by
foreign multinational corporations (MNCs). All
states were implored to "encourage African owner-
ship of industry" and to "make full use of state
resources to ensure national participation in
industry."[38] On the face of it, these recommendations constituted sound economic advice but,
given the overwhelming economic dependence of
African states on the developed countries coupled
with the peripheral position of the continent in
the world capitalist economic system, they were

clearly unrealistic. Consequently, the impact of
the declaration on the process of industrialisation and economic development of member states
was nil.

Notwithstanding this, a similar conference
was held two years later in Abidjan in 1973.
There the OAU Ministers approved a "Declaration
on Cooperation, Development and Economic Independence."[39]  Like the "Addis Ababa Declaration",
the Abidjan document was also advisory.  For
example, it drew-up guidelines for Africa's ties
with the enlarged European Economic Community (EEC).
It also directed that in future all "international
negotiations, whether held within internatinal
organisations, whether they concern relations
between Africa and groups of developed countries,
or simply relations with these countries taken
individually, Africa should not be subservient to
any economic power bloc."[40]  This Abidjan Declaration was not binding but we should not under-
estimate its limited efficacy.  As the two Lome
negotiations with the EEC have shown, African and
developing countries constitute a rather formid-
able force in bargaining with the developed
countries only when they act as one bloc; although
from the African point of view even then the Lome
II document is far from being a perfect agreement.[41]

The Abidjan Declaration had a number of
shortcomings.  For example, the clause which urged
African states to "defend energetically, continually and in solidarity", their right and sovereignty over their own national resources, did not
reflect the real economic situation on the continent.  Because of their financial bankruptcy
and almost total absence of indigeneous technical
expertise, most African countries have had to
enter into unequal concessionary agreements with
western-based MNCs for the exploitation of their
natural resources.  Except for the few oil-export-
ing states (and even for them only recently) much
of the profit from such exploitation is retained

by the multinationals.  Liberia is perhaps the
most clear-cut example of such a situation.[42]
Until African states can raise enough domestic
capital for development and until they have
enough skilled manpower available, this deplorable
economic plundering will continue.  In that regard,
collective self-reliance may be an appropriate
development strategy for Africa.

The issue of buying crude oil at concessionary prices from the Arab oil-producing
countries, was perhaps the only occasion when the
OAU attempted to achieve some economic order in
the continent.  The four-fold increase in the
price of crude oil as a result of the Middle East
war of October 1973 adversely affected the already-
fragile economies of African states.  OAU members
were therefore forced to try and secure some concessions from the Arabs.  The long negotiations
between the Arab states, the Arab  League and the
African states under the umbrella of the OAU are
outside the scope of this chapter.[43]  Suffice it
to say that by tring to get oil at less than the
market price for its badly-hit members, the OAU
tried to ensure that the economic crisis-which
the high prices of oil had provoked in most of
its members - did not degenerate into political
crisis and chaos.

When, after long and frustrating negotiations,
the Arabs refused to sell oil at concessionary
rates to African states, the Organisation turned
its attention to other means of alleviating the
crisis.  It succeeded in procuring limited financial assistance from the Arab oil-producers:
some $200m for use by the African states.[44]  To
prevent a scramble for these meagre funds, the
Ministerial  Council established criteria for
distribution.  Oil-producing African countries
were automatically disqualified from using the
facility, but special consideration was given to
landlocked and drought-stricken countries, also
the hardest hit by the international economic
crisis.  In the end, 35 states were eligible.

Ethiopia and Tanzania got the largest portion of
the money - $14.7m each - followed by Zambia with
$12.7m, Zaire $12.4m, and $11.8m, $11.3m and $10.6m
for Morocco, Uganda and Sudan, respectively.[45]

The OAU's role throughout the oil crisis was
largely "regulatory"; ie. to ensure that African
states did not rush individually to the Arabs to
strike unfavourable oil deals. When the Organisation failed to secure preferential treatment
from the Arabs, African countries were released
to negotiate bilateral agreements with the oil
producers. Nevertheless, it is arguable that
the OAU's insistence on criteria and/or a ceiling
for borrowing, prevented a rush for the limited
funds and ensured that those states which were
worst hit by the oil embargo got a fair share of
the money. In this way, the impact of the oil
crisis on the landlocked and drought-stricken
states was eased somewhat.

It is also significant to point out that the
OAU failed to get special price concessions from
the Arabs not because it did not press its case
well enough but because its plea for preferential
treatment was made from a position of weakness.
Having already severed diplomatic relations with
Israel in the aftermath of the October war,
African states were left with a very strong moral
case but with no political trump card to use
against the Arabs in the bargaining for special
treatment. In the end, the Arabs were able to
separate morality from the sale of crude oil,
which they considered as a purely economic trans-
action. This of course, raises the question of
"Arab imperialism" or what can be called the
imperialism of the fourth world - the oil rich
countries. In our example, there is no doubt
that the Arabs wanted to use oil as a lever
against the Africans in their struggle with Israel
or, indeed, on other political matters. The oil
problems and the subsequent negotiations are also
closely linked with the whole issue of global

economic problems which have severely hit African
states. These have highlighted the precarious
position of Africa at the periphery of world
capitalism.[46]

The devastating economic effects of the oil
crisis on African states forced them to pay more
attention to substructural rather than to superstructural matters. It was a reminder that
Africa's salvation lies only in concerted efforts
aimed at solving the continent's perennial economic problems. It was a crude hint to all
Africans that for the continent to be in a stronger
bargaining position vis-a-vis other actors in
the world it must be economically viable and
united. This last point constitutes perhaps the
most important and lasting effect of the oil
embargo on the perceptions of the continent and
its leaders. Not surprisingly, 1976 saw the
first special session of the OAU's Ministerial
Council meeting which was devoted entirely to
economic issues.[47] Held in the Zairean capital
of Kinshasa, the meeting, among other things,
recommended the creation of an African Economic
Community. A resolution put forward by the
Zairean Foreign Minister Karl Bond, called upon
the ECA and other international institutions
interested in the economic advancement of the
continent, to work towards the realisation of an
economic union in Africa over a 15-25 year period.[48]

This conference renewed hopes that at long
last the African continent was bracing itself for
the enormous task of restructuring its economic
future to meet the challenges of the last lap of
the twentieth century. This optimism was also
reflected in the speeches of some of the delegates
at Kinshasa. For example, the Gabonese Foreign
Minister said that the main achievement of the
gathering was that it prepared a "solid and irreversible basis for economic cooperation and
integration" among African states.[49] Such optimism
turned out to be premature, however. No signifi-

cant progress has been made towards Pan-African
economic integration. Most of the subsequent
progress has been limited to regional integration
and has been confined mostly to West Africa.
What the conference achieved, therefore, was
merely to renew interest in the idea of Pan-
African economic integration at some future date.
More significantly, the OAU and the ECA became
interested in the future of the continent with
respect to its social and economic development
and industrialisation.

Three years after the Kinshasa meeting, in
February 1979, a "futures" conference was sponsored by the ECA in Monrovia. This symposium was
mainly concerned with Africa's future social and
economic development as well as its industrialisation. In particular the meeting examined such
issues as the type of developmental patterns that
Africa needs in the decades ahead and how they
could be achieved.[50] The ideas from the symposium
were later submitted to the 16th annual summit of
the OAU held in the Liberian capital that July.
The proposals were adopted by the heads of state
and a document called the "Monrovia strategy for
economic development of Africa" was scheduled to
be discussed at a special session of the heads of
state in Lagos. The ECA conference and the document which emerged from its deliberations - the
Monrovia strategy - undoubtedly increased the
interests of African decision-makers in the
issues affecting the continent's social and economic development. They paved the way, therefore,
for the historic Lagos economic summit which was
held in April 1980.

(a)   The Lagos Economic Summit

The Lagos summit scheduled for late 1979 was
postponed because of the change of government in
Nigeria in October. However, the meeting was held
in April 1980. At their preparatory meeting held
the week before the summit, the OAU's Foreign

Ministers painted a very gloomy picture of the continent's economic future. Paradoxically, this was, perhaps, a very positive sign because it indicated at least that the decision-makers were aware of the tremendous task before them. Edem Kodjo, the Organisation's Administrative Secretary-General, gave the most pessimistic of all the speeches at the meeting. He said that if the current worsening economic plight of the continent vis-a-vis other regions of the world was not corrected quickly enough, then "the future has no future" for the majority of African states. He predicted that of the 50 or so members of the OAU, "only eight could survive the next few years" if the present adverse economic trends continued. Kodjo made a number of recommendations which, if adopted, might help to improve the gloomy economic picture. These included a unitary monetary system for the whole region, a maritime and transport commission and, or course, a common lingua franca.[51]

The Executive Director of UNIDO, Dr. Khanae, noted in his speech at Lagos that after two decades of political freedom and efforts to promote economic development in Africa, no positive results had been obtained. This is reflected in the region's share of world industrial production, which rose only martinally over three years, from 0.7 per cent in 1975 to 0.9 per cent in 1978. Khanae attributed the dismal record of the continent to lack of skilled manpower and to the low level of technology.[52]

The Council of Ministers made a number of wide-ranging recommendations to the subsequent Heads of State economic summit. These included the division of Africa into four economic zones and the establishment of an African common market as well as an energy commission.[53] After three days of deliberations, which were marked by some eloquent speeches from African leaders, the OAU adopted what has become known as the "Lagos plan for the implementation of the Monrovia strategy

for the economic development of Africa." This
is a massive 140-page document which covers every
conceivable aspect of economic activity:  from
human resources, science and technology to the
protection of the natural environment.  Its introduction sums up the salient reasons for holding
the extraordinary economic summit.  These included
the "unfulfilled promises of global development
strategies" which have made the continent even
more "susceptible than other regions to the economic and social crisis suffered by the industrialised countries."[54]  Consequently, Africa's
economy has stagnated and her growth rate fallen
far behind that of other regions of the world.
"Faced with this situation and determined to
undertake measures for the basic restructuring
of the economic base of our continent, we resolve
to adopt a far-reaching regional approach based
primarily on collective self-reliance."[55]

The major concern of the summit was thus
the economic and social development of the African
continent as it enters the last two decades of
the twentieth century.  The message was obvious:
given their overwhelming dependence on the
industralised countries for food, technology,
financial assistance and, in fact, for virtually
every other economic activity, African states
must try and disengage themselves from the tight
economic embrace of the industralised nations of
both the east and the west.  Instead, emphasis
was to be placed on agriculture and, in particular,
Africa would strive to achieve self-sufficiency
in food production at a cost of some $22 billion.[56]
The overall objective was the setting-up of an
African common market in phases through a twenty-
five year period.  Between now and 1990, African
countries would strive to strengthen existing
regional economic groupings on the continent, promote sectoral integration, coordinate and harmonise
existing and future economic groupings, promote
joint schemes, and harmonise their financial and
monetary policies.  These policies, it is hoped,

would pave the way for the successful creation of
a continental common market by the turn of the
century.

The Lagos plan of action is obviously a
beautiful blue-print for the future economic and
social development of Africa.  It has all the
ingredients which should make for the successful
economic "take-off" of the continent.  For example,
on food production, the document stated that any
improvement would require "a strong political will
to channel a greatly increased volume of resources
to agriculture, to carry through essential reori-
entations of social systems, to apply policies
that will induce small farmers and members of
agricultural co-operatives to achieve higher levels
of productivity."  It then went on to list about
fifty ways which would eventually lead to a 50
per cent decrease in post-harvest food losses,
one of the main causes of food shortages in the
continent at the moment.[57]  On the question of
Africa's energy problems and how to combat them
in the future, the African states proposed the
establishment of "an African Nuclear Energy
Agency with a view to follow development in
nuclear technology, formulate and harmonise
nuclear energy development programmes in Africa
and provide manpower training in the nuclear
field."[58]  If carried out, the "Lagos plan" would
put the continent in a much stronger economic
position to face the challenges of the twenty-
first century.  It would also enhance the position
of Africa vis-a-vis other regions especially with
regard to political-cum-economic bargaining, such
as the continuing NIEO negotiations.

Nevertheless, like all blue-prints, the
Lagos Plan of Action has a lot of weaknesses.
Some of these have already been pointed out.
One of the most immediate ones is that involving
political heterogeneity.  There is no gain-saying
that the successful implementation of the plan
would very much depend on the political climate

amongst African states. At the moment, the var-
iegated political map of the continent has made
cooperation very difficult even at the sub-
regional level:  the break up of the East
African Community is a clear case in point.  This
problem is magnified many times over when Pan-
African cooperation is considered in both the
poltical and economic spheres.  Without political
harmony and trust among African nations, it would
be difficult, if not entirely impossible, to
realise the "Lagos dream" of African states cooperating together in a continental common market.

This political obstacle is what has given
rise on several occasions, to the argument that
Africa must have a continent-wide philosophy capable of providing "a cohesive political religion
or world view" for African states; "otherwise
even an African Common Market may become a feasting
ground for economic vampires like the Trilateral
Commission."[59]  While the above statement is
obviously an overly-pessimistic view of the future
of African economic integration, there is no doubt
that continental political diversity has been in
the past and still is a serious barrier to cooperation.  This was evident at the Lagos summit
meeting, when a group of Arab states - the rejectionists[60] - walked out in protest against the
presence of the Egyptian delegation.  Again, the
meeting spent a good proportion of its time discussing the military coup in Monrovia in which
the then-current chairman of the OAU, President
William Tolbert, lost his life.  Any successful
execution of the Lagos blue-print would therefore
require a lot of patience, maturity and strong
political will from the majority of African states,
especially from the more influential ones like
Nigeria and Tanzania; such states will have to
put the interest of Africa before individual and
ideological considerations.  But at the moment
not many African states are  prepared to make such
apparent sacrifices.

The Lagos Plan emphasised regionalism as the basis for the eventual creation of an African Common Market. However, it did not state how this regionalism would come about. It seemed to have ignored the incompatible political, ideological and personality factors which have made cooperation even on the level of bilateral relations very hard to forge. At present, only ECOWAS is of much interest and relevance with regard to the broad objectives of the Lagos summit. Apart from that, other regions have not yet appreciated the need for such regional integration ventures even to start talking about their establishment. For example, how would the North Africans cooperate in regional enterprises when the whole area is divided between the so-called rejectionist bloc on the one hand and Egypt and Sudan on the other? Until the Middle East crisis is solved, or pending a change of regime in Cairo which would be acceptable to the majority of North African states, a regional economic scheme there along the lines of ECOWAS is quite unlikely.

Another difficulty arises from the very nature of the Lagos strategy itself. Many of the objectives expressed in the summit document seem sound on paper but are difficult to bring to fruition in practice. As Kenneth Mackenzie has rightly pointed out, "when the document filters out to civil servants who do the work, some paragraphs will give them ideas for things they can do; many paragraphs will cause them to nod gently off to sleep."[61]

This situation arises because most of the prerequisites for the successful implementation of the plan are lacking in most African states. For instance, agricultural development alone would require some $22 billion in a continent where the average GNP is less than $500. The implication is that most of the money would have to come from outside sources, from the same countries in the developed north-the west in particular-from which

Africa is trying to free itself. In the past and
even today, these western countries have benefited
from the extreme economic and, in some cases,
political dependence of Africa on them. They
would surely be reluctant to create a situation
which would in the long run create a continent
viable enough politically and economically to pose
a serious challenge to their established economic
and political pre-eminence. In fact, paradoxically,
the success of the plan is either directly or
indirectly, predicated on collaboration with the
developed North. The Lagos document contains a
lot of seeds for the frustration and disillusion-
ment of African policy makers in the future.

Finally, there is the question whether
African leaders are prepared to make the necessary
sacrifices to see through such a project. Moreover, doubts have also been raised as to whether
those very leaders even grasp what development is
all about: "Many African leaders have no proper
conception of development even at the individual
national levels, or, are afraid of what it may
take to organise a good life in their societies".[62]
It is therefore doubtful if the very leaders are
prepared to make the relevant sacrifices or have
sufficient political will to implement a continental development strategy.

In spite of the many shortcomings of the
Lagos document, it has at least highlighted what
has perhaps been the main challenge to the
African nations since independence:  how to create
a viable society free from the current economic
deprivations which its citizens suffer every day.
"What happened in Lagos is functional in the sense
that it may generate more serious discourse, even
if the summit may be viewed as a false start, and
even if the plan of action may be one that is full
of sound and fury with little long-term significance.  There has to be a start from somewhere."[63]
The Lagos summit constitutes, therefore, a step in
the right direction, although the road is obviously

rough, circuitous and full of hard challenges. There is surely no going back. Even if the plan is not implemented in its entirety, Africa may yet be better-off in the year 2000 as a result of the Lagos conference.

(iii)   The Past and the Future:   Problems and Prospects

        Attempts to assess the performance of the OAU in its seventeen years' history are of necessity fraught with enormous difficulties. This is so for a variety of reasons. First the Organisation is relatively "young" compared with other regional institutions like the Arab League and the Organisation of American States (OAS). Second, views differ greatly as to which of the Organisation's functions are most important. This is because any assessment of the OAU's role in the political, social and economic well-being of the continent is by and large shrouded in the assessor's ideological colours.[64] This situation makes any evaluation of the institution's activities subjective, to say the least. What we have been doing in previous paragraphs and what we intend to do in this concluding section is, therefore, to "identify those fetters which affect its pursuit of goals as laid down in the Charter... or to be inferred from its resolutions and actions ..."[65] In brief, we can assess the OAU by juxtapositioning its Charter with its actual performance. By comparing theory with practice, it is hoped to isolate some of the obstacles which have hindered the effective and efficient functioning of the institution to date.

        Prominent among the factors which have frustrated the activities of the OAU are the political ones. As already pointed out, the Organisation is made up of "equal" and "independent" states with varying types of economic development, ideological orientations and political systems. Besides this, there are the problems raised by an

obstinate adherence to eurocentric concepts such
as state sovereignty and its corollary, non-
interference in the domestic affairs of other
members. Both principles are given a prominent
place in the Charter. Unfortunately, the Charter
did not specify which issues fall within the
exclusive purview of state sovereignty. Not surprisingly, African states and leaders have continued to exploit the all-embracing protective
shield of the two clauses to forestall the operations of the Organisation. This has been so notwithstanding the "goodness" or "badness" of the
issues involved or whether they constituted a
threat to the peace and stability of the continent
or not.

Closely related to the above problem are the
different ideological backgrounds and allegiances
of the membership. As already indicated, the
50-odd members of the OAU have heterogenous socio-
political and economic systems. For example, some
have embraced an economic system based on the
capitalist variety and maintain close links with
the west. Others have self-declared socialist
economies and political systems and have maintained
close links with the east. In-between, we have
what have been loosely called "African socialist"
or "Arab socialist" development strategies and
political systems. The implications of such
political and economic fragmentation within the
membership have had far-reaching consequences for
the performance of the Organisation. It has been
very difficult and sometimes impossible to reach
a consensus even over issues on which the Charter
is very unambiguous, such as opposition to apartheid[66] in South Africa and external military intervention. Understandably the OAU has not been able
to transcend the clash of national interests among
its members. Such a situation has further ham-
strung its activities. This is of particular
importance given the fact that the Organisation is
composed of states with comparable power and influence, at least until the oil boom saw the emer-

gence of Nigeria as a regional power.[67]

But besides the existence of political
factions within the OAU, its economic-cum-financial
weakness has also frustrated its activities.  The
OAU lacks economic and financial resources to make
its will felt and respected by its members and by
states outside the region.  In the past, for instance, the Organisation has not honoured many of
its decisions and resolutions because it lacked
either the financial means or the logistics to
do so.  The current civil war in Chad is a clear
case in point.  The OAU summit in Lagos decided to
send a peace-keeping force to the war-torn territory but lacked the men as well as the money
and logistical support.[68]

The OAU has on many occasions lived on borrowed funds because the majority of the membership could not make its budgetary contributions
on time.  For example, Diallo Telli, the first
Administrative Secretary-General, revealed in
1965 that of the then-36 member states, 24 had
not paid their annual budgetary quotas either in
full or in part.  The Secretariat had to incur a
$2m debt to keep it functioning.[89]  Ten years
later, the financial situation was the same.  The
London Guardian revealed that of 42 members only
five had paid their financial quotas to the OAU's
Liberation Committee.[70]  While the financial difficulties of the Organisation are in part due to
lack of political will amongst members to make
hard sacrifices, they are, above all, the result
of the sheer poverty of most African nations.  Of
the 25 poorest nations in the world, Africa alone
boasts of 16.  This situation, plus the four-fold
increase in the price of crude oil, has led to
very serious balance of payments problems for most
African nations.[71]  The result has been tight
budgeting and less money devoted to international
commitments.

Perhaps one of the most serious limitations

on OAU effectiveness is the absence of a standing
army.  The OAU does not have a stand-by force
which it could deploy at very short notice to
troubled areas to keep the peace.  The inability
of the institution to contain or solve African
disputes stems mainly from this fact.  It is thus
ironic that Africa, which is militarily the
weakest of all the world's regions, has also been
the area where moves to strengthen its defence
capabilities through the projected African High
Command (AHC) have been vigorously resisted.[72]
More than any other issue, the AHC has been bedeviled by political, technical and financial considerations.  Paradoxically, while many African
states are against a regional defence force, they
have nevertheless been active supporters of an
extra-continental peace-keeping force which would
be mainly controlled from Europe.

At present the absence of the necessary
political will to surrender what most African
states and leaders consider to be an important
aspect of sovereignty - control over their armies
- has made the AHC proposal a thing of the dis-
tant future.  Moreover, the low level of functional
interdependence amongst members of the African
subsystem makes the AHC idea suspect to most of
them, particularly to the very small ones.  They
fear the use to which such a standing force might
be put in the future.  Would it be used for the
supression of extra-regional aggression or would
it be used to muffle popular movements within
menber states?  These are all issues which have
not been resolved and which would continue to
dominate any discussion of an AHC structure.

At the moment, most African countries are
more or less, at a similar level in their development.  This means that none of them with the exceptions of Nigeria and Libya - could shoulder
the financial and technical burden of an AHC,
even if it were to be set up.  When a regional
power eventually emerges which would assume a role

similar to that of the USA in the Americas, it
would perhaps be possible to have an AHC. But
even then its role would have to be acceptable to
the small members if such a force were to be
effective. This presumes that the regional or
hegemonial state would be largely responsible for
logistical and financial support while the smaller
nations would provide the manpower, much like UN
peace-keeping operations. Before this could be
practicable, however, the notion of primus inter
pares, which is rejected at the moment by the OAU,
would have to be incorporated into its Charter
policies to reflect the real world situation.

What are the prospects for the future? Discussion of the future of the OAU as a problem-
solving regional institution must take into consideration its legal, political, economic, administrative and even structural shortcomings. Some
of these we have exposed in the foregoing paragraphs. In fact, most of the discussion about the
Organisation's future must bear in mind the obsole-
scence of its Charter and, therefore, the need for
its amendment. The African states will have to
accept that all states are not equal. Once that
is done the way will then be open for the revision
of the Charter. The principle of "equality" would
have to give way to a hierarchical arrangement of
member states. The principle of "non-interference"
would also yield to a situation whereby the OAU
would be able to intervene in conflicts which are
perceived to be a threat to the security and peace
of the continent. This would, of course, require
radical admendments to the functions of the
"Administrative" Secretary-General to give him
powers similar to those of the UN Secretary-
General.

The 1973 oil crisis should already have demonstrated to the African nations, as well as to the
rest of the world, that many of the traditional
functions of the state such as defence of territor-
iality and the promotion of citizens' welfare are
becoming increasingly elusive. Even the super-

powers have had to team up with their allies to
meet their defence and even economic needs.[73]
The world is being drawn together daily and is
getting "smaller". More than ever, there is
increasing "interdependence" in the economic,
social and even political spheres among members
of the world system. This phenomenon is no less
true for African states and the continent in
general.

This development has also tended to de-
emphasise, albeit very slowly, eurocentric concepts such as boundaries and sovereignty. New
doors for mutual influence and penetration are
opening up at all levels throughout the coninent.
Looked at from such a perspective, African nationalism and Africa's eurocentrism as hindrances to
intra-African integration are merely transitory
phenomena. "The African nationalism of today will
leave room for something larger..."[74] in the
future thus making the functions of the OAU much
easier and more effective. The Lagos economic
summit has paved the way for such a prospect.

If we accept the above then the future becomes more optimistic and predictable. The problems of the OAU could be seen as being only temporary. The obstinate adherence to the Charter
by member states especially over such principles
as non-interference in the internal affairs of
others, would give way to a more "realistic"
formula in intra-African diplomacy which would
promote greater cooperation and integration among
Africans. How long it would take to reach such a
stage is another thing altogether. Already, there
is talk about drawing up an African Charter of
Human Rights. That is surely a step in the right
direction.

In short, given time it may still be possible
to achieve supranationalism in Africa. That is
the lesson from the long experience of the EEC.
With time, selfless sacrifice and good planning,

there is no reason why the projected African Common Market should not take-off in future. The long-term prospects for the OAU and the continent look bright. How "long" is "long term" is difficult to say. For the time being, the OAU "is the only thing we have got that unites us"[75] despite its numerous shortcomings. We must endeavour to make it work efficiently if it is to meet the challenges of the twenty-first century. For this to be possible the 50-odd members must be prepared to yield some of their powers to a central African authority. This is the central challenge facing every African state and regime in the last 20 years of the twentieth century.

Notes

1.  See Samuel P. Huntington Political Order in Changing Societies (New Haven: Yale University Press, 1968).

2.  Emphasis is mine.

3.  Julius Gould and William L. Kolb (eds) A Dictionary of the Social Sciences (London: Tavistok, 1964) 489.

4.  For a comparison of the OAU and the UN see B. Andemicael The OAU and the UN (New York: Africana, 1976). For a detailed and illuminating treatment of the OAU and its institutions, see Z. Cervenka The Unfinished Quest for Unity, (New York: Africana 1977). See also Immanuel Wallerstein, Africa: The Politics of Unity (New York: Vintage, 1967), Jon Woronoff Organising African Unity (Metuchen, New Jersey: Scarecrow, 1970), Yassin El-Ayouty The Organisation of African Unity After Ten Years (New York: Praeger 1975) and Y. Tandon "The OAU: a forum for African international relations" Round Table, 246, September 1972, 221-30.

5.  Huntington , op. cit. 2-5.

6.  See the Charter and T. O. Elias "The Charter of the OAU", American Journal of International Law, 59(2), April, 1965.

7.  Articles 2(c) and 3, of the Charter.

8.  Onyeonoro S. Kamanu, "Secession and the right of self-determination: an OAU dilemma", Journal of Modern African Studies, 12(3), September 1974, 355-76.

9.  The 1960 Republican Constitution of Ghana specifically made provision for the surrender of Ghana's sovereignty to a Pan-African government or central authority.

10. Kamanu op. cit. 264.

11. Report on the OAU Consultative Mission to Nigeria, (Lagos: Government Printer, 1967) 1. See also Africa Research Bulletin, henceforth (ARB) November 30, 1967, 901 and West Africa, December 2, 1969, 1561 for more details of the Mission's work. For a good treatment of the civil war itself, see John J. Stremlau The International Politics of the Nigerian Civil War 1967-70 (Princeton: Princeton University Press, 1977).

12. Report on the OAU Consultative Mission op. cit. 3.

13. Ibid 4.

14. Ibid 6

15. Ibid 6

16. Ibid 12

17. See Guardian (London) July 21, 1975. The Tunisian Charge d'Affaires in Addis Ababa paid the price for his intrasingence over the issue when he was given 24 hours to quit Ethiopia.

18. West Africa, July 30, 1979, 1357.

19. A. Bolaji Akinyemi, "Can the OAU Lead to African Unity?" Afriscope, 2(6), June 1972, 24.

20. For a compilation of inter-African disputes
    from 1963-74, see B. David Meyers, "Inter-
    regional conflict management by the OAU",
    International Organisation, 28(3), Summer
    1974, 345-75, and also Robert O. Mathews,
    "Interstate conflicts in Africa: a review"
    International Organisation, 24 (2), Spring
    1970, 335-60.

21. For more details on the Algero-Moroccan con-
    flict, see ARB, June 1-30 1972, 2502, Saadia
    Touval, "The Morocco-Algeria border dispute",
    ARB October 1-31, 1966, 632, Patricia Berko
    Wild, "The Organisation of African Unity and
    the Algerian-Moroccan border conflict,"
    International Organisation, 20(1) Winter 1966,
    18-36, and Saadia Touval, The Boundary
    Politics of Independent Africa, (Cambridge:
    Harvard University Press, 1972) 258-59.

22. ARB, June 1-30 1972, 2502.

23. We must bear in mind also that recently non-
    state actors have increasingly used force to
    bring about desired changes within states
    and between states. The activities of the
    Palestine Liberation Organisation (PLO) and
    various other guerrilla movements throughout
    the world are good examples of such activities.

24. ARB, October 1-31 1965, 379.

25. This was clear from the division within the
    Organisation over the recognition of the
    MPLA in Angola and the Soviet-backed Cuban
    military intervention in that country, in
    1976.

26. See Africa (London) 101, January 1980, 30.

27. The conference started on May 22 1978. After the meeting, President Houphouet-Boigny told the Press that the French members of the West African Economic Community (CFAO), hoped to expand their mutual defence pact to include French-speaking countries in Central Africa. See ARB, May 1-31, 1978, 4860.

28. ibid 4839.

29. ibid 4860.

30. See ARB, December 1-31, 1970, 1949.

31. Nigeria: Bulletin on Foreign Affairs 1(2), 1971, 47-48.

32. For instance, at the eighth annual summit in Addis Ababa, the Organisation once more re-affirmed the determination of African peoples and states to take all necessary measures to eradicate from the African continent the scourge that the mercenary system represents," Africa Contemporary Record, Volume 3, 1970/71 (London: Rex Collings, 1971)C4.

33. Africa Diary (New Delhi) September 24-30 1978, 9192.

34. The FAO in its 1977 Report, for instance, stated: "of all the developing regions, Africa is the only one where food production has grown less than population in the 1970s." See "Africa" in FAO, The state of food and agriculture (Rome, 1977) quoted in Timothy M. Shaw "On Projections, Prescriptions and Plans: Towards an African Future," Quarterly Journal of Administration, and also Timothy M. Shaw (ed) Alternative Futures for Africa, (Boulder: Westview, 1981).

35. See Shaw "On Projections, Prescriptions and Plans," 22.

36. See Timothy M. Shaw "EEC/ACP interactions and images as redefinitions of Eur-Africa: exemplary. exclusive and/or exploitative?" Journal of Common Market Studies 18(2), December 1979, 159-74.

37. For instance, a conference on African Telecommunications 1966, Pan-African Highway 1969, Organisation of African Trade Union Unity, 1973 and many others.

38. For more details see ARB, (Economic and Technical Series) April 15 - May 14 1971, 2007.

39. ARB (Economic and Technical Series) April 15 - May 14 1971, 2709.

40. ibid  May 15 - June 14  1973, 2739.

41. Shaw, "EEC-ACP interactions and images".

42. See MOJA's letter to President Tolbert of Liberia protesting against the visit to Liberia of Henry Kissinger April 1976, and also Greg Lenning and Marti Mueller's chapter on "Liberia and the Mining Companies," in their Africa Undermined (London: Penguin, 1979) 257-73.

43. For details of the negotiations see Sola Ojo, "The 1973 oil crisis and Black Africa's Relations with the Arab World,"Nigerian Journal of Political Science, (Zaria), ARB (Economics and Technical Series) January 15 - February 14, 1974, Ali Abusin The Launching (sic) of Afro-Arab Cooperation:  an experiment in inter-regional solidarity (Cairo: League of Arab States General Department of Information, nd) and Sola Ojo's contribution to this collection.

44. See Africa Newsletter, (Cairo), 7 July 15, 1974.

45. <u>ARB,</u> August 15 - September 14, 1974 3223 and January 15 - February 14, 1974 3002.

46. Shaw, "On Prescriptions, Projections and Plans".  For the impact of the oil crisis on some African economies, see <u>UN World Economic Survey, 1976</u> (New York) and <u>Trade and Development Council, East Africa and the Sudan: Report of the Trade Development Council Mission to Kenya, Tanzania, Zambia and Sudan,</u> Australian Department of Overseas Trade, May-June, 1975.

47. See <u>Africa Contemporary Record, Volume 9,</u> 1976/77, A74, and <u>ARB</u> (Economic and Technical Series) November 15 - December 14, 1976, 4087.

48. <u>ibid.</u>

49. <u>ibid.</u>

50. See <u>West Africa</u>, "Towards the Year 2000", August 6 and 20 1979, 1411 and 1501 respectively.

51. See <u>Daily Times</u> (Lagos), April 24, 1980.

52. <u>ibid.</u>

53. <u>ibid</u>, April 25, 1980.

54. <u>West Africa</u>, May 19, 1980, 870

55. <u>ibid.</u>

56. <u>Daily Times</u>, May 2, 1980.

57. Robert Mackenzie "Africa needs the economic plan", <u>Daily Times,</u> May 9, 1980.

58. <u>West Africa</u>, June 2 1980, 961-2.

59. Yima Sen, "False start at Lagos?", West
    Africa, June 2 1980,963.

60. The Arab rejectionist states are those states
    which are totally opposed to the Egyptian
    Peace initiative with Israel.  They include
    Libya, Algeria and Tunisia.

61. Daily Times, May 9, 1980.

62. Sen, op. cit. 963.

63. ibid.

64. For a practioner's assessment of the OAU's
    performance, see Okoi Arikpo, "The OAU and
    the UN:  have they succeeded?", Nigeria:
    Bulletin on Foreign Affairs 1(2), October
    1971, 48-54.

65. Richard A. Fredland; "The OAU after ten years",
    African Affairs, 72(288), July 1973, 309.

66. The dialogue debate in the early 1970s and
    the division it engendered among African
    states was a clear case in point.  This was
    in spite of the Lusaka Manifesto (1969) which
    came out strongly in favour of South Africa's
    diplomatic, political, economic and social
    ostracisation both in Africa and the world at
    large.

67. See for instance; Sandy Feustel, "Nigeria:
    Leadership in Africa", Africa Report, May-June
    1977, 48-50, and Olajide Aluko    "Nigeria's
    initiative in the West African Economic Com-
    munity", Societe d'Etudes et d'Expansion Revue
    (Liege), November-December, 1977, 870-880.

68. See "OAU grapples with Chad problem", Daily
    Times, April 25, 1980.

69.   ARB, October 1-31 1965, 375.

70.   Guardian (London), May 14 1975.   The paper
      disclosed that Egypt was owing the Committee
      over $1,600,000 and Nigeria was in arrears
      to $1,400,000.   20 other states were in
      arrears of over two years.

71.   See Ojo, op. cit.

72.   See O. Iyanda and J. Stremlau, "The dilemma
      of the African High Command", Nigeria:
      Bulletin on Foreign Affairs 1(2), October 1971,
      10, for more details.

73.   The abortive US rescue mission in Iran in
      April 1980 to free the American hostages held
      in that country was a vivid illustration of
      the limitations even on the world's most
      powerful country.

74.   See W.A.E. Skurnik, The Foreign Policy of
      Senegal (Evanston: Northwestern Unversity
      Press, 1972) 289-90.

75.   Brigadier Joseph Garba of Nigeria, quoted in
      African Development, 10 (9), September 1976,
      856.

Chapter Eight

## Conflict and Cooperation in Southern Africa

Adekunle Ajala

Southern Africa, for the purposes of this chapter, is comprised essentially of the following territories: Angola, Botswana, Lesotho, Malawi, Mozambique, Namibia, South Africa, Swaziland, Zambia and Zimbabwe. While these territories present a relatively compact geographical region there are a few other territories which, for political reasons, can be looked upon as forming part of the Southern African sub-region even if on a marginal basis.[1] The latter include Tanzania which is a leading member of the Front Line States, Zaire whose role in the Angolan independence struggle contributed in no small measure to the course of events in the sub-region and also the Malagasy Republic which has, in recent years, been gradually turning its attention from Europe and is now "beginning to play an increasingly crucial part in African and Southern African affairs".[2] Nevertheless particular attention will be paid to the first group of territories which for the purposes of this chapter will be regarded as the 'core' area while mention will be made of the 'marginal' territories whenever necessary.

The most distinctive features in the structure and processes of Southern Africa sub-region when compared with the characteristics of other regions are concentrated in the discontinuities of scope and membership between issue areas. The central issues of course are racism in all its manifestations and applications as practised by an entrenched group of white minorities and decolonisation and self-determination

as demanded by the oppressed majority. Other
issues either merely revolve around these major
ones or serve as their manifestations or even
aberrations . They have not only been responsible
for the conflict in the sub-region but also determined the level of cooperation in the area.

i)  Background

South Africa, the dominant state actor in
the sub-region, formally institutionalised racial
discrimination in the form of apartheid in 1948
when the Nationalist Party came into power.
Through a series of legislation the South African
regime took measures to perpetuate white minority
rule, deny the majority African populace their
basic human rights, render any existing organised
African resistance ineffective and divide the
Africans into "Bantustans" meant to provide the
white South Africans with the much needed manpower
in the mines, farms, factories etc.  African
resistance to such measures had led to the formation and now the growth of both the African
National Congress (ANC) and the Pan-African Congress (PAC) - both dedicated to bring about a just,
multi-racial, humane society in South Africa where
all races would, as of right, be able to participate in the social, economic and political development of the country.

Meanwhile the process of decolonisation had
started to gather mementum in the rest of Africa.
Since the Manchester Pan-African Conference of
1945 the nationalist movements had made "independence" their target in the colonies.  The achievement of independence by the Gold Coast under the
name of Ghana in 1957 was Pan-Africanism's first
success and it spurred other nationalist movements
on to victory.  By 1960 the colonial powers -
Britain, France and Belgium - had come to terms
with the aspirations of the African people and
granted independence to most of their colonies.
While Britain was trying to disengage itself from

Southern Rhodesia by hook or by crook, Portugal
refused to budge from her African colonies. It
then looked as if the process of decolonisation
would be halted along the Zambezi since South
Africa was also resisting any attempt to grant
independence to South West-Africa (Namibia).

1960 - which was declared "Africa's Year" -
was remarkable in many ways. At the beginning of
that year the then British Prime Minister, Harold
Macmillan undertook a tour of several Anglophone
African countries. Addressing members of the
South African parliament on February 3 he spoke,
inter alia, about the strength of African national
consciousness as follows: "In different places
it takes different forms. But it is happening
everywhere. The wind of change is blowing throughout the continent".[3] A few weeks later the South
African regime's forces gunned down many innocent
Africans who were demonstrating against the pass
laws in Sharpeville. This awful experience,
coupled with the ruthless suppression of any form
of nationalist expression forced the Africans to
recognise that their objectives would never be
realised by peaceful means. The Africans suddenly
became aware of the fact that the protagonists of
apartheid would stop at nothing in order to maintain that abominable system. They were prepared
to take up the challenge.

Portugal, in an attempt to stem the wave of
African nationalism, decreed in 1951 that her
African colonies would henceforth be regarded as
"overseas provinces". All efforts to make her
see the futility of such a policy were brushed
aside and African yearnings for self-determination
were met with brutal repression. While Portugal
was employing the services of the PIDE, its secret
police, to oppress, imtimidate and incarcerate any
African who "dared" to talk of independence in her
colonies the UN General Assembly adopted on 14
December 1960 the Declaration on the Granting of
Independence to Colonial Countries and Peoples

which solemnly proclaimed the necessity of bringing colonialism in all its forms and manifestations
to a speedy and unconditional end.[4]  The impact of
this declaration on the struggling masses in the
remaining colonies - the Portuguese included -
was tremendous for it gave them the moral courage
to continue fighting until their birthright was
secured.

Before the adoption of the Declaration many
former mandated territories of the UN were either
already independent or were about to attain that
status.  The only exception was South West Africa
which South Africa wanted to incorporate as its
"fifth province".  In view of South Africa's
defiance of world opinion over the issue both
Liberia and Ethiopia instituted proceedings on
4 November 1960 in the International Court of
Justice against her concerning her administration
of the territory and her failure to fulfil her
international obligations as the mandatory power.
While the legal battle raged on there was a great
expectation throughout the world that, in view of
the previous advisory opinions handed down over
the years over the issue, the Court would come
out in favour of the applicants.  But to the con-
sternation of everybody the Court on 18 July 1966
ruled against both Ethiopia and Liberia.[5]  This
unexpected decision led immediately to two major
activities.  Firstly the UN General Assembly
adopted a resolution terminating South Africa's
mandate over the territory and declaring that
"henceforth South West Africa comes under the
direct responsibility of the United Nations".[6]
Secondly SWAPO embarked on an armed struggle in
order that the Namibian people might achieve their
birthright.

Meanwhile the Pan-African movement, which
had been beset by internal wrangling and division
into the Brazzaville, Casablanca and Monrovia
groups, had succeeded in overcoming most of its
difficulties.  As a result all independent African

states (with the exception of South Africa) gathered
in Addis Ababa in May 1963 to form the Organisation
of African Unity (OAU). At that summit all African
leaders were unanimous in their desire to rid
Africa of colonialism and racial discrimination.
Consequently they established a Coordinating
Committee charged with the responsibility of
"harmonizing the assistance from African states
and for managing the special fund to be set up"
for the total liquidation of colonialism on the
African continent and also decided on measures to
bring apartheid and racial discrimination to an
end. This Coordinating Committee, which later
became known as the OAU Liberation Committee,
constituted the instrument for formulating OAU
policies on the inter-related problems of Southern
Africa. The independent African states in the
sub-region which are also members of the OAU in
most cases react to the situation in accordance
with the guidelines, strategies and parameters
set by the continental organisation.

ii)   Conflict

From this brief background it is clear that
a number of actors operate to bring about and
influence the situation in Southern Africa. These
range from the OAU, nation-states, political
parties, liberation movements, trans-national,
multi-national and state corporations as well as
trade unions and even the churches.[7]  An attempt
will be made in this chapter not only to examine
the inter-play between these different actors but
also to analyse what policy choices are open to
them.

At the inaugural meeting of the 1963 certain
special resolutions were adopted. The first two[8]
aimed at bringing both colonialism as well as
apartheid and racial discrimination to an end on
the African continent. Both spelt out how this
objective was to be achieved. Besides, both made
it clear that South Africa, in view of her abomin-

able apartheid policy in South Africa and her
intransigence  over South West Africa, Portugal,
because of her dubious and futile policy of
"overseas territories" and the United Kingdom,
which was finding ways to shirk her responsibility
to the majority African populace of Southern
Rhodesia, were the main targets.  All independent
African states endorsed the resolutions while
those which later became independent gave their
assent to it on joining the continental organisation.  African unanimity was therefore, maintained
over the issue.

But how did these target states react to the
OAU resolutions?  By and large their reactions,
which in varying degrees centred on indifference,
formed the bedrock of conflict in the sub-region.
While the United Kingdom embarked upon an ingenious
design to comouflage its real intentions in Southern
Rhodesia both South Africa and Portugal ignored
the OAU call for a change in their respective
policies.

By the time the OAU was established there
were indications that if the British Government
did not take drastic measures in good time the
minority regime in Southern Rhodesia might take
the laws into its own hands and unilaterally
declare independence in the territory.  In view
of this, the resolution adopted by the assembled
heads of states and government specifically called
on Britain the colonial power "not to transfer the
powers and attributes of sovereignty to a minority
government imposed on African peoples by the use
of force and under cover of racial legislation".

In response to this call the British government arranged talks with the leaders of the
Rhodesian Front in London but nothing was achieved.
Although the Rhodesian leader Ian Smith left Sir
Alec Douglas-Home in no doubt that if no agreement
was reached Rhodesia would go ahead with a Unilateral  Declaration of Independence (UDI) the

British took no steps to pre-empt such a move.
Instead, the British government changed tactics in
an effort to exonerate itself from any eventuality
and also to appear to be doing something about
the on-coming revolt.  In one breath it insisted
that the Rhodesian problem was a colonial question
for which only the United Kingdom must bear final
responsibility but at the same time not only
agreed to discuss the issue at Commonwealth meetings but also suggested to the "Rhodesians that a
Commonwealth delegation might be able to mediate
in the constitutional dispute".[9]  Nobody was left
in doubt as to the British Government's real intentions.  While the illegal minority regime in
Salisbury saw this as a green light to go ahead
with its preparations for a UDI the African
nationalists too realised that they could not
count on the British sense of fair play.  They
had to get ready for any eventuality.

Two reasons could be adduced for the British
move.  Firstly, the British were confident that
if it came to the crunch the white minority regime
could easily take care of African "agitators" in
the territory.  And secondly, they were well
aware of the military and economic weakness of
the OAU.  The British reckoned therefore that
the whites in Southern Rhodesia would easily get
away with UDI if the British Government gave
spurious reasons for non-intervention.  What they
failed to realise, however, was that the wind of
change which was blowing in other parts of the
continent might later turn into hurricane pro-
portions at the Zambezi.  But this eventuality
did not cross their minds at the time they inevitably laid the foundation for a future bloody
confrontation in Southern Rhodesia.

So the Southern Rhodesian regime, confident
that the British Government had given it a blank
cheque for rebellion, went ahead to implement its
UDI plans.  A clamp-down on all nationalist
activities was high on its agenda; as such, many

nationalist leaders were rounded up and put in
detention while the final touches were put to the
Unilateral Declaration of Independence which was
announced on 11 November 1965.

Meanwhile, Nationalist activities too have
been undergoing some changes. Divergent views of
how best to tackle the problem had led to a split
in the Zimbabwe African People's Union's (ZAPU)
hierarchy. Reverend Ndabaningi Sithole supported
by Robert Mugabe and other like-minded members
who favoured a more radical approach broke
away to form the Zimbabwe African National Union
(ZANU) in 1963. It was this group that took the
initiative in getting ready for the subsequent
liberation struggle. Between September 1964 and
March 1965 about forty ZANU members were sent to
various places outside the country for training
in guerrilla warfare, sabotage and the manufacture
of explosives. ZAPU soon followed suit.[10] By
April 1965 some of these nationalist fighters
started to return to the territory in order to
embark upon the struggle for their birthright.
With the illegal declaration of independence in
November 1965 they stepped up the armed struggle.

In the Portuguese colonies the situation
remained tense. The armed struggle which began
in both Guinea-Bissau and Angola in 1961 had
spread to Mozambique by 1964. Nevertheless
Portugal which depended on these colonies for
"her economic strength, strategic potentiality
and political dimension"[11] remained as obdurate
as ever since her NATO allies were supplying the
hardware with which to prosecute a war she could
never win. While the struggle in both Guinea-
Bissau and Mozambique was spearheaded by single
liberation movements - PAIGC and FRELIMO - respectively the situation was slightly different
in Angola. There three liberation movements -
MPLA, UNITA and FLNA - were in existence. We
examine the effect of this multiple existence of
liberation movements on the situation in Southern

Africa later on.

South Africa for her part appeared unruffled by the activities of the international community to force her to change her policy. This apparent act of indifference forced the OAU Administrative Secretary-General to report to the 1964 OAU Summit in Cairo that the offensive "did not have the slightest effects on the regimes" in Southern Africa and also to come to the conclusion that "all avenues for peaceful and legal means to alleviate the intolerable conditions have been progressively eliminated by the South African Government". In the meantime South Africa had started to implement its Bantustan policy,[12] in spite of African opposition while the pass laws and the other paraphernalia of apartheid continued to be implemented.

Southern Africa was thus in a state of heightened tension when the white minority regime of Rhodesia proclaimed UDI. Spontaneous and immediate hostile reaction greeted the declaration throughout the world. African reaction was succintly put by a senior Tanzanian Minister when he vowed that "No power on earth will stop us from a final duel with the forces of white racism in Southern Africa".[13] Thus the battleline was drawn in Southern Africa.

Frantic efforts were made at the UN to isolate Rhodesia economically and diplomatically. Several resolutions were adopted and sanctions imposed in order to achieve this objective.[14] But before these sanctions could be effectively applied the cooperation of both Portugal, which controlled the adjoining territories of Mozambique as well as Angola, and South Africa was absolutely necessary. This they refused to give. Instead the three recalcitrant states cemented their pre-UDI working arrangement in an "unholy alliance".

What were the reasons for this unusual
alliance? Could it simply rest on the fact that
all three seemed to have been threatened by the
black populace in their respective territories?
To answer these and other related questions it
must be pointed out that the racial policies of
the three regimes were not quite the same. Even
if one does not entirely agree with the altruism
said to be the basis of Portuguese racial policy,
it could not be equated with apartheid as
practised by the South African regime in both
South Africa and South West Africa. The essential
common denominator was, however, that the white
minority was in power in each of the territories
controlled by these governments. Each had done
everything possible to exclude the indigenous
African people from participation in the government of these territories. Besides, Africans in
each of these territories were more or less
regarded as beasts of burden and condemned to
menial jobs. Jobs requiring skilled manpower
were reserved for the whites either by legislation
or by the type of education available to the
different races. But were these the only reasons
for the alliance? Certainly not. Each member
had other motives for joining the club of pariahs.

South Africa's response to UN actions over
UDI stemmed from a statement made by Verwoerd to
the effect that "our strength lies in isolating
outselves from those policies in which we do not
believe, and which we believe will lead to the
disappearance of the white man's rule in South
Africa".[15] This line of thought had always
determined South Africa's approach to the events
in Southern Africa. According to Strijdom: "Our
task in South Africa is to maintain the identity
of the white man; in that task we will die fighting".[16]

Two vital points emerge from these statements. Firstly, South Africa regarded herself
as a bastion of white rule. Wherever there was

any indication, however remote, that the security
of South Africa might be adversely threatened
South Africa would not hesitate to take necessary
measures to nip such a threat in the bud.    There
was no doubt that both the Portuguese territories
and Rhodesia provided South Africa with the necessary cordon sanitaire.   No price was too high
to pay in order to maintain this status quo.   So,
secondly, as both Portugal and Rhodesia were
threatened by the liberation fight they had no
other alternative but to seek assistance from
their powerful neighbour.   There was therefore a
tacit understanding amongst them that an attack
upon any of the territories should be regarded as
an attack upon them all.

        While the white minority regimes of Southern
Africa were coming much closer together the
liberation movements in Rhodesia - ZAPU and ZANU -
were in open and serious conflict with one another.
The Salisbury regime capitalized on these differences and banned both of them.   They had to
operate from exile by the time the UDI was declared.
All OAU initiatives to reconcile them met with
failure.   Nevertheless each continued to intensify
its preparations for an armed struggle.   By August
1967 a combined force of ZAPU and South Africa ANC
liberation fighters had started operations in
Rhodesia.   For about four weeks they seriously
harassed white infantry and police in the Wankie
district.   The Europeans were at times so pinned
down that they were unable to evacuate their
wounded.   White officers lost their lives for the
first time since the anti-colonial war of 1896.
When the situation appeared so grim the Rhodesian
Hawker Hunter jets had to join in the battle,
using rockets and napalm to set fire to grasslands
in an effort to dislodge the freedom fighters.   As
a result, Prime Minister Ian Smith was forced to
call for South African assistance.[17]

        Meanwhile the liberation struggle was hotting
up in the remaining parts of white redoubts of

Southern Africa. In Angola various areas had become combat zones. On Christmas Day 1966 UNITA forces raided the town of Teixeira de Sousa and they derailed several trains on the Benguela Railway by mid-1967. At the same time the FLNA/ GRAE supporters kept up a steady string of small but deadly ambushes in the North while the MPLA was engaged in operations in Eastern Angola. They were "successful in ambushing enemy forces and sabotaging roads, bridges, and river barges along the upper Zambezi and Lunguenvungue Rivers".[18] As for Mozambique events had even moved much faster. FRELIMO had by 1966 not only carried the struggle deep into the enemy's camp but had been firmly entrenched in the Cabo Delgado, Niassa and Tete provinces.[19]

South West Africa was not left out. When the process of international and legal pressure had been tested and found wanting following the abortive 1966 judgment of the ICJ the Namibian nationalists took arms to liberate their father- land. On 2 August 1966 the first confrontation between the nationalists and the South African police occurred. Although the former suffered initial setbacks, within a month they were back in business. This time they attacked the admin- istrative post at Oshikango which was used by the South African Commissioner for part of Ovamboland, killed many South African soldiers and caused a lot of damage.[20] Scared by this event the South African Parliament passed the Terrorism Act which provided harsh penalties in an effort to prevent the armed struggle in both South Africa and Namibia. But in spite of this the struggle con- tinued unabated.

In an effort to contain the situation South Africa immediately rushed her troops and police to Rhodesia. These were initially mandated to patrol the "Zambezi Line" in order to prevent the in- filtration of men and arms from Zambia. The South African air force embarked upon high-altitude

photo-reconnaissance flights over Zambia and
Southern Tanzania. However all this reaction
notwithstanding the freedom fighters kept up the
pressure. Besides, borrowing a leaf from the
white racists, the liberation movements entered
into a form of transnational coalition. This was
easy to achieve since all of them were based
either in Zambia, Tanzania, Congo (Kinshasa) (now
Zaire) or the neighbouring Democratic People's
Republic of the Congo. ANC of South Africa
formed an alliance with ZAPU of Rhodesia while
there was a loose working arrangement between PAC
of South Africa and ZANU of Rhodesia. The liberation movements in the Portuguese colonies also
met regularly within the forum of CONCP to exchange views and ideas. The only exceptions were
both UNITA and FLNA. But later on these groupings
were determined by their chief sources of external
aid. While ANC, ZAPU, MPLA and SWAPO, originally
received their external non-African aid from
Moscow, PAC, ZANU and FLNA had China as their
chief benefactor. This realignment of forces and
the impact it had on the liberation struggle in
Southern Africa forced Britain to embark on the
abortive "Tiger" and "Fearless" talks.

The OAU for its part did not relent in its
efforts to secure united fronts of the liberation
movements in each of the territories concerned.
But it had to content itself with the above-
mentioned groupings. While the OAU continued to
provide the necessary assistance to the liberation
movements in their legitimate struggle for their
people's birthright both Zambia and Tanzania
agreed to convene good neighbourliness meetings
amongst the leaders of East and Central African
States. This series of meetings produced the
Lusaka Manifesto of 1969 which spelt out clearly
how they thought the problems of South Africa
could be solved. In it the African leaders made
it absolutely clear that there could be no
surrender or compromise on the issue of liberation
in the region. The Manifesto declared that:

We have always preferred and we still
prefer to achieve it without physical
violence. We would prefer to negotiate
rather than destroy, to talk rather
than kill. We do not advocate violence; we advocate an end to the violence against human dignity which is
now being perpetrated by the oppressors of Africa. If peaceful progress
to emancipation were possible, or
if changed circumstances were to
make it possible in the future, we
would urge our brothers in the re-
sistence movements to use peaceful
methods of struggle even at the cost
of some compromise on the timing of
change. But while peaceful progress
is blocked by actions of those at
present in power in the States of
Southern Africa, we have no choice
but to give to the peoples of those
territories all the support of which
we are capable in their struggle
against their oppressors".[21]

This document received both OAU and UN endorsement
later that year.

However, convinced of their own invincibility
the outcasts of Southern Africa simply ignored
the olive branch thus held out to them by the
African leaders. Instead they embarked upon
various manoeuvres through third parties - France,
Britain and the United States - to buy off certain
African leaders who later came out to plead for
"Dialogue with South Africa".[22] Although this
issue generated a lot of debate it did not take
long before the idea was thrown into the waste
paper basket of history during the OAU Summit held
in Addis Ababa in June 1971. In a 'Declaration on
the Question of Dialogue' adopted at the conference
the African heads of states and government rejected
dialogue which was described as a "manoeuvre by

South Africa and its allies to divide African
States, confuse world opinion, relieve South
Africa from international ostracism and isolation,
and obtain an acceptance of the status quo in
South Africa". It reiterated Africa's total commitment to the principles of the OAU Charter and made
it abundantly clear that the Lusaka Manifesto was
the only basis for a solution to the problems of
apartheid, racial discrimination and colonialism
in Africa. Besides, it stipulated that if there
was going to be any dialogue at all it should be
held between the minority regime of South Africa
and the people the racists were oppressing and
exploiting. Furthermore it forbade OAU members
from initiating or engaging in any type of
activity that would undermine or abrogate the
solemn undertakings of the OAU Charter.[23]

While the dialogue conspiracy was being
hatched by South Africa the Portuguese for
their part indulged in assassinations. On 3
February 1969 Dr. Edwardo Mondlane who had been
FRELIMO's leader since 1962 was killed by a bomb
wrapped in a book. A few weeks earlier the deputy
military commander of FRELIMO forces, Samuel
Kankonbe, was assassinated in Southern Tanzania.
However all these acts notwithstanding the armed
struggle was stepped up throughout the whole of
Southern Africa.

The Rhodesian freedom fighters managed to
fuse their armies into the Front for the Liberation
of Zimbabwe (FROLIZI) in 1971 in order to be able
to face the enemy more effectively. The outcome
of this was the constitutional proposals hastily
agreed upon by Alec Douglas-Home and Ian Smith in
that year. But due to the efforts of the African
National Council under the leadership of Bishop
Abel Muzorewa these proposals were subsequently
turned down by the African people. And of course
the fighting was stepped up further as a result.

In the Portuguese colonies the situation was
getting so desperate for the racists that a change
of policy was being advocated. As a result
Caetano, Salazar's successor, agreed to certain
verbal changes in the constitution of Portugal.
These changes allowed that the "overseas provinces"
might look forward to some kind of identity of
their own, and might even in due course be per-
mitted to call themselves "autonomous states".[24]
The changes envisaged were, however, minimal since
the real authority in financial, military and
administrative matters was to remain in Lisbon.
Even if there were majority African representation
in the proposed legislatures of the "overseas
provinces" their powers were scarcely widened
from the purely decorative nature they had before.
As such, and also because the changes came at
least a decade too late, they made no impression
on the Africans who knew full well that they were
meant to undermine militant African nationalism.
Instead, their reply to these manoeuvres was
increased armed struggle which finally led to the
coup in Portugal on 25 April 1975[25], an event
which had such an impact on the situation on
Southern Africa that even the most ardent sup-
porter of the white regimes must have come to the
conclusion that that was the beginning of the
end of "white power".

Before we examine the implications of this
event on the Southern African situation one thing
must not be forgotten. That is the OAU's "Accra
Declaration on the new Strategy for the Liberation
of Africa" of January 1973 and its impact on the
subsequent overall Southern African development.
The thrust of this Declaration, after recognising
that the liberation of Africa was a collective
responsibility of all African states, was to accord
priority to the liberation of Portuguese territories before tackling the remaining problems.
It reaffirmed the determination of the Liberation
Committee to make the second decade of the OAU a
decade of the armed struggle with tangible and

decisive victories. In order to achieve this
objective increased aid was put at the disposal
of the liberation movements in the Portuguese
colonies while armed struggle was intensified in
Rhodesia (especially in the north-eastern part
of the territrory) and Namibia where the strike
weapon had become an added factor. The impact of
these activities was such that it made Ian Smith,
out of desperation, to commit the colossal
blunder of closing the border with Zambia and
also served to open the eyes of the Portuguese
to their futile military adventures. And so the
inevitable happened on 25 April 1974, thus bringing Portuguese fascism to an end. But more
importantly the white redoubt in Southern Africa
was thrown into disarray and each leader began to
think seriously about how to save his own neck.[26]

     The immediate outcome of the coup however
was the Portuguese recognition of self-determination in her African colonies. Immediate steps
were taken to implement this new awareness. As
a result the independence of Guinea-Bissau was
recognised by the Portuguese Government on 9
September 1974 while others were to attain that
status as follows: Mozambique on 25 June 1975,
Cape Verde on 5 July 1975 and Sao Tome and Principe
on 12 July 1975. It was relatively easy to
arrive at these dates since only one liberation
movement had been carrying on the struggle in
each of those lusophone territories. In the
remaining case of Angola, however, it was not so
easy. But after negotiations had been successfully completed it appeared as if it might be
possible to achieve a peaceful transfer to the
African nationalists there too before the end
of 1975. However this was not the case.

     Angola's independence was tentatively
scheduled for 11 November 1975. The Alvor
Accord not only provided for this but also ensured the setting up of a transitional tripartite
coalition - made up of MPLA, FLNA and

UNITA - to lead the territory to independence.
However this optimism was short-lived as serious
disagreements soon led to civil war in the
territory.  It is common knowledge that non-
African powers played prominent roles in fuelling
the fire of the Angolan civil war.  However, we
shall be concerned here mainly with the part
played by some African states in the sordid affair.

Shortly after the transitional tripartite
coalition was set up in Luanda FLNA started from
its base in Zaire to infiltrate into Angola with
a view to attacking the MPLA in Luanda and
northern Angola.  Early in March FLNA gunned down
fifty unarmed MPLA activists.[27]  From then on
Zaire became not only the conduit for US hardware
to FLNA in prosecuting the war[28] but also became
involved in the actual fighting.  On 11 September
Mobutu sent his elite Fourth and Seventh Commando
battalions into action.  A week later a consolidated task force made up of Zairian, FLNA and
dissident Portuguese troops were engaged in serious
combat against the forces of the MPLA.  At the
same time another Zairian force joined the Front
for the Liberation of the Enclave of Cabinda (FLEC)
since Mobutu had always nourished the idea of
annexing the oil-rich enclave.  While the FLNA
and Zaire were prosecuting the war from the North
both UNITA and the South African forces were
ravaging Southern Angola on their way to Luanda.
With the situation so grim MPLA had no alternative
but to call for Cuban assistance.  The most extra-
ordinary aspect of the Angolan debacle was however
the role played by Zaire, Zambia,[29] Senegal and
the Ivory Coast especially in relation to South
African involvement.[30]

In spite of everything the MPLA was able to
take over the reins of government when the
Portuguese finally pulled out on 11 November 1975.
An extra-ordinary session of the OAU dealt with
the issue but it was deadlocked.  Nevertheless
Angola was admitted to the Organisation shortly

afterwards as more member states came to recoznise
the government of the MPLA based in Luanda.

The independence of Portuguese colonies,
although the most immediate and most spectacular
effect, was not the only outcome of the April
coup. When that issue became a foregone conclusion South Africa suddenly realised the futility
of her actions and the hollowness of her "cordon
sanitaire" approach as the liberation movements
could now surround Rhodesia and even get to South
Africa's borders as well. That of course was
why she became involved in the Angolan civil war
so that at least a manipulable leadership might
be installed in Luanda. But in April 1974 the
immediate question was simply how could the fences
with black Africa be mended? What options were
now open? Should Ian Smith and his fellow-
travellers be sacrificed in Rhodesia and moves to
grant independence to Namibia be started so that
the apartheid system might, at least, be granted
some period of grace even if the on-coming onslaught could not be resisted forever? How and
where does one start? It was in an attempt to
answer these and many other questions that South
Africa began its policy of detente which had its
origin in the "outward-looking" policy.[31]

South Africa took refuge under the Lusaka
Manifesto and let it be known in Lusaka that she
was prepared to renew the contacts which had been
broken off after Vorster's misguided indiscretion
over exchange of correspondence between himself
and President Kaunda.[32] Assurances were given
this time that South Africa was genuinely interested in exploring the possibility of achieving
better relations with black Africa. As a result
a series of exploratory talks took place in many
places between Zambian and South African officials.
It was while these talks were at an advanced stage
that the whites in Mozambique revolted and staged
an insurrection aimed at achieving their own UDI.
South Africa could therefore not contemplate

giving them any support at that stage.  President
Kaunda, seeing South Africa's action as an act
of faith, jumped to the conclusion that South
Africa would keep to her promise not to interfere
adversely again in the independence process in
Southern Africa.  This assumption was however
later proved false especially when South Africa
ordered her troops to march into Angola when it
was becoming clear that MPLA would form the
government in Luanda.

By September 1974, however, President
Kaunda was able to convince Presidents Nyerere of
Tanzania, Khama of Botswana and Mobutu of
Zaire as well as the FRELIMO Leader, Samora
Machel of South Africa's sincerity.  So  the
first of the Front Line States (FLS) meetings was
scheduled for 21 October 1974.[33]  To buttress
this point Vorster led a delegation to the Ivory
Coast on 21 September 1974.[34]  Although this
visit was kept secret at the time Kaunda must
have known about it and used it to influence
the other FLS presidents.

While the presidents were holding their
meeting in Lusaka, Vorster delivered a speech
in the South African Senate[35] in which he
advocated a peaceful solution to the problem of
Southern Africa for, according to him, the costs
of continued confrontation were "too high to contemplate".  Kaunda for his part responded by
claiming that Vorster's speech amounted to "the
voice of reason for which Africa and the rest of
the world have been waiting for".[36]  While
President Kaunda was expressing his satisfaction
over Vorster's speech Pik Botha, then the South
African UN representative, was admitting to the
world body his government's realisation of its
past misdeeds and assuring it of a desire to "do
everything in our power to move away from discrimination based on race or colour...".[37]  All
these well-orchestrated speeches gave rise to
moments of hope and optimism although these were

soon proved to be groundless and short-lived,
especially when the antics of Ian Smith came
into play and South Africa invaded Angola.

Initially, however, "dialogue" appeared to
be the beginning of what everybody had always
wanted. Within a few months an agreement had
been reached to release the leaders of the
Rhodesian African political parties - ZAPU and
ZANU - from detention to participate in an all-
party round-table conference to discuss Zimbabwe's
independence. This was due to the efforts of
Vorster who persuaded Smith to see the need for
such a move and to Kaunda as well as other FLS
leaders who prevailed upon the Zimbabwean African
nationalists who were very sceptical of the Smith
whom they knew to be a slippery character. As a
sequel to this all Zimbabwean nationalist groups
agreed early in December 1974[38] to unite under
the umbrella of the African National Council in
order to present a united stand at the forthcoming
constitutional talks. But no sooner had they
agreed to go along with this arrangement than
Smith started to show his true colours. First of
all he went back on his promise to release all
detainees immediately. Then to complicate matters
still further he detained Ndabaningi Sithole on
a flimsy and unproved charge and later had to
rescind that decision.[39] Nevertheless the damage
had been done to "dialogue".

In an effort to repair the damage and also
show its determination South Africa began to withdraw its police units from duty on the "Zambezi
Line" to rear-area camps inside Rhodesia. At
about the same time Vorster assured President
Tolbert of Liberia of his desire to see a peaceful solution to the Rhodesian problem,[40] when he
paid a secret visit to that country. But the
Zimbabwean nationalists remained unconvinced since
they had no faith in the ability of Vorster to
force Smith against his will. They were, however,
not alone in this regard as the proceedings of

the OAU Council of Minister's extra-ordinary
session summoned especially to deal with the
issue showed in Dar-es-Salaam in April 1975.[41]
At the end of the session the Ministers adopted
the Dar-es-Salaam Declaration[42] which was endorsed
by the OAU Summit held in Kampala in July 1975.

This Declaration made it clear that as long
as the objective of majority rule before independence was not compromised the OAU would support
all efforts made by the Zimbabwe nationalists to
win independence by peaceful means.  The holding
of constitutional conferences where the nationalist forces could negotiate with the Smith regime
was not ruled out.  "If that takes place", the
Declaration maintained, "the OAU has the duty to
do everything possible to assist the success of
such negotiations, in constant consultation with
the nationalists  until and unless the Zimbabwean
nationalists themselves are convinced that talks
with Smith have failed".  If that happened, however, "the freedom fighters will have to intensify
the armed struggle with the material, financial
and diplomatic assistance of independent Africa".

Having thus given the green light the FLS
made up of Tanzania, Zambia, Botswana and Mozambique, continued to explore with South Africa the
possibility of convening a Rhodesian constitutional conference.  The Victoria Falls Conference of
August 1975 was the outcome of these efforts. In
spite of the presence of both Kaunda and Vorster
the conference ended in failure.  To say that
Smith's intransigence was responsible for the
fiasco would be an understatement.[43]  On his
return to Salisbury, Smith made it absolutely
clear that he would arrest any of these nationalist leaders, whom he described as "convicted
criminals" who dared to return there.  Besides,
he admitted openly that Vorster's pressure had
led him to the conference table and he was not
likely to have a repeat performance for some
time to come.

The breakdown of the Victoria Falls talks
soon led to the break-up of the fragile coalition
of the Zimbabwean nationalist leaders. While
both Muzorewa and Sithole went to Lusaka where
they formed the Zimbabwe Liberation Council and
declared their opposition to future negotiations
and their support for an intensification of the
armed struggle, Nkomo organised in Salisbury a
congress which elected him president of the ANC.
To counter this dubious move the supporters of
both Muzorewa and Sithole organised a rally in
Salisbury in October 1975 which attracted more
than 40,000 people.[44]  From then on the ANC became
split into the so-called 'internal' and 'external'
wings especially when Nkomo embarked upon his
internal settlement talks with the Smith regime.
Although Nkomo was given every possible assistance
and encouragement by Kaunda these talks also
failed to achieve any settlement by the time they
finally broke down in March 1976.  Meanwhile South
Africa had invaded Angola and the other Zimbabwe
African leaders had come to the conclusion that
Nkomo could at best be regarded as an opportunist.
In any case the armed struggle had been intensified and this subsequently led to the Geneva talks
which also failed to produce any settlement.[45]

The immediate outcome of the Geneva talks
was a further realignment of forces among the
Zimbabwean African nationalists.  Both Magabe,
who had taken over the leadership of ZANU from
Sithole, and Nkomo came together to form the
Patriotic Front while Sithole and Muzorewa later
returned to Salsibury to lead ZANU (Sithole) and
UANC respectively.  Besides it had become absolutely clear to them all that "the only way left
for the Africans to win political power was
through a guerrilla war".[46]  The subsequent recognition of the Patriotic Front by the OAU as the
only "fighting force" drove both Muzorewa and
Sithole into Rhodesia and forced them to cooperate
with Smith to achieve the Internal Settlement
Agreement of March 1978.  But while the Internal

Arrangees were getting on with the negotiations and the formation of a transitional government[47] the Patriotic Front was demonstrating its fighting capabilities. This performance coupled with the stand of the African Commonwealth members before,[48] and during the Lusaka Commonwealth Conference of 1979 finally forced the British Government led by Mrs. Thatcher to change its previously stated course and go to the conference table.[49] Although the Patriotic Front could not be regarded as absolutely perfect the cooperation of both ZANU and ZAPU, its two components, helped in no small measure to attain independence for Zimbabwe on 17 April 1980.

Although the Rhodesian situation had over-shadowed other developments in Southern Africa since the Portuguese coup of 1974 there was no standing-still in either South Africa itself - where the most significant occurrence was the Soweto students' uprising of June 1976 - or in Namibia. As a matter of fact the South African policy on Namibia had taken on some new character-istics and urgency since that coup chiefly because of the massive emigration of the Ovambos into Angola and Zambia. It can however, be categorically stated that the greater part of the battle against South Africa's intransigence and defiance over Namibia took place at the UN where the Republic was disallowed from taking part in General Assembly deliberations from 1974. Nevertheless, SWAPO con-tributed immensely in the efforts of the inter-national community to get South Africa totally out of Namibia.

To this end SWAPO on 17 January 1975 gave the following conditions for talks with South Africa on the future of Namibia: South Africa must recognise the right of the Namibian people to independence, national sovereignty and ter-ritorial integrity; South Africa must accept that SWAPO is the sole authentic representative of the Namibean people; all political prisoners

should be released and the banning order on SWAPO
acting President Immanuel Gottlieb Nathanael
Nacuilili must be set aside; the so-called R17
Emergency Regulations still operating in Northern
Namibia should be revoked; all Namibians in exile,
irrespective of their political leaning, should be
allowed to return freely to their country without
fear of arrest or any other form of victimization;
South Africa should also commit herself to the
withdrawal of her troops and police from Namibia.[50]

It took South Africa five months to give
any reply to these conditions and the demands
contained in the UN Security Council Resolution
of 366 of 13 December 1974. Even then the
response was a negative one. In a speech delivered on 20 May 1975 at Windhoeck Vorster made
it clear that South Africa would not accept UN
supervision in Namibia's journey to independence.
He gave every indication that the territory
would continue to be administered under the
Bantustan policy and also that the Bantustan
leaders of the territory would work out an independence timetable. Within a few months afterwards South Africa had handpicked 156 agents
drawn from eleven ethnic groups to attend a so-
called constitutional conference at Windhoeck.
That was the beginning of the "Turnhalle Conference" which on 18 March 1977 approved a constitution submitted to it by South Africa. A
referendum was to have taken place on the so-called
constitution in May 1977 but because it was unanimously rejected by the international community
the representatives of USA, Britain, France,
Canada and West Germany - the Contact Group -
began their negotiations over the future of
Namibia on 7 April 1977. Since then the Group has
acted as an intermediary between South Africa on
the one hand and the international community as
represented by both SWAPO and the UN on the other.
It has worked out the modalities for achieving
Namibia's independence and these have been endorsed
by the UN[52] after SWAPO had given its tacit

acceptance.[53]   South Africa has since put many
obstacles in the way of the implementation of
these proposals and seemed to be buying time by
adopting such delaying tactics like securing an
internal settlement agreement similar to that
achieved in Zimbabwe in March 1978 and recently
setting up a so-called Council of State in Namibia.
All indications, however, point to the fact that
South Africa can no longer have its own way in
Namibia.  South Africa is bound to suffer the same,
if not even worse, fate in Namibia as Smith and
his fellow travellers in Zimbabwe and the consequences would be even more bitter for her in the
long run if she fails to read the handwriting on
the wall in good time and grant independence to
the Namibian people with SWAPO as their authentic
representatives.

It is evident from the above analysis that
attention has so far been paid to what could be
easily described as conflict situations between
black nationalists backed by African organisations
and independent African states on the one hand and
the white racists of Southern Africa on the other.
Sight has , however, not been lost of conflict
situations which arose among the liberation movements themselves, chiefly in Angola and Zimbabwe.
Mention has also been made of the military cooperation between the three racist minority regimes
and sometimes among the liberation movements as
well.  Cooperative efforts especially between
Zambia supported by Tanzania, Mozambique, Botswana
and lately Angola - and South Africa in an effort
to bring both Ian Smith and the Zimbabwe liberation
movements to the conference table had also been
outlined.  An attempt will now be made to examine
other cooperative ventures especially in the economic and other previously unexamined spheres, at
least in this chapter so far, between the white
racist regimes and independent African states of
Southern Africa.  So far, priority has been given
to the conflict situations because they serve to
determine the level of any cooperative ventures

in the region except those inherited from colonial era; and even these have been subjected to reviews because of the above-mentioned conflict situations.

iii)  Cooperation

It has already been established that South Africa is the dominant state actor in Southern Africa.  Most of the conflict situations already discussed revolve round it.  And when the region is also viewed in economic terms South Africa's position towers above the rest.  In can be claimed categorically that were it not for the "herrenvolk" mentality of her leaders, South Africa could even have conveniently been in a position to lead the whole of Africa in view of her industrial and economic capabilities and natural resources.  But instead she has become the most hated pariah on the continent.  No black African state is willing to be publicly identified with her while those which are so identified have either been forced into such a position either by accident of colonial history or by expediency.  And they always try to wriggle out of such a position as quickly as possible.

Nevertheless there exists a complex web of economic relationship in the region which cuts across racial lines.  This stemmed from the British colonial policy which laid the foundation for a custom's union and equally ensured a steady stream of cheap labour by contract agreements to South Africa from the neighbouring colonies such as Nyasaland (Malawi), Northern Rhodesia (Zambia), and Tanganyika (Tanzania).  Such contract agreements signed by Portugal also facilitated the steady flow of unskilled manpower in quantum to South Africa from both Angola and Mozambique. Besides, the transport system in the region is such that most independent African states had no choice but to rely on routes passing through the white redoubts in order to export most of their commodities or to import most of their needs.  The foundation for this was laid during the colonial era for as Grundy puts it "from 1889 to 1906 inter-territorial relations in southern Africa were largely pursued by means of negotiations, com-promises, agreements and disagreements over rail-way routes and rates, and customs tariffs".[54]

As far back as 1910 South Africa has had a customs union agreement with the then three British High Commission Territories which on the attain-ment of independence in the 60s became known as Botswana, Lesotho and Swaziland (BLS). The British government had originally planned that these territories would later become part of South Africa and so provided in the Act of the Union of 1909 for such eventuality.[55] South Africa's policy of apartheid however put an end to any such dream. Nevertheless the three territories had become so 'protected' by the British colonial authority that on their attainment of independence they had no choice but to continue in this association of dis-parities which had its origins in the Potchefstroom Agreement of 29 June 1910.[56] This Agreement was revised in order to achieve better terms for these territories after they had become politically inde-pendent.[57]

The economic cooperation which results from this Agreement can be compared to that between an elephant and three little rats. Although the renegotiation of the Agreement in 1969 helped to improve the benefits accruing to these three states it has not in any way reduced their depen-dence on the South African economy.[58] It is true that the three countries can now levy additional duties on imports to meet South Africa's com-petition in the customs area and are also per-mitted to establish specified industries con-sidered essential for their development. It is also true that, in accordance with the new arrange-ment, they have a right to be consulted on duties before these are imposed by South Africa for the customs area. But they are still linked to the

South Africa Rand currency area, to her postal
and telecommunication services, and Jan Smuts
as the main regional airport.  They continue to
"export" labour to the South African mines while
Swaziland still uses South Africa's citrus board
as its export agent.  Besides, the three remain
tourist attractions for the white South Africans.
Although they are making frantic efforts to get
out of their inherited economic stranglehold
their external trade is still lumped with that
of South Africa.

Namibia's situation is not different from
that of BLS.  It is a member of the customs union
and its external trade is also lumped with that
of South Africa.  Its economy is controlled predominantly by South Africans and multinational
corporations while the territory is preserved as
a market for South African manufacturers.[59]
About 90% of Namibia's imports come from South
Africa while its exports provide the foreign exchange to pay for part of South African imports.

As far as Zimbabwe is concerned her economy became more or less an extension of the South
African economy following UN sanctions.  South
Africa thus provided a conduit for Zimbabwean
goods despite the UN boycott and bought about a
third of these exports.  South African firms,
especially the Anglo-American Group and their
multinational corporate allies have been deeply
involved in the territory's economic life.[60]

Between 1964 and 1974 Portugal almost
vitually depended on South Africa for new investment in its African colonies.[61]  The reason for
this is not far to seek.  In the first place the
pressure from the African nationalists had ruined
the Portuguese economy which at the best of times
was nothing to reckon with.  In the second place
Mozambique had long provided one of the most
important sources of cheap labour for the South
African mines and a quarter of their annual

earnings of 60 million dollars were usually paid
directly to the Portuguese Government in gold at
the official rate.[62] South Africa was therefore
the most important financier of the Cabora Bassa
dam. Before embarking upon that project the
Anglo-American Corporation of South Africa had
been the most important investor in Mozambique
having invested about US $30 million in various
projects. It was closely followed by the
Industrial Development Corporation owned by the
South African government. This explains why
trade between South Africa and Mozambique grew
by leaps and bounds during the period. Mozambique
therefore became an important and growing market
for South African manufactured exports especially
of machinery and equipment. Although changes are
now envisaged these will take a long time to
materialise since the economy of both countries
became so intertwined before independence. The
FRELIMO government has imposed restrictions on the
recuritment of migrant labour for the South African
mines but agreements have been signed by both
countries for the purchase by South Africa of
about 1000 megawatts of power from the Cabora Bassa
dam.

The picture in Angola is not very different
from that of Mozambique before the 1974 coup except
that Angola is rich in oil. But like Mozambique,
Angola's economy became increasingly enmeshed in
the South African economy. The Anglo-American
Corporation is equally involved in Angola while
South Africa was also financially responsible for
the construction of the Cunene hydro-electric
project.[63] Many other South African firms are involved in the economic life of Angola. It is, however, clear that because of South Africa's involvement in the Angolan civil war and its continued
occasional raids on the territory the relationship
between both countries would not be as cordial as
that between Mozambique and South Africa.

Zambia and Zimbabwe were members of the
defunct Central African Federation and their
economies were closely interwoven. Both jointly
built the Kariba Dam while Zambian exports and
imports relied chiefly on the Benguela and
Rhodesia Railways - both in the hands of racist
regimes. Zambia, therefore, felt the pinch of
the situation in Southern Africa, especially after
UDI, more than any other state in the region.
This might have been responsible for her ambivalent
policies during the period, especially for the
growing cooperation between the Zambian Government
and the white South African regime.[64] Zambia's
role in efforts to get a peaceful settlement of
the Rhodesian crisis might account for this but
how does one explain her questionable policy over
Angola? That single act caused her untold hard-
ship when the Benguela railway was closed down
for a time after MPLA had come to power. Zaire,
of course, suffered the same fate as a result of
her involvement in the Angola civil war. It is,
however, noteworthy that relations amongst the
three states have been normalised and both
Angola and Zambia have since cooperated as members
of the FLS to solving the remaining problems of
southern Africa.

It must also be mentioned that Zambia has
done a lot to disengage herself from her national
dependence on the white south. This has been
achieved by the construction of Tan-Zam railway
and an all-weather road linking Zambia with
Tanzania. The achievement of independence in
Zimbabwe is going to help further in this direction.
Renewed cooperation in all fields of human endeavour is likely to occur once more between the
two states within a larger community, one made up
of all independent African states in the region
leaving out only South Africa in the cold when
Namibia has achieved independence.

Malawi's relations with the white racist
regimes of Southern Africa has been dictated solely

by economic considerations. Like the other
neighbouring states in the area Malawi depends
largely on the money remited home by her people
working in the South African mines. But more
importantly Banda's ambition to build a new
capital and the need to find the monetary and
other necessary assistance drove him into the
arms of the South African leaders.[65] Banda
started his secret contacts with the South
African regime in an effort to secure a loan for
Malawi's development projects in 1966.[66] As
South Africa let it be known that this financial
aid would be forthcoming Banda started to rain
insult of his fellow African leaders. His tirade
was rewarded with an offer of a trade agreement
signed in March 1967 as well as financial and
material aid for installing transmitters. From
then on South African aid began to come in leaps
and bounds as long as Banda kept on the pressure
to break OAU unanimity over the dehumanising
policy of apartheid. Eventually loans for building railway lines linking Malawi with Mozambique
and to the new capital Lilongwe were forthcoming.
This had led to the establishment of diplomatic
relations and even the exchange of high-ranking
visitors including a visit by respective foreign
ministers and heads of states.[67] At the same
time Malawi was not only cultivating but also
cooperating with the Portuguese colonial regime[68]
during its criminal war in her African colonies.
However the coup of 1974 caused Banda to have
second thoughts about Malawi's relations with
the remaining white redoubts of southern Africa.
Malawi is therefore making frantic efforts to
improve relations with the black states in the
region as well as cutting down on the numbers of
its citizens working in the South African mines.[69]

As for the Malagasy Republic she was initially excited by South Africa's 'generous offer
of financial aid to Malawi' before she put out
secret feelers to the South African regime in
1968. This move encouraged the South African

regime to set up a special foreign loans fund to
promote economic cooperation with well-disposed
African states.  At this stage France stepped in
to give the Malagasy Republic, which had started
to develop cold feet, the stimulus to go ahead
and open talks over the issue with the South
African regime.  As a result of these moves a
financial agreement was signed between South
Africa and the Malagasy Republic at Tananarive
on 20 November 1970.  More aid was promised by
both the South African government itself as well
as the South African Industrial Development
Corporation and the Southern Sun Hotel Group.[70]
Extensive trade relations also developed between
the two countries.  All these manoveures were
responsible for the Malagasy Republic's membership
of the "Dialogue Club".  With the overthrow of
President Tsirariana, however, all links were cut
off and the Republic returned to embrace the
orthodox OAU policy on apartheid and racial discrimination.

iv)  Conclusion

        The coup of April 1974 that toppled the
Portuguese fascist regime had a decisive impact
on the situation in Southern Africa.  It brought
about the independence of both Mozambique and
Angola sooner than the white racist regimes of
Zimbabwe and South Africa had hoped for.  It made
possible the Dar es Salaam Declaration of April
1975 in which the OAU decided to concentrate the
liberation struggle on both Zimbabwe and Namibia.
Now that since April 1980 Zimbabwe's independence
has become a reality there is no doubt that the
effects of this achievement have been shattering
for South Africa both in Namibia and South Africa
itself.

        The conflict situation in the region will
continue.  The OAU will concentrate all its
resources - financial, material and diplomatic -
on the attainment of Namibia's independence.  This

will be equally true of the UN. So no matter
however long South Africa drags her feet Namibia
will be free and the DTA will become a disposable
commodity in the waste paper basket of history.
This will expose South Africa's vulnerability
and she will not be in a position to withstand
the ensuing hurricane.

The struggle for human dignity and fundamental human rights will have to be waged from
two fronts. The activities of the liberation
movements will have to be stepped up after they
have been reorganised to really face the enemy
and stop their internal feuds. At the same time
the cooperation of all nationalist forces which
do not necessarily belong to either the ANC and
the PAC would be needed. South Africa is too
strong militarily to be faced by any or all the
neighbouring states in any conventional warfare.
Although it is true that South Africa was forced
to retreat from Angola, when it comes to the final
onslaught on the Republic itself she would stop
at nothing to maintain the status quo; that is,
unless a new type of leadership has by then
emerged which would read the handwriting on the
wall and probably bring in the necessary changes,
educationally, socially, politically and economically.

Independent African states have a duty to
help create an atmosphere which would be conducive
for the emergence of such a leadership in South
Africa. This they could do by assisting South
Africa's neighbours to be economically less dependent on the Republic. Since the black South
Africans have no tangible purchasing power because
of the apartheid system South Africa depends
chiefly on the markets of the neighbouring states
for the sale of her finished goods. If these
neighbouring states are in a position to close
their markets to such goods the consequences would
be disastrous for the Republic. The economy would
experience an unprecedented slump. And those

foreign powers whose policy towards South Africa
has been dictated by the amount of profits their
nationals make from the degradation and other by-
products of apartheid would realise that it is
not enough to indulge in platitudes and mere
assertions of their adhorrence of the system.
Rather they would be forced to take necessary
actions not only to stop further investments but
to see that the system is liquidated.

The possibility of South Africa's neighbours taking such an action cannot be ruled out.
They have started to seek ways of achieving their
economic liberation from their inherited depen-
ence on South Africa. At a meeting held recently
in Lusaka the leaders of Angola, Botswana, Lesotho,
Malawi, Mozambique, Swaziland, Tanzania, Zambia
and Zimbabwe as well as representatives of Namibia
explored the possibility of increased economic
cooperation and adopted a Programme of Action to
achieve their objective.[71] Although it will take
some time to achieve this objective it could certainly be done. When that happens then the economic cooperation of these states will come to
play a decisive role in finding a solution to
the conflict situation in Southern Africa.

Notes

1.  "Southern Africa" has been defined by many
    writers in different ways. For some of those
    definitions see Larry Bowman "The subordinate
    state system of Southern Africa" International
    Studies Quarterly 12(3), September 1968, 231-
    261; Margaret Doxey "Alignments and coalitions
    in Southern Africa" International Journal
    10(3), Summer 1975, 535; E. A. Gross "The
    coalescing problem of Southern Africa" Foreign
    Affairs 46(4), July 1968, 743-757, Ann Seidman
    and Neva Seidman "Southern African contradic-
    tion: Part II, South Africa's outward reach"
    Contemporary Crises 1, 1977, 371-401; Kenneth
    W. Grundy Confrontation and Accommodation in
    Southern Africa (Berkeley: University of
    California Press, 1973) xiv-xv; Timothy M.
    Shaw "Southern Africa: co-operation and con-
    flict in an international sub-system" Journal
    of Modern African Studies 12(4), December 1974,
    636; Richard Dale "Southern Africa: research
    frontiers in political science" in Christian
    P. Potholm and Richard Dale (eds) Southern
    Africa in Perspective (New York: Free Press,
    1972) 3-15; and Leonard Harding Die Politik
    der Republik Suedafrika (Munich: 1975) 117.

2.  Grundy Confrontation and Accommodation in
    Southern Africa, xv.

3.  Rand Daily Mail, 4 February 1960.

4.  UN General Assembly (UNGA) Resolution 1514
    (XV).

5.  For discussion and analysis of the Court
    judgment see C. J. R. Dugard "The South West
    Africa cases, Second Phase, 1966" South African
    Law Journal 83, 1966, 429-460; Richard A. Falk
    "The South West Africa cases: an appraisal"
    International Organization 21(1), Winter 1967,
    1-23; Brian Flemming "South West Africa cases:

Ethiopia v. South Africa, Liberia v. South
Africa, Second Phase" Canadian Yearbook of
International Law, Volume 5 (Vancouver:
University of British Columbia Press, 1967)
241-253; Ernest A. Gross "The South West
Africa case: what happened?" Foreign Affiars
45(1), October 1966, 36-48; and Paul van der
Merwe "South Africa and South West Africa"
in Potholm and Dale (eds) Southern Africa in
Perspective 69-76.

6.  UNGA Resolution 2145 (XXI) of 27 October 1966.

7.  For an analysis of the strategy adopted and
    the roles played by some of these actors see
    Ernst-Otto Czempiel Friedenspolitik in
    Suedlichen Afrika: Studien zum in Südlichen
    Afrika, Volume 10 (Munchen: Kaiser Verlag,
    1976).

8.  For the text of both resolutions, see
    "Appendix 6: resolutions adopted at the Addis
    Ababa Summit of May 1963" in Adekunle Ajala
    Pan-Africanism: evolution, progress and
    prospects (London: Andre Deutsch, 1973)
    378-381.

9.  James Barber "The impact of the Rhodesian
    crisis on the Commonwealth" Journal of Common-
    wealth Political Studies 7(2), July 1969, 88.

10. Basil Davidson, Joe Slovo, Anthony R. Wilkinson
    Southern Africa: the new politics of revolution
    (London: Penguin, 1977) 230.  See also New
    Africa, April 1980, 17.

11. Quoted from Pan-Africanism 210.

12. For the details of the Bantustan policy see
    Barbara Rogers Divide and Rule: South Africa's
    Bantustans (London: IDAF, 1976) and Sam C.
    Nolutshungu South Africa in Africa: a study of
    ideology and foreign policy (Manchester: Man-
    chester University Press, 1975) 116-121.

13. Quoted from Robert C. Good UDI: the international politics of the Rhodesian rebellion
(Princeton: Princeton University Press, 1973)
21.

14. For details of these measures see ibid.;
Davidson, Slovo and Wilkinson Southern Africa;
and R. B. Sutcliffe "The political economy of
Rhodesian sanctions" Journal of Commonwealth
Political Studies 7(2), July 1969, 113-125.

15. Assembly Debates, vol. 3, cols. 3761-2.

16. Quoted in William Henry Vatcher Jr. White
Laager: the rise of Afrikaner nationalism
(New York: Praeger, 1965) 149.

17. Petersen "Military balance in Southern Africa"
in Potholm and Dale (eds) Southern Africa in
Perspective 313. See also Grundy Confrontation and Accommodation in Southern Africa 191.

18. Petersen "Military balance in Southern Africa"
312; Grundy Confrontation and Accommodation
in Southern Africa 174-175; Basil Davidson
In the Eye of the Storm (Harmondsworth:
Pelican, 1972); and Davidson, Slovo and
Wilkinson Southern Africa 61.

19. Eduardo Mondlane The Struggle for Mozambique
(Harmondsworth: Pelican, 1969) 154-162, and
John Paul Mozambique: memories of a revolu-
tion (Harmondsworth: Pelican, 1975) 121-123.

20. Petersen "Military balance in Southern Africa"
314.

21. For the full text of the Lusaka Manifesto see
Ajala Pan-Africanism 393-400.

22. For details of this move see ibid. 245-246;
Nolutshungu South Africa in Africa 268-295;
Zdenek Cervenka The Unfinished Quest for
Unity: Africa and the OAU (London: Africa
Books, 1977) 116-119; and Grundy Accommoda-

<u>tion and Confrontation in Southern Africa</u>
141-151 and 274-275.

23. CM/St. 5 (XVII) 1971.

24. Davidson, Slovo and Wilkinson <u>Southern Africa</u>
77.

25. For the scenarios that led to this event see
<u>ibid</u>. 66-94.

26. See Colin Legum <u>A Republic in Trouble: South
Africa, 1972-73</u> (London: Rex Collings, 1973)
and Cervenka <u>The Unfinished Quest for Unity</u>
122-139.

27. John Stockwell <u>In Search of Enemies: a CIA
story</u> (London: Norton, 1978) 67-68.

28. <u>Ibid</u>. 86.

29. For Zambia's role see Douglas G. Anglin and
Timothy M. Shaw <u>Zambia's Foreign Policy:
studies in diplomacy and dependence</u> (Boulder:
Westview Press, 1979) Chapter Eight. My
impression of this chapter, however, is that
the authors were too sympathetic to the
Zambian cause and therefore glossed over her
role in the Angolan crisis.

30. See John A. Marcum "Lessons of Angola" <u>Foreign
Affairs</u> 54(3), April 1976, 420.

31. See David Hirschmann "Pressures on Apartheid"
<u>Foreign Affairs</u> 52(1), October 1973, 168-179,
O. Geyser "Detente in Southern Africa" <u>African
Affairs</u> 75(299), April 1976, 182-207 and
Douglas G. Anglin "Zambia and the Southern
African 'Detente'" <u>International Journal</u>
30(3), Summer 1975, 471-503.

32. For the details of this exchange of correspondence see "Dear Mr. Vorster" (Lusaka:
Government Printer, 1971).

33. See Table 7.1 for the list of the meetings of Front Line States, 1974-75, in Anglin and Shaw Zambia's Foreign Policy 274.

34. Geyser "Detente in Southern Africa" 203-204.

35. South African Senate Debates, 23 October 1974, and To the Point, 1 November 1974.

36. For the full text of President Kaunda's response see "Southern Africa: a time for change. Address by His Excellency the President, Dr. K. D. Kaunda, on the occasion of the conferment of the degree of LL.D. (Honoris Causa) University of Zambia, 24 October 1974" (Lusaka: Government Printer, 1974).

37. The Argus, Rand Daily Mail and Die Burger, all of 25 October 1974.

38. Colin Legum "Southern Africa: the secret diplomacy of detente" African Contemporary Record, Volume 7, 1974-1975 (London: Rex Collings, 1975) A11-13.

39. See Stanley Uys Sunday Times (London) 9 March 1975, 3.

40. The Star 17 February 1975, 25.

41. See Cervenka The Unfinished Quest for Unity 128-130.

42. For the full text of the Declaration see OAU Resolution ECM/St. 15 (IX) 1975, or "The Dar es Salaam Declaration" (Addis Ababa: Organisation for African Unity, 1975).

43. See Geyser "Detente in Southern Africa" 206, and David Hirschmann "Southern Africa: Detente?" Journal of Modern African Studies 14(1), March 1976, 113.

44. John Day "The Divisions in the Rhodesian

African nationalist movement" <u>World Today</u>
33(10), October 1977, 387.

45. See "Negotiating the End of Conflicts:
Namibia and Zimbabwe - a report by the International Peace Academy" (New York: 1979)
12-16.

46. Day "The Divisions in the Rhodesian African
nationalist movement" 388.

47. See K. Nyanayare Mufuka "Rhodesia's Internal
Settlement: a tragedy" <u>World Today</u> 78(313),
October 1979, 439-450.

48. Nigeria's nationalization of British Petroleum
played a major and decisive role in shaping
British policy over Rhodesia.

49. See Martyn Gregory "Rhodesia: from Lusaka to
Lancaster House" <u>World Today</u> 36(1), January
1980, 11-18.

50. <u>Namibia Bulletin</u> (New York) 1, 1975.

51. See Cervenka <u>The Unfinished Quest for Unity</u>
152-154, and Geyser "Detente in Southern
Africa" 196-199.

52. For details of the proposals see "Negotiating
the end of conflicts" 35-46.

53. Roger Murray "Namibia's elusive independence
- a contest between African nationalism and
South African interests" <u>Round Table</u> 265,
January 1977, 42-49.

54. Grundy <u>Confrontation and Accommodation in
Southern Africa</u> 49-50.

55. For the historical development of these
territories see Jack Halpern <u>South Africa's
Hostages</u> (Harmondsworth: Pelican, 1965). See
also Part Three of Potholm and Dale (eds)
<u>Southern Africa in Perspective</u> 96-155.

56. For an account of how the system worked under the 1910 Agreement see Peter Robson "Economic integration in Southern Africa" Journal of Modern African Studies 5(4), December 1967, 469-490.

57. For an analysis of the arrangement see P. M. Landell-Mills "The 1969 Southern African Customs Union Agreement" Journal of Modern African Studies 9(2), August 1971, 263-281.

58. For an analysis of South Africa's involvement in the affairs of the three states see John Seiler "South African perspectives and responses to external pressures" Journal of Modern African Studies 3(3), September 1975, 456-458.

59. UN Council for Namibia (1975) "Report" UN Official Records 29th Session, Supplement 24 (A/19024), New York.

60. See Anglo-American Corporation Annual Report, 1974 (Johannesburg: 1974).

61. Basil Davidson "South Africa and Portugal" UN Unit on Apartheid Notes and Documents 7/74(1974).

62. See Economist Intelligence Unit Quarterly Economic Review, Third Quarter 1974.

63. UN Council for Namibia "Report."

64. See Douglas G. Anglin "Confrontation in Southern Africa: Zambia and Portugal" International Journal 15(3), Summer 1970, 497-517.

65. Philip Short Banda (London: Routledge & Kegan Paul, 1974).

66. See Ajala Pan-Africanism 240-241.

67. Anthony Hughes "Malawi and South Africa's co-prosperity sphere" in Zdenek Cervenka (ed)

Landlocked Countries of Africa (Uppsala: Scandinavian Institute for African Studies, 1973) 212-232, and Carolyn McMaster Malawi: foreign policy and development (London: Julian Friedmann, 1974).

68. See Robert D'A Henderson "Relations of Neighbourliness - Malawi and Portugal, 1976-74" Journal of Modern African Studies 15(3), September 1977, 425-455.

69. Ibid. 454-455.

70. Ajala Pan-Africanism 241-242.

71. "Union of the Southern Nine" Africa (105), May 1980, 43-45.

# Chapter Nine

## Transnational Corporations and Regional Integration in West Africa

### Ralph I. Onwuka

The continued expansion in the activities of Transnational Corporations (TNCs) in the West African sub-region has been significant and controversial. This is mainly because of divergencies in the interests of the two dominant parties concerned: the centre-based TNCs and their host countries in the West African periphery. If the latter intend to develop their weak and unstable economies through self-reliance, they will inevitably need capital and technology which are not easily available within the periphery. If, on the other hand, the host countries decide to welcome the TNCs, which most do, then the profit-motivated interests of the foreign investors are likely to run into conflict with the development-oriented motives of their hosts. This is the dilemma confronting West African leaders.

Regional integration in West Africa can be seen, then, as a collective response to this dilemma. The development problems of the sub-region include how to acquire, organize and utilize, needed external resources whilst seeking to minimize external intervention in the development process. Regional integration, not in the orthodox Mitrany[1] sense, is an approach to collective development which simultaneously seeks to minimize foreign involvement.

Reasoning almost along the same line with Aaron Segal,[2] Richard Lipsey[3] and Philip Ndegwe,[4] various United Nations (UN) agencies (particularly the Economic Commission for Africa (ECA)), the

European Economic Community (EEC), and the Organisation of African Unity (OAU), have variously
regarded regional integration and sub-regional
economic integration as a necessary condition
for achieving self-sufficiency in food production,
in generating appropriate technology and in
realising industrial development. Furthermore,
integration is seen as a way to control the
exploration and extraction by TNCs of natural
resources of a given area. Thus the general
belief has spread that regional integration
creates the potential for self-generating development. In a region at the periphery like West
Africa regional integration is also expected to
lessen the prevailing high level of dependency on
the developed economies, especially on the market
economies of the former colonial powers, and on
the TNCs.

The purpose of this chapter is to assess
the role of the TNCs in the West African development-oriented integration processes, and thus to
confront the question: Are the TNC's propellers
of economic advancement or agents of affliction
in the West African political economy? Precisely
put, are the TNCs, on the one hand, and the West
African economic organisations (or their participating states), on the other hand, "partners in
development"? It is difficult to give a definite
and clinical answer to this rather complex and
intricate question. But in the process of attempting to analyse the role of the TNCs in West African
integration for development, I hope to advance to
the debate to which Samir Amin, Joseph Nye,
Robert Keohane, Immanuel Wallerstein and more
recently, Sanjaya Lall, Paul Streeten, Tim Shaw
and a host of others, if not the animateurs,
have already in various disguises contributed.
In treating the above posed question, the chapter
will, in a rather moderate tone, conclude pre-
scriptively by suggesting ways of curbing, and
where necessary controlling, the excesses of
the TNCs in the bid to achieve more inward-looking

development in the sub-region. And given this concern, the Economic Community of West African States (ECOWAS) should be recognised and treated as the most powerful organ available to effect more truly regional control of the activities of the TNCs.

a) Development, integration, and transnationals in West Africa

Regional integration deals predominantly with a hierarchy of issues, interests, and institutions, and sometimes the input of transnational actors to the process are underrated. Shaw has observed that dependentistas are critical of integration and the notion of unilineal progress and so advocate disengagement as a prerequisite for development. What seems to be a weakness of an orthodox approach to regional integration is its neglect of "the political economy of outcomes and distribution."[5] We shall return to this later.

Regional integration in West Africa, as in other developing areas, is development-oriented integration in the sense that development goals constitute the central objective as well as the driving force in all joint economic activities in the region. Thus the concern of this chapter is not "political" but "economic" integration in the region. The latter, economic, integration involves "the suppression of discrimination between economic units".[6] Such a dynamic process "presuppose(s) the unification of monetary, fiscal, social and counter-cyclical authority whose decisions are binding for member states".[7] The level and scope of economic integration depends, therefore, on the nature of the "restrictions" removed, so that the more restrictions that are removed between component units (states) the higher the level of economic integration. Conversely, the fewer restrictions removed the lower the level of integration.

The existing economic interactions in West Africa could be classified into three.[8] The lowest level is the co-operation level where various joint implementation programmes and policies are executed. At this level there is a cluster of such integration activities as the Cocoa Producers Alliance (CPA), African Groundnut Council (AGC), West African Development Association (WARDA), Inter-African Coffee Organisation (IACO), Organisation pour la mise en valeur du fleuve Senegal (OMVA), Lake Chad Basin Organisation, and River Niger Basin. At this primary level, the organisations are principally formed in order to confront collectively common development problems such as the provision of energy, paucity of food supply and production, increasing the fertility of arid land and enhancing the navigability of rivers. Actions taken against these difficulties include the co-ordination of study programmes for the development and rational exploitation of basins' resources or (in the cases of AGC, CPA, and WARDA) to ensure through joint action remunerative prices for the export products of the participating states.

In the second group are found a few economic organisations, some of which are now defunct, aimed at promoting intra-regional trade by excluding third parties through the erection of tariff walls. The interim organisation of 1965 and the Articles of Association of 1967 were attempts which failed to materialise into a free trade area. But alive and effective is the Communaute Economiques de l'Afrique de l'ouest (CEAO) and its monetary wing, Union Monetaire Ouest Africaine (UMAO). In article 2 of the Treaty establishing the CEAO the members agreed to instal a common external tariff with regards to both the customs and fiscal duties levied by states.

In the third group is ECOWAS, which is designed to mature into a common market by 1990. This is the highest level of integration when compared with the other two types discussed above.

In this regard constant reference will be made to
ECOWAS because it is the only truly region-wide
economic organisation in West Africa due to its
wide spread of membership in both linguistic and
geographical senses.

The objectives of ECOWAS range from the
liberalisation of quantitative and qualitative
restrictions on trade, capital and labour to the
harmonisation of agricultural, economic, industrial,
and monetary policies; as well as the joint implementation of programmes to be financed from
the Fund for Co-operation, Compensation and Development. From the nature and content of the objectives of the above-mentioned economic ventures
in West Africa, it becomes obvious that a number
of strategic factors still belie the implementation
of the set intentions. These factors include
finance to carry out the various development
programmes, technology capability to manufacture,
handle and transport products, and securing access
to large markets for particular products, as well
as the organisational setting necessary for the
efficient performance of the above.

b)   Before independence

Those corporations with subsidiaries in the
West African periphery, with headquarters in one
or two of the centres of the world system, and
engaging in transnational interactions of various
types - for example in information, labour,
capital, management and marketing - are for the
purposes of this chapter regarded as TNCs. The
early colonial powers in the region (Britain,
France, Portugal and Spain) dominated the business
activities in their respective areas of governance.
So that, in the former British West Africa, for
example, other than the Royal Niger Company, such
Manchester-based companies as John Walkden and
Liverpool-centred John Holt dominated business
activities particularly in distribution and
industry.[9]   Aside from distribution and trade,

there was a marked interest in mining and through
such large concerns as the Ashanti Goldfields
Corporations (1897), the Sierra Leone Consolidated
African Selection Trust (1932) (later the Sierra
Leone Selection Trust (1935)), and Amalgamated
Tin Mines of Nigeria Limited (1939), monopoly
super-profits were guaranteed for the imperial
centres at the expense of the colonies.[10]

In French West Africa a similar but more
centralised pattern of domination over the colonies prevailed. Mining, manufacturing and distribution activities were dominated by either the
government aid agencies, such as Fonds d'Aide et
de Co-operation (FAC) and Caisse Centrale de la
Co-operation Economique (CCCE), or by other Paris-
based corporations that benefited directly from
these aid agencies. Liberia, though not offi-
cially colonised has had a business life equally
dominated by an American-based firm, Firestone
Rubber Company, which has run the country's rubber
plantations and various manufacturing and distribution enterprises. Thus the period before
the independence of most West African states in
the 1960s was the high watermark in the era of
bilateral and very unequal center-periphery connections.

c)    After independence

From the 1960s onwards, non-colonial OECD
countries, notably Japan, emerged as serious
competitors to the established imperial centres
of Paris, London and Lisbon. Between 1960 and
1971 Japanese overseas direct investment in Africa
increased fifteen times, from $30m to $45m.[11]  It
is notable that Japan, as a resource-deficient
country, concentrated larger percentages of its
direct investment in Africa in extractive industry than did other centre states. And by 1970
the value of the foreign subsidiaries and branches
of the United-States - based corporations was more
than $65 billion.[12]  Petroleum, copper, iron,

bauxite, phosphate, and gold operations have been
the major targets of transnational activity in
Nigeria, Ivory Coast, Liberia, Sierra Leone,
Ghana to mention a few (see Table 1). In the
early years of independence, the monopoly of the
TNCs in extractive businesses was first threatened
and then broken by most participating governments.
Mining of non-renewable resources became a sensitive issue in the exercise of sovereignty of the
new nations; hence the patriotic wave of nationalisation or indigenisation policies in the region.[13]
In service or distributive areas - particularly in
petroleum distribution, banking and insurance -
foreign participation is conceded only where
foreign technical input is imperative. This is
the case in petroleum distribution in Nigeria and
Sierra Leone where continued reliance on foreign
expertise has made a ridicle of the apparent
government take-over of the dominant shares in the
respective mining industries. In terms of the
manufacturing sector, the TNCs usually establish
subsidiaries in the sub-region which are operated
within a wider global framework in a vertical
monopoly position. Thus products manufactured
elsewhere are found readily in many West African
markets. This is the case with a number of house-
hold goods (e.g. Omo washing powder, Blue Band
margarine, Astral soap, Gibbs toothpaste) distributed in the sub-region by numerous subsidaries
of Unilever.

In post-colonial West Africa it could be
said that the activities of the TNCs have intensified, instead of diminishing, as their direct
investment met in most cases with investment conditions perceived as favourable by themselves.
This positive attitude can be attributed to two
major features. First, members of the ruling
class have happily become "agents" or "carriers"
for the TNCs in the area. Wallerstein[14] has
argued, supported by Cooperstock, that the central
prevailing contradiction is "between the interests
organised and located in the core countries and

Table 1

Some Transnational Corporations
In West Africa

| Host Country | Enterprises wholly - or partly - owned or controlled by TNCs | Nature of Enterprises |
|---|---|---|
| Liberia | The Liberian American Swedish Minerals Company (LAMCO), The Deutsche Liberian Mining Company (DELIMCO), Liberian Iron and Steel Corporation (LIMSCO), Liberia Mining Company, National Iron Ore Company | extractive (iron ore) |
| Mauritania | Compagnie Miniera du fe Mauritanie (Iferma) controlled by the Bureau Francais de Recherches Geologiques et Miniere (Bram) and Societe Miniere de Mauritania (Somina) | extractive (iron and copper) |
| Guinea | Companie des bauxite de Guinea, des Mines de fer de Guinea | extractive (bauxite and iron ore) |
| Nigeria | Shell/BP, Esso, Mobil, Agip, Safnap, Minatone | extractive (petroleum and uranium) |

Table 1 (cont'd)

| Host Country | Enterprises wholly – or partly – owned or controlled by TNCs | Nature of Enterprises |
|---|---|---|
| Nigeria | Coutinho, Caroy & Co., ITT, Julius Berger, Soleh-Boneh, Dumez, U.A.C. (Nigeria) | manufacturing (construction, telecommunication, distribution) |
| Senegal | Taiba | extractive (phosphates) |
| Ivory Coast | Energie electrique de Cote d'Ivoire | extractive |
| Ghana | Lonrho, CAST, Union Carbide, Aluminium Company of America (ALCOA), The Volta Aluminium Company (VALCO) | extractive (gold, bauxite, diamonds, aluminium, manganese) |
| Sierra Leone | Sierra Leone Petroleum Refining Co., National Diamond Mining Co., Sierra Leone Rufile, Sierra Leone Ore and Metal Co. | refining extractive (petroleum, diamonds, iron ore) |
| | NATCO-member of T. Choitran Group of Companies, Sierra Leone Oxygen Factory, Aureol Tobacco Company, Freetown Cold Storage. | manufacturing |

Sources: L. Rood "Nationalisation and Indigenisation in Africa" Journal of Modern African Studies; African Contemporary Record, 1975/76 and 1977/78; African Research Bulletin, 1971; West Africa, March 31, 1980.

their local allies on the one hand, and the majority of the population on the other". Cooperstock[15]
rightly observed, in support of such established
views, that "the subordination of African states
to the requirements of the world economy represents the familar pattern of the 'development of
underdevelopment' ". These "agents" of "underdevelopment" have been vexatiously referred to by
Shehu Umar Abdullahi in a recent lecture, as those
who

> do everything within their ability to
> justify even the unjustifiable as
> long as it can help the western world.
> They are mentally sick and intellec-
> tually dwarf. They employ their
> intellect to defend whatever they
> know can help their western material
> masters even when that can clearly
> wreck or weaken the economy of their
> fatherland.[16]

The second factor is not unconnected with
the first: namely, TNCs ahve relative monopoly
of supply of both capital and technology. Thus,
with an efficient network of marketing and organisational facilities, they acquire the capacity to
spread a capitalist mode of production in the sub-
region, most times on their own terms. And because
their activities are profit-based they tend to concentrate more in areas of high returns than those
more functional for development. Thus in 1971
there were more transnational activities in
Liberia than Mali. Table 2 shows that direct
investment in West Africa, as a percentage of
Gross National Product, is highest in the former
and lowest in the latter. Also in 1972, direct
investment in Nigeria, which is the fourth on the
ranking scale, totalled $2.1 U.S. billion. The
largest single piece of this was held by Shell-BP
whose investment in the country at the time
amounted to 7 per cent of all foreign investments
in Africa.

Transnationals also dominate in all stages of scientific and technological processes. They invest extensively in Research and Development (R & D) and own most of the patents granted and registered in periphery countries. The dominance relationship between the TNCs and West Africa is reinforced by the superior management, distributive network, and bargaining power of the former over the latter. The TNC's have gained an efficient organisational network through experience and research and a high entrepreneurial ability through their international operations. These attributes are very significant compared with developing countries' standards. The resulting asymmetrical relationship between the parties - the sellers and buyers of technology - is perpetuated further by the buyer's inability to "clarify supply and demand conditions in the international flow of advanced knowledge or to articulate their requirements adequately",[17] an issue well treated by Leff in his recent study.

In West Africa, many of the transnational interactions are with states themselves rather than with particular organisations. This is because until the recent past when ECOWAS was formed, there was no truly West African economic community capable of providing the point dappu for the needed action and discourse on the TNCs. Thus one could safely say that regional integration in West Africa has not matured into a condition comparable to that in Central America or Europe where collective measures are readily applied towards foreign corporations. The prevailing "low" level of integration in West Africa has made bargaining with TNCs state-centric to date. Because of this characteristic of regional integration in West Africa much of the discourse in this chapter will be based on state-TNC relationships. But where and when necessary, references will be made to the CEAO or ECOWAS or to other economic organisations in the development integration process.

d)  Growth:  rationale for co-existing with TNCs

Some renowned and consistent nationalists
have acknowledged their helplessness in operating
an open economic policy towards the TNCs.  This
is because, it is argued, they are eager to
develop their economies, and so a measure of
dependence on the transnationals for capital and
technology is almost inevitable.  President
Nkrumah of Ghana, despite his socialist leanings
rationalised his dealings with western capitalism
thus:

> It was considered in the circumstances
> of the time that the undertaking of
> joint ventures with already operating
> capitalist concerns was better than
> the alternative of economic blockade
> by the West and the consequent lack
> of development until the assistance
> of the socialist States could be pro-
> cured and become operational.[18]

To Nkrumah, therefore, intercourse with the western
based TNCs was temporary and functional.  In his
book, Neo-Colonialism,[19] Nkrumah further explained
how development-oriented and independent actions
are constrained and indeed determined by international finance.  For instance, his desire to
develop the Volta River multi-purpose scheme which
was regarded as essential to the overall industrialisation of Ghana, forced Nkrumah into accepting the technological and financial services of
the United States-based consortium, the Volta
Aluminium Company (VALCO).  Nkrumah and Ghana
are not alone in this reluctant admission of the
inevitability of international technology and
finance in national or regional growth processes.
Each West African government has tended to welcome
foreign investments (both direct and portfolio),
based on the argument it was in a hurry to develop.
Having argued that capital and technology are the
major determining factors in coexisting with the

Table 2

Stock of Foreign Direct Investments
as Percentage of GNP in West African States
(1967 & 1971)*

| COUNTRY | YEAR | | RANK |
| | 1967 | 1971 | |
| | % | % | |
| --- | --- | --- | --- |
| Liberia | 125 | 100 | 1 |
| Mauritania | 65 | 73 | 2 |
| Guinea | 30 | 39 | 3 |
| Nigeria | 21 | 22 | 4 |
| Togo | 21 | 21 | 5 |
| Senegal | 19 | 20 | 6 |
| Ivory Coast | 19 | 17 | 7 |
| Ghana | 15 | 15 | 8 |
| Sierra Leone | 18 | 13 | 9 |
| Benin | 10 | 8 | 10 |
| Gambia | 10 | 6 | 11 |
| Niger | 8 | 6 | 12 |
| Upper Volta | 6 | 5 | 13 |
| Mali | 2 | 2 | 14 |

* Compiled from Carl Widstrand (ed.), Multinational Firms in Africa, (Stockholm: Almqvist
& Wiksell, 1975) 84.

TNCs, it is necessary to explore how these resources relate to the economic growth of the sub-region.

e)  Dependence on international finance and
    technology:  who gains?

It would seem that development integration will be slowed down without international capital and technology.  This is sometimes true.  For example both the expertise and the capital needed to produce a detailed map of Lake Chad and its perimeter were supplied by Britain in 1972.  And it was France that has supplied much of the financial, technological and administrative backbone needed by OMVS.  And when French assistance was incapable of satisfying all OMVS needs, advances were made to Abu Dhabi, Saudi Arabia, and other countries.  This was the case, for instance, in the $1 billion U.S. needed for the construction of two dams.[20]  In similar manner, the World Bank has supported the activities of the inter-governmental cement industry, Cimens de l'Afrique l'Ouest (CIMAO).  Also Air Afrique established in 1961 by eleven OCAM States in partnership with a French consortium (SODETAF),[21] one of the TNCs that has undertaken joint ventures with mainly francophone West African economic organisations.  It would seem that at the inter-governmental level, TNCs' involvement in the provision of capital and technology is less significant that their involvement at national level.  Examples abound in TNCs' involvement in national growth as opposed to regional development.

We have argued that most leaders in West Africa regard the role of international finance and technology (supplied by TNCs, governments or international financial institutions) as a necessary condition for national economic growth.  This is so particularly when the foreign corporations supply the initial capital outlay for the operations of various development ventures.  The

TNCs also contribute, as in the case of Nigeria
for example, in providing or aiding in the supply
of additional revenue from profit-sharing, taxation
and royalties, and customs, excise and sales duties.
With respect to those TNCs - and they are plentiful
- involved in mining operations, Greg Lanning and
Marti Mueller have rightly observed that "taxes are
the main linkage between the mines and host economy."[22]  For the 1979/80 financial year, for instance, Nigeria realised a sum of over ₦ 12 billion
from customs and excise, petroleum profit tax, mining royalties and company earnings tax.  Of course,
revenue from petroleum profit tax yielded the dominant share of over half of the grand total as
shown in Table 3.

Table 3

Nigeria's Revenue (Estimated and Collected) from Direct

Taxes, and Customs and Estimates 1979/80

| Revised Estimates | | Approved Estimates | Collected Revenue |
|---|---|---|---|
| Customs and Excise | ₦1,429,798,323 | 1,240,639,190 | 1,208,004,000 |
| Direct Taxes | | | |
| Petroleum Profit Tax | 6,098,029,044 | 4,784,500,000 | 6,687,350,000 |
| Mining, Rent and Royalty | 2,217,175,000 | 1,552,545,000 | 2,122,180,000 |
| Earnings and Sales | 27,897,370 | 27,897,370 | 1,737,888,000 |
| Company Tax | 525,182,000 | 525,182,000 | 540,002,000 |
| | | | ₦12,115,424,000 |

Source:  Business Times (Lagos), April 22, 1980, p. 1.

It is noteworthy that the realised petroleum profit tax jumped to a higher total than
either the revised or approved estimates, an indication that with an increase in petroleum mining
activities and indeed price, the profits of the
producing companies rose by an even greater percentage, a possible indication that the corporations
benefitted more than the host country.  Thus an
ex post facto argument could be raised:   that
Nigeria could have benefitted more without (rather
than with) international finance and technology.
Perhaps the incentive outlays could be delayed if
not halted but in the process the host country may
be forced to generate locally "embodied technology"
adapted to the extractive circumstances of the
area.  In the end, an external dependence relationship with the TNCs would have been replaced by one
of interdependence, so that the terms for TNC
participation would be determined by internal not
external factors.

f)   Terms of agreement between TNCs and host West
     African countries

     Whatever a West African host country
realises from direct taxes and customs and excise
depends on the prevailing tax regime and on-going
agreements between the host country and the TNCs
concerned.  Sometimes the host country has had
reasons to seek revision of the on-going agreement.  In French West Africa, the French metropolitan agencies FAC and CCCE were useful in
transferring capital from France to West Africa
through the TNCs.  By 1970 eight large French TNCs
had procurred 50 per cent of the CCCE's development fund.  In course of time this triangular
relationship met with the disapproval of such
countries as Benin, Guinea and Mauritania.[23]

     This system of tripartite deals compli-
cated the relationship between the host country
and the TNCs.  In addition, it introduced political consideration in the operation of the system.

Understandably, Niger[24] preferred a direct partner-
ship with such TNCs as Esso and Texaco for oil
exploration and with SOMAIR, a French-German-
Italian consortium, for uranium prospecting.
Senegal, a democratic socialist state, would like
indigenes to take a more active role in the
private sector which is strongly tied to French
multinational concerns operating basically in the
French industrial zone in Dakar. Senegal has a
50-50 per cent interest in most of its venures
with TNCs (e.g. MIFERSO); Guinea has a more radical
relationship with the TNCs within its borders. It
has 51 per cent in the Boke mining project vested
in the Compagnie des bauxite de Guinea. The
Mauritania Peoples Party (PPM) has a "Party Charter"
which enumerates the government's policy towards
TNCs. This charter, inter alia, provides for the
nationalisation of key sectors in the economy. And
in keeping with the PPM doctrine, SOMINA[25], a largely
British-owned company, was nationalised in 1975.

Nigeria has developed more stringent rules
guiding foreign participation in businesses than
either Liberia or Nkrumah's Ghana. Under the 1977
Nigerian Enterprises Promotion Decree, oil milling,
mining and quarrying fall under enterprises in
Schedule 2 in respect of which Nigerians must have
at least 60 per cent equity interest.[26] Such a
decree should, allowing for the international financial practices of foreign investors, reduce the
"take home" or the net transfers of these TNCs
operating in the mining sector.

Sometimes the superior bargaining power of
the participating TNC or the eagerness of the host
country to harness international finance can result
in unequal contracts. The Ghana-VALCO agreement
seems to fall into this type. The agreement made
provisions that compelled the Ghanaian government
to institute fiscal provisions which allowed VALCO
a long-term tax relief which in effect allowed the
company "to operate outside the general legislation
of the country"[27] for the euphemistic reason of
attracting foreign investment. The London-based

weekly, <u>West Africa</u>, has revealed in detail that
the:

> Tax relief under the Pioneer Industries
> and Companies Act permitted VALCO to
> avoid tax for up to ten years either
> to recover an amount equivalent to the
> paid-up shares capital ($12m) or an
> amount equal to half of the total
> capital cost of the smelter. Schedule
> C dealing with tax stabilisation, was
> even more generous. When income tax
> did become payable, it was to be cal-
> culated at the rate applicable in 1961
> and it was to be fixed at this rate
> for the duration of the contract. The
> rate was to be 40 per cent on retailed
> profits and 2.5 per cent on retailed
> profits transferred out of Ghana.[28]

The position in Liberia was similar to that
in Ghana. In addition to a generous tax regime,
the agreements establishing the principal mining
concessions in Liberia ranged between 30 and 80
year term periods. LAMCO, a joint venture between
the Liberian, American and Swedish Mineral Company
and Bethlehem Steel Corporation was to pay 50 cents
per ton royalty in 1963-4 and thereafter 50 per
cent of the net profit.[29]

The Ghanaian and Liberian concessionary
agreements are good examples of unequal contracts
which were detrimental to the development effort of
the countries concerned. It would seem that
though these two agreements had almost identical
effects, they were prompted by different motives.
On the one hand, Nkrumah was perhaps influenced
by a genuine desire to industralise Ghana and in
the process was hoodwinked by subtle bargaining
techniques of the foreign corporations involved.
On the other hand, the two recent Liberian regimes
of Tubman and Tolbert were functioning essentially
as the comprador agents of the American-based

company. In effect the Liberian leaders functioned as allies of the TNCs in "undeveloping" the country.

Profit is the sine qua non of continued operations by the TNCs in the world system, including the West Africa sub-culture. Thus where the host government, as in the case of Nigeria, adopts strict rules guiding the operation of TNCs, the concerned transnational might intensify any irregular financial policies in order to reduce risks and uncertainty. Based on a global business strategy the foreign company readily manipulates

> international differences in tax and
> tariff rates, multiple exchange rates,
> quantitative restrictions on profits
> remission, existence of local share-
> holders, exchange rate instability
> and the overstating of apparent costs
> as a means to obtain higher pro-
> tection against imports.[30]

Where in spite of these "financial business practices" the corporation is confronted with the possibility of nationalisation the TNC concerned might decide to go into liquidation or at least curtail operations. The Sierra Leone Development Corporation (DELCO), then a subsidiary of William Baird of Scotland which began mining iron ore in the country as far back as in 1933, was liquidated in 1972. Also under the intense pressure of the threat of being nationalised as in the Sierra Leonean case, bauxite mining companies in Guinea were forced to cut down operations. Generally, a foreign corporation desiring to commence, expand or liquidate operations in any part of the region usually considers the prevailing investment conditions before making any decision; these include political stability, currency stability, and government policies towards investment and trade. The utility of international finance and technology, particularly in the short-run is indisputable, but in a development-oriented integration process they

are like a two-edged sword, serving two parties in
opposite directions. It is possible that the side
serving the central interests of the TNCs is
sharper and more purposeful than that serving the
region and here lies the contradictory or problematic impact of the role of TNCs.

g)   Impact on employment and welfare position

We have established that international
finance and technology are usually in the service
of multiple interests; thus the contradiction in
the role of the TNCs in the region. Their impact
on the employment and welfare position in the host
region is equally contradictory, because of the
diverse goals pursued by the parties involved:
the TNCs, its subsidiaries, and the host country.
The TNC determines the mode of production, which
determines the technological and capital input
and consequently the number of nationals to be
employed. Depending on the orientation and intention of the host government, it will hope for
a reduction in unemployment and in welfare problems
with the operations of TNCs within its borders.
But invariably such transnational activities are
not directed towards solving these domestic ail-
ments, although it is possible that they could be
minimised (and sometimes complicated) as a consequence of extractive or industrial activities of
the foreign companies.

With regards to mining, it has been force-
fully argued that:

> The promised direct benefits of mining to
> employment are reduced by the trend to
> massive open-cast mines, with their smal-
> ler unit production costs and increased
> capital intensity. The investment of
> two or three hundred million dollars
> will establish a mine employing only a
> few hundred workers.[31]

Thus the mining company referred to above chose to
strike a favourable balance between capital and
labour in order to lower costs, not to improve the
lot of the indigenes of, in this case, Liberia.
Employment possibilities are further reduced by
the fact that the TNCs for their global operations,
need a highly specialised cadre of managerial and
technical staff not readily secured locally. What
are generally recruited around the operating areas
are poorly-paid unskilled workers needed for construction and allied unskilled processes. Their
services are cheap and their employment temporary.

So, in terms of offering either qualitative
or quantitative employment to the host country,
the effect of the TNCs' presence is questionable.
Qualitative employment effects of transnational
operations are beginning to be positive in those
countries (for example, Ghana and Nigeria) where
the governments and the foreign companies, under
the pressure of the former and the expense of
possibly both, have embarked on joint or private
technical programmes for the nationals of the host
country. Such an understanding could institution-
alise dependence on the TNC concerned if the accord
does not result in more self-reliant production.
Although, as we have argued, the TNCs are not
basically concerned with the welfare and employment
problems of their host West African countries,
nevertheless export-oriented production could still
lead to infrastructural development around the
industrial or mining zones. This is particularly
so in areas such as petroleum mining in Nigeria,
copper operations in Mauritania, or iron-ore and
bauxite mining in Liberia and Ghana respectively.
It is possible for the local communities to benefit
(though this seems to be a somewhat marginal spill-
over) from such facilities as good road and railway
systems, and electricity, port and water facilities,
which otherwise would not have been readily available. Thus Ghana's Volta Scheme, despite its
neocolonial contents, had led to increased fishing
and agricultural activities and thus to valuable

food protein. However, national policies could
negatively affect the net employment results as
in Ivory Coast where the country's "dual nation-
ality"[32] policy, which accords citizenship rights
to Voltaic migrant labour numbering over half
total labour force, has aided in reducing the
employment and welfare advantages of transnational
activities. In the commercial section in 1979
there were 455 Ivorian directors as against 1572
non-African directors and 2 non-Irorian African
directors.[33] Thus in the Ivorian case, it could
be confidently said that TNCs' operations have
had a negative impact on the employment position
of the country.

Despite fringe benefits arising from most
operations of TNCs, it is possible for these
companies to constitute a threat to the lives of
the local inhabitants in special or general circumstances. For instance, the oil spillage in
the delta region of Nigeria which occurred in
early 1980 threatened the lives and livelihood
of over half a million people. Equally threatened
were people's cultural and pastoral traditions
when the mining companies deprive villagers of
their land, on which their livelihood wholly depends. In most cases no resettlement exercises
could adequately repay the loss.

Other than having destablising effects on
the social and cultural order, the TNCs have
aided in maintaining and intensifying the unequal
distribution of income in each West African state.
Before the dramatic execution of President Tolbert,[34]
Liberia had remained a classic case of a few
families[35] dominating the economic and political
life of the country at the expense of the majority
of the population. At the locus of economic and
political power in almost all West African states
is a few people who maintain a symbiotic relationship with the TNCs. These compradors sustain and
nourish the dominant position of the TNCs vis-a-
vis the host country. It could also be argued

that though TNCs contribute to the provision of
the international finance and technology needed
in most "plant" projects, these are sometimes
isolated and uncoordinated in both time and space
with the general development programmes of the
nation or region.

As already indicated, TNCs are mainly
interested in maximising returns and minimising
costs rather than in the development of the host
country per se. In addition, a West African integration process that does not duely recognise the
impacts (both negative and positive) of the
activities of TNCs is bound to be frustrated by
the TNCs' extraneous actions. Thus to make self-
generated development possible ECOWAS, as the
rallying point, should attempt to establish and
effect regional policies for the control of TNC
activities. In particular it should regulate the
generation and utilisation of technology and adopt
other necessary steps that would create propitious
conditions for more autonomous development.

h)  Regional policies on TNCs and technology

There is a need, then, to establish in
West Africa more equitable societies where there
is no undue concentration of a country's wealth
in the hands of a few. Clarence Zuvekas[36] has
suggested a number of consistent income redistribution measures which developing states might
take. These include fiscal policies, increases
in the level of education, agrarian reforms, and
industrial development and population policies.
Sometimes these policies have proved difficult to
pursue due to their related social and political
effects. For example, the 1977 Nigerian Land
Decree, a positive redistribution policy, was
still attracting criticism three years after its
promulgation. Changes such as those suggested
above would require fundamental and courageous
shifts in leadership behaviour and content at the
national level. Towards this end, and indeed in

the absence of any such changes, ECOWAS could act as the nerve-centre for encouragement and possible action.

ECOWAS itself should be directly concerned with the control of TNC operations and in the adoption of integrated common investment policies in the region. The founding fathers in the Lagos Treaty made inadequate provisions for an evolving Community economic policy. Chapter VII of the ECOWAS Treaty expects a common transport and communication policy to evolve gradually. Article 48 specifically envisages "consultation" and "co-operation" in energy and mineral resources while Article 59 permits (economic) relations between member states and third parties, if such links do not "derogate from the provisions of the Treaty". It seems that it was not the intention of the founding fathers of the Community to evolve an integrated common economic policy other than t. suggest ad hoc provisions that would enhance in-frastructural links and encourage the co-ordin-ation of policies on energy and mineral resources.

ECOWAS could learn from the Andean Pact[37] about establishing integrated common investment policies. For the multilateral control of foreign investments in the Andean Community, a common code - Decision 24 - was ratified in June 1971. Article 18 of this Decision regulates that

> any contract regarding importation of
> technology or regarding use of patents
> and trademarks shall be reviewed and
> submitted to the approval of the pertin-
> ent agency of the respective member
> country, which shall evaluate the
> effective contribution of the imported
> technology by means of an appraisal of
> its possible profits, the price of the
> goods embodying technology or other
> specific means of measuring the effect
> of the imported technology.[38]

In addition, licensing agreements for the exploitation of foreign trade marks in the Andean Group
cannot contain restrictive[39] clauses (e.g. pro-
hibition or limitation to export or sell products
manufactured under respective trademarks or its
products in some given countries). Importantly,
it is a breach of Decision 24 to grant foreign
investors more favourable treatment than that
granted to national investors. A policy such as
that of the Andean Pact will minimise undue com-
petition among the West African countries for
foreign investments. Another goal of Community
policy towards the TNCs should be not only to
avoid inappropriate technology, but also to ensure that the "appropriate" forms are marketed
under acceptable conditions. Such conditions,
given an appropriate bargaining situation,would
minimise the much-talked about "exploitation" of
the host country by the TNCs.

Collateral to the above step to curb the
excesses of the TNCs is the need for an ECOWAS
technology policy to ensure the generation and
assimilation of technology resources within the
region. Although considerable emphasis has been
placed on technology planning at both national
and regional levels, very few African countries
have integrated technology policies in practice.
Rather, most have science and technology policies
as integral parts of their respective development
plans, whilst their technical and manpower development programmes are defused into several related
ministries. Except for Ghana and Nigeria in 1980
there has been no frontal programme in the region
to generate technology internally. The Andean
Pact is instructive in regard to adopting an
integrated regional plan for technology generation.
The group's Decision 24 stipulates measures aimed
at sub-regional technology development under conditions of high unemployment. In addition, according to this landmark decision, any imported or
locally-generated technology should be evaluated
in terms of its effect not only on employment but
also on technical development, on specific develop-

ment plans, on the balance of payments and on the
environment.

i)  Problems of Policy Implementation

A major problem to be envisaged in the implementation of any agreed common investment and
technology policies in the West African region is
that of building the necessary technical resources-
engineers, architects, accountants and others who
would have to conduct negotiations with foreign
as well as Community corporations.  Without this
cadre of technical experts a second problem - of
having a clear grasp of regional technological
problems with regards to specific programmes or
projects - would persist for a long time.  Because
of the proven paucity of technical staff required
in regional technology building, the initial problem
of trying to attract Community-trained personnel
for this purpose could generate controversy and
continued debate.  Member states are bound to
weigh their national needs against those of the
Community as a whole.  Other than this, problems
rooted in the distribution of costs and benefits
are bound to arise in the implementation of any
Community economic policies.  Evidence has shown
so far that much of the internal bickering with
ECOWAS, particularly in its inceptive years, was
centered around "which" state gets or loses "what"[40]
particularly in the areas of Community finance,
staffing and sectoral programmes.

Another problem likely to surface from
Community efforts to control and direct the use
of international finance and technology is the
danger of overbureaucratisation evident in the
functioning of the Andean Pact.  Overbureaucratisation arises from the multiple layers of
decision-making whcih are unavoidable in cases
where the Community has to interact with both the
TNCs and with such international institutions as
the ECA, IBRD, and IMF, as well as with the member
states.  This problem also results from the fact

that "most of the bureaucratic apparatus lacks understanding of the content and scope of the decisions"[41] of the Community as is the case in the Andean Pact. However, the merits of instituting regional technology and investment policies outweigh the demerits of such action.

In conclusion, some observations need to be made. First, regional integration in West Africa is at a "primitive" stage still. Until 1975, there was not a truly regional common market and now ECOWAS is in a vulnerable state, somewhat tottering given prevailing circumstances in the region. The result is that many transnational interactions are in fact state-centric. Second, as the result of an absence of strong multilateral economic activities in the sub-region, there exist multifarious rules and regulations guiding international investments. Third, it is obvious that the TNCs, aided by resident compradors have in most cases continued to exploit the economic deficiencies of the host countries. The TNCs have used various oligopolistic advantages (e.g. possession of international finance and technology) in exerting in West Africa a dominance relationship with the host countries. Finally, fourth, strong centralizing and coordinating action by ECOWAS is imperative: i) to minimise the effects of the prevailing high dependence on international capital and technology and consequently ii) to eliminate the negative impact of TNCs on the development of the regional economy to date.

296

Notes

1.  Cf.David Mitrany, The Functional Theory of Politics (London: Martin Roberts, 1975).

2.  Aaron Segal, "The Integration of Developing Countries: some thoughts on East Africa and Central America" Journal of Common Market Studies, 5 (4), 1967, 252-282.

3.  Richard G. Lipsey, "The Theory of Customs Union: a general survey" in Melvyn B. Krauss, (ed) The Economics of Integration (London; George Allen and Unwin, 1973), 57.

4.  Philip Ndegwa, The Common Market and Development in East Africa (Kampala: East African Publishing House, 1968).

5.  Timothy M. Shaw, "Dependence to (Inter) Dependence: review of debate on the (new) international economic order," Alternatives, 4(4), March 1979, 562.

6.  B. Ballasa, The Theory of Economic Integration (London: George Allen and Unwin, 1973).

7.  Ibid.

8.  See details in Ralph I. Onwuka, Development and Integration in West Africa: The Case of ECOWAS (Ile-Ife: University of Ife Press, forthcoming)

9.  Anthony G. Hopkins, An Economic History of West Africa (London: Longman, 1975) 210.

10. Ibid.

11. Patrick F. Wilmot, "Multinational Corporations in Africa" New Nigerian, Tuesday 18 April 1978, 5.

12.  P.B. Evans, "National Autonomy and Economic Development" in Robert Keohane and Joseph S. Nye (eds) Transnational Relations and World Politics (Cambridge: Harvard University Press, 1973) 325.

13.  See the penetrating study by L. Rood, "Nationalisation and Indigenisation in Africa," Journal of Modern African Studies, 14(3), 1976.

14.  Immanuel Wallerstein, "Class and Class-conflict in Contemporary Africa" Canadian Journal of African Studies, 7 (3), 1973,380.

15.  Henry Cooperstock "Some Methodological and Substantive Issues in the Study of Social Stratification in Tropical Africa" in Timothy M. Shaw and Kenneth A. Heard (eds.) The Politics of Africa: dependence and development (London: Longman & Dalhousie University Press, 1979) 24.

16.  Shehu U. Adbullahi, "The Role of the Nigerian Intellectuals in Nation-building," New Nigerian, Tuesday 18 April 1978, 5.

17.  N. Leff, "Technology Transfer and U.S. Foreign Policy: the developing countries" Orbis, 23 (1), Spring 1979, 146.

18.  Quoted in West Africa, 3271, 31 March 1980,571.

19.  Kwame Nkrumah, Neocolonialism: the last stage of imperialism (New York: International, 1966)

20.  West Africa, 3284, 30 June 1980, 1173.

21.  Each member state contributed 6 per cent of the share capital with the balance held by SODETRAF, Africa (London) 52, December 1975, 117.

22. Greg Lanning and Marti Mueller, _Africa Undermined_ (Harmondsworth: Penguin, 1979) 21.

23. A. Oke, "The Nation-State and Multinational Corporations: the West African experience" Unpublished M.A. Thesis, Department of International Relations, University of Ife, 1979.

24. _African Contemporary Record, Volume 8, 1975/76_, B778.

25. _Ibid_. B762.

26. _Nigerian Enterprise Promotion Decree (1977): Promotion of Nigerian Enterprises_ (Lagos: Nigerian Enterprises Promotion Board, July 1977) 10.

27. _West Africa_, 3271, 31 March 1980, 573.

28. _Ibid_.

29. Lanning and Mueller, _Africa Undermined_, 262.

30. Sanjaya Lall and Paul Streeten, _Foreign Investment: Transnationals and Developing Countries_ (London: Macmillan, 1978) 59.

31. Lanning and Mueller, _Africa Undermined_.

32. Alex Rondos, "Ivory Coast: the French factor" _West Africa_, 3224, 30 April 1979, 743.

33. _West Africa_, 3222, 16 April 1979, 657.

34. On 12 April 1980, President Tolbert was killed in a _coup d'etat_ which installed Master Sergeant Samuel K. Doe as the Head of State and Chairman of the Peoples Redemption Council (PRC). See _West Africa_, 3274, 21 April 1980, 689.

35. See the analysis in J. G. Liebenow, <u>Liberia:</u>
    <u>the evolution of privilege</u>   (Ithaca:
    Cornell University Press, 1969).

36. Clarence Zuvekas, <u>Economic Development</u>
    (London: Macmillan, 1979) 287-290.

37. The Cartegena Agreement was signed on 26 May,
    1969 by Bolivia, Chile, Columbia, Ecuador
    and Peru.  On 13 February 1973 Venezuela
    acceded to the Treaty.  The "Commission",
    the "Junta" and the "Board" are respectively
    the plenipotentiary, the decision-making and
    the technical institutions of the Pact.  See
    Junta del Acuerdo de Cartegena, <u>Technology</u>
    <u>Policy and Economic Development</u>   (Ottawa:
    International Development Research Centre,
    1976) 7.

38. <u>Ibid</u>.37.

39. Article 25, Decision 24.

40. See Ralph I. Onwuka, "The ECOWAS Treaty:
    inching towards implementation", <u>World</u>
    <u>Today</u> (London) 36 (2), February 1980, 52-64.

41. Rafael Vargas-Hidalgo "The Crisis of the
    Andean Pact:  lessons for integration among
    developing countries" <u>Journal of Common</u>
    <u>Market Studies</u>, 8 (3), March 1979, 220.

Notes on Contributors

ADEKUNLE AJALA is a Research Fellow, specializing in Southern African affairs, with the Nigerian Institute for International Affairs in Lagos. Dr. Ajala has a doctorate from the Free University of West Berlin and is author of Pan-Africanism: evolution, progress and prospects and other papers.

OLAJIDE ALUKO is Professor of International Affairs at the University of Ife, the first full professor in this subject in black Africa. Dr. Aluko holds a doctorate from the LSE and is author of numerous articles in African Affairs, Millenium and Quarterly Journal of Administration as well as of two books: Ghana and Nigeria, 1957-1970 and Essays on Nigerian Foreign Policy. He is also editor of and contributor to The Foreign Policies of African States.

'SOLA OJO is Lecturer in International Relations at the University of Ife. A specialist in Middle Eastern affairs, Dr. Ojo holds a Ph.D. from the LSE and has published articles in Africa Quarterly, Nigerian Journal of Political Science, International Studies and Quarterly Journal of Administration. He is co-editor (with Olajide Aluko, Amadu Sesay and Timothy M. Shaw) of Southern Africa in the 1980s.

AMECHI OKOLO holds a Ph.D. from Purdue University and is a Lecturer in International Relations at the University of Ife. A student of political economy, Dr. Okolo has published review articles in the Korean Journal of International Affairs and Quarterly Journal of Administration.

RALPH I. ONWUKA is Senior Lecturer and Acting Head in the Department of International Relations at Ife. Dr. Onwuka holds a Ph.D. from the LSE and has been an editor of Africa, Quarterly Journal of Administration and the Ife Papers on International Affairs. His essays have appeared in Quarterly Journal of Administration and World Today. Dr. Onwuka is author of Development and Integration in West Africa and co-editor (with Timothy M. Shaw) of Africa and World Politics: independence, dependence and interdependence.

GILBERT A. SEKGOMA is a doctoral student in the Department of History at Dalhousie University in Nova Scotia. He comes from Botswana and is working on decolonization and the political economy of Sierra Leone.

AMADU SESAY is a Sierra Leonean scholar with a Ph.D. from the LSE. Dr. Sesay is a Lecturer in International Relations at Ife and author of essays in Africa Quarterly, Africa Spectrum, Politique Africaine and (with Orobola Fasehun) in Shaw and Onwuka (eds) Africa and World Politics.

TIMOTHY M. SHAW is Associate Professor of Political Science at Dalhousie University in Nova Scotia. He has a doctorate from Princeton University and was a member of the Department of International Relations at Ife from 1979 to 1980. Dr. Shaw is co-author of Zambia's Foreign Policy, editor of Alternative Futures for Africa and co-editor (with Olajide Aluko) of The Political Economy of African Foreign Policy: comparative analysis and Nigerian Foreign Policy: alternative perceptions and projections.